W9-AOY-888

Almost Like a Song

Almost Like a Song

by
Ronnie Milsap

with Tom Carter

McGRAW-HILL PUBLISHING COMPANY
New York St. Louis San Francisco Bogotá Hamburg Madrid Mexico
Milan Montreal Paris São Paulo Tokyo Toronto

4 5 6 7 8 9 DOC DOC 9 5 4 3 2 1 0

ISBN 0-07-042374-1

Library of Congress Cataloging-in-Publication Data

Milsap, Ronnie.
    Almost like a song / Ronnie Milsap with Tom Carter.
        p.   cm.
    ISBN 0-07-042374-1
    1. Milsap, Ronnie.   2. Country musicians—United States—
Biography.   I. Carter, Tom, 1947–   . II. Title.
ML420.M514A3   1990
782.421642'092—dc20
[B]   90-5530
                                                             CIP
                                                             MN

To my wife Joyce and my son Todd,
to the memory of my Grandmother Phenia,
and to my Grandfather Homer, who died August 31, 1989,
while this book was nearing completion.

Acknowledgments

I want to give special thanks to
Joyce Milsap, Donald Reeves, and Nancy Overbey.
Without their help this book would never have been written.

I also want to thank Tom Carter
for his passion and dedication to this project.

Special thanks, also, to my editor,
Dan Weaver. He's a genius at helping new writers.

Foreword

When I was approached with the idea of writing my autobiography, one question came to mind immediately: "Why would I want to do it now?" I'd always thought that one's autobiography should be similar to one's memoirs, coming near the end of life. God willing, my life isn't near its end. It seemed like a highly premature idea.

It was pointed out that I've lived more during my young life than most men do in several lifetimes. And it wasn't written anywhere that I could do only one autobiography.

I began to soften. What sold me on the idea of writing the book was that it might inspire others who have faced adversity. I was born virtually blind and into poverty, abandoned by my mother, forced out of my home, and placed in the custody of strangers by the age of six. In many ways, those were the least of my travails.

I have a confession. People think I have a lot of willpower, and I do. But its formation wasn't entirely voluntary. I have it because I had to. I had willpower because at times I had nothing else. Quitting wasn't an option. If it had been, perhaps I would have taken an easy road to failure over the harder one to success. Humans have a tendency to take the path of least resistance. And as you'll read, I'm highly human. And, doing what I had to taught me a lesson: I could do almost anything if I wanted to.

I think anybody can do virtually anything if he or she wants to badly enough. I did, and I don't have a patent on determination. I just have a desire to share its effects.

Millions of folks have contributed money, good thoughts, and fine deeds to my life. Sharing my life story will, I hope, reciprocate some of those contributions.

A lot of people have jarred their memories and mine to bring forth this book. It isn't sugarcoated. I can't say I've told you everything about me. There are some things I honestly don't think would interest you. But what's here is said truthfully, sometimes painfully. There are things in here that have never been told before—not even to my closest friends.

I thought at first that putting forty-six years into 100,000 words would be fun, and at times, it definitely was. But some memories hurt a lot to recall. They hurt a lot more to say out loud and put on paper. In the interest of my own sanity, I had forgotten a lot of things—until I became involved with this book. In many ways, the recall was like spending two years on an analyst's couch.

I'll tell you about my boyhood home, a quarter mile from the nearest dirt road, straight up a mountain, and buried so deep in wilderness it was visible only by air. To recall what it was like living there four decades ago, I went back. I climbed the mountain I climbed as a child. I stood in the country general store that was the source of my boyhood needs. I knelt in the chapel that was my childhood church.

I walked the halls of my primary and secondary school house in Raleigh. I looked up classmates I hadn't seen in years and laughed with them for hours about things that time and trauma had all but erased.

You're going to be surprised, perhaps astonished, regarding some of the things you're about to read. Some of you who thought you knew me will wonder if I knew myself when I did certain things.

I've recorded twenty-one albums, and averaged 150 personal appearances annually, for the past sixteen years. I know the meaning of hard work. I've never, however, applied myself more seriously to anything than I have to the writing of this book. At times I took a break from it because I had to. I was emotionally taxed. I'd get to where I dreaded thinking about my past.

I didn't think I should be dreading the truth, so I left the project in body, but never in spirit.

In rereading these pages, I've been inspired myself. I have to thank God and a lot of good friends and relatives, but most of all my wife, Joyce, for getting me through some things I thought I'd never get past.

I hope this book helps each of us get on to better lives.

1

It had been a routine press conference. Weary reporters asked the usual tired questions.

"Mr. Milsap, were you born blind?"

"Ronnie, have you abandoned your country music roots by recording songs that are more accepted by pop music audiences?"

"Ronnie, why do you treat your mother like shit?"

The room became an instant symphony of coughing and throat clearing. Amid all the squirming, the reporter who had posed the question rose from his chair, presumably to repeat the inquiry as a challenge.

"Why do you treat your mother like shit?"

After members of my entourage removed him, I learned that he was not a reporter. I was told that he escorts a woman who identifies herself as my biological mother.

I believe she is.

The woman supposedly knows intimately the formerly unpublished account of how my mother gave me away when I was one year old.

My grandparents and daddy explained to me years later that my mother did not want her baby because I was blind. They led me to believe that she was ashamed of her sightless firstborn. She apparently thought she had fallen into disfavor with God, and that my birth was her divine punishment. She had given birth to a stillborn baby before me. According to her twisted thinking, my blindness indisputably confirmed God's anger toward her. Religious fears were as perverse as

1

they were common at that time in rural western North Carolina. Misguided fundamentalist teachings were the way of life and the only hope for eternal life among the Appalachians of the Smoky Mountains.

Daddy told me how my mother spent much of the first twelve months of my life sobbing and blaming him for me. He endured a year of hysterical rantings. She demanded that if he really loved her, he would find a way to rid her of this pitiful disaster in diapers.

"Take away God's punishment," she thundered. My daddy finally had all he could take, and when I was one year and one day old, he jerked me into his arms and stormed out through the door. He said my mother yelled after him: "Don't you take that baby out of this house without a blanket."

Funny; the woman who put me out in the cold wanted me to be warm.

Daddy took me twenty miles to live with his mother and stepfather, Phenia and Homer Frisby. They raised me lovingly until I was sent away to the state school for the blind at the age of six. My grandmother became my substitute mother, and all the feelings one has for a mother, I had for her. I called her "Mama."

Not long after my real mother put me out, she put Daddy out of her life, too. She divorced him.

My daddy (James Millsaps), Uncle J.C. (Phenia and Homer's son), my grandparents, and I all lived inside a four-room cabin. It was built of undressed lumber, and like the people who lived inside, it was humble yet sturdy. The way my grandmother kept it so clean and orderly was a symbol of their pride. It provided a sense of security to a blind boy who needed things to be in their places so he could find his way around.

We began each day with a farm breakfast that would make modern continental diners cringe. The menu included fried chicken, fried pork loin, fried apples, fried eggs, grits, hot biscuits, and sawmill gravy. The hard-working mountain folks wanted substance in their stomachs to begin the exhausting days. Today, as I travel around America on a tour bus, I often have to eat greasy and spicy food. I've had tacos for breakfast and buckwheat pancakes for supper, and I have no trouble with the unusual diet. That might have something to do with the way I learned to eat a lot, and eat it when it was served as a child.

My grandmother cooked those starchy, cholesterol-rich feasts, did the dishes, cleaned the house, and virtually did a full day's work before she started the next meal. We had no freezer, so we preserved home-grown vegetables in mason jars.

Meat was preserved in a smokehouse or left alive until it was time for a meal. It takes a long time to prepare fried chicken when you have to kill and dress it as well. The water had to be boiled after she walked a quarter mile to a spring to fetch it.

My Grandma Phenia did it all. She worked as hard as the men she served, and they worked like there was no tomorrow.

They tell me she had raven hair that time turned to gray. She was slightly overweight and had a heart condition. She wasn't healthy enough to work as hard as she did. The first time I heard Merle Haggard's "Mama's Hungry Eyes," I thought of Phenia. The song goes:

Mama never had the luxuries she wanted,
But it wasn't 'cause my Daddy didn't try
She only wanted things she really needed
One more reason, for my Mama's hungry eyes.

Truly, one of my greatest regrets in life is that she passed away before I became prosperous. I had a lifelong fantasy that someday I would buy my grandmother nice things.

Phenia officially died from a heart impairment. I believe the heart failure was induced by hard work. She suffered from pelagra, and not knowing any better, she ate all the wrong foods for her condition. More about her and her death later.

My daddy was six feet, two inches tall, yet he weighed only about 160 pounds. I think his slenderness was the result of back-breaking work as a manual laborer, the only job he ever knew because of his fourth-grade education. I was a five-year-old who idolized the man who went to work before daylight and came home after dark. People told me his body was brown from the sun. I could feel its firmness from the toil. I coveted his muscles.

He always smelled of stale sweat and fresh tobacco. I loved the scent. He'd smoke two packs of Camels a day. Sometimes he rolled his own blend from a Prince Albert tobacco can.

Living with my real daddy and Grandpa Homer was like having two daddies. I was close to Homer, too, whose stature was markedly different from my real daddy's.

Homer was only five feet, eight inches, dipped Bruton snuff, always wore a bearded stubble, and often reeked of a working man's odors. I don't remember him ever wearing anything during those days except bib overalls. Their frayed pockets were deep. There were lots of secret compartments for pencils, a pocket watch, and other things that I searched for in his clothes. To a child, his clothes were a mystery, like the covering on a walking attic trunk.

Our house was at the end of a dirt path, a half mile from the nearest road, and directly up a steep mountain. The road connected to a buckling, two-lane asphalt highway laid down during mountain improvements by the Tennessee Valley Authority around the time of the Great Depression. We didn't have electricity, plumbing, a telephone, or a car when I came to live with my grandparents. The day I left that house at seventeen, we still didn't have any of those conveniences.

In doing research for this book, I returned home in the summer of 1988. Three men came with me, all of whom were in their thirties and forties. None was overweight, and one was a former professional football player.

We had to push ourselves up that mountain, a slant of at least forty-five degrees. Waist-high weeds, so dense we couldn't walk through them, hid deadly cottonmouths and rattlesnakes, and the angle of that hill forced us to stop for rest many times.

I thought of Homer, who in his prime, never weighed more than 150 pounds. I remember how he hefted our food and living supplies up that bank to the tiny house. One day, he hoisted a 100-pound sack of fertilizer on his bent and bony back and scaled that treacherous terrain, let the bag fall from his aching shoulders, and then repeated the haul—sixteen times. In one day, Homer carried 1,700 pounds of fertilizer up that path to our cabin.

Calling that kind of labor "hard" is about as much of an understatement as calling an ocean a pond. But for Homer, hard work came without question. It was as natural as loving the family for whom he did it.

*   *   *

My blindness was diagnosed when I was five months old. I was four years old the first time I remember being examined by Dr. Nettie Perrett.

She was the doctor who delivered me in my natural parents' living room. Months later, she reaffirmed her initial diagnosis of congenital glaucoma.

I should make it clear that, although it has been said that I was born totally blind, I had what is called "light vision" in my left eye. I couldn't see forms or tell distances, but I could detect light, very, very slightly, if I looked into direct sunlight.

To call that "sight" may be misleading, but it was hope to a little boy. I was, at the bottom of my heart, positive that someday my light vision would be surgically improved, and I eventually would see.

Dr. Perrett was a caring and sincere country practitioner who tended people who could pay, as well as those who could not. She and her husband, Dr. Dick Perrett, lived in Robbinsville, North Carolina, and she often walked or rode a mule to the mountain homes of her patients. During her forty-seven-year career, she delivered over 3,000 babies. That figure is about four times the number of people who live in Robbinsville's city limits today. In one high school yearbook, it was noted that Dr. Nettie delivered every player and every coach on that season's football team. For a delivery, she charged $25. The fee included prenatal care, the birth at home, and two postnatal appointments for mother and child. Despite the nominal charge, she often was paid in home-grown vegetables or slaughtered livestock.

I visited Dr. Nettie in June 1988, seven years after her retirement. It was only then I learned that she was never paid for my birth. My father couldn't afford the doctor's services so he got a midwife for the delivery. During the procedure, the midwife decided that my head was too large, and she was afraid to try to remove me from my mother. Dr. Nettie told me that my daddy rushed to her house, desperately seeking help. She was taken in somebody's car to my mother's house in Robbinsville.

As a child, I overheard adults talk of medical breakthroughs and how modern science was searching for cures for blindness. About that time, Dr. Jonas Salk discovered the polio vaccine. I thought to myself, if a crippling disease could be wiped out, why not someday something as comparatively minor as my blindness? I wanted nothing more then, or now, than to simply look at this world before I leave it.

When I was young, I may have encountered my mother a half-dozen times. The first time was when I was five or six. She surprised me by bringing along a baby daughter. I thought she was trying to be kind when she put my fingers on her daughter's eyes. Then she said something I will never forget.

"Feel her eyes, Ron. They're real clear, not like yours. She's not like you, and she didn't shame me. She can see."

You can imagine how words like that would break the heart of a little boy. I can still remember holding back the tears. But I wasn't about to let myself cry in front of a stranger.

Those early attempts at controlling my emotions proved to be rehearsals for the way I am today. I'm not as emotional as some people, perhaps because I developed the habit at that impressionable age of suppressing my feelings.

Today, I can remember days and dates surrounding events of long ago very well. But I can't always remember how I felt at the time. Maybe, subconsciously, I don't want to. As a grown man, I haven't cried very often. A few of the times have been around people I'm really close to, but most often I've been able to control it until I could get somewhere to cry alone.

Another time, when I was still a preschooler, my mother came to visit and gave me a dollar. In those days, a dollar was a lot of money. You could buy a Coca-Cola for a nickel or a loaf of bread for fifteen cents. To a six-year-old, paper money, even one dollar, seemed like a fortune. I put the dollar beside the big family Philco radio where I could feel for it and find it. I was mighty proud of that dollar. I would check regularly to make sure it was safe. It was the most money I'd ever had, and I didn't have it very long. My mother stayed for two days, then before she left, she asked me for the dollar back!

But, I have to say, these stories about my mother are uncharacteristic of my life. Today, after much soul-searching, I feel I am a positive person who thrives on optimism, and I hold no bitterness about the past. Yet my past is part of my story, and if you cared enough about me to pick up this book, I want you to know the whole story. The lingering effects of feeling unwanted by my mother will always be with me.

I have heard psychologists claim that ninety percent of a child's personality is formed by the age of seven. If that is true, my psychological scars are deep. I was taught to feel guilt and inferiority because I was blind. Sometimes, instead of trying to compensate for blindness, I tried to punish myself. I was a small child trying to achieve atonement for an affliction over which I had no control. My mother actually made me feel, in my young mind, that I was responsible for my own blindness.

I started kindergarten later than most kids because I couldn't go to public school, and there was a delay in the welfare process to get money for clothes so I could attend a special school.

My mother managed to visit me once at school before I graduated at nineteen. I didn't hear from her again until I was twenty-five. She wrote a letter to her "beloved" son. She didn't ask how I'd been. She didn't ask if all was forgiven. She asked for money. There are few things I enjoy more than sharing my God-given prosperity. My mother must have heard about that.

She resurfaces every so often trying to steer my generosity in her direction. In 1975, after I'd had a few hits for RCA Records, she turned up again. She wanted money.

There have been other requests through the years for me to open my heart to her by first opening my wallet. But I have never given her money, and I have always refused to see her. Maybe that's why she sent her boyfriend, the "reporter," to the press conference that day. She may have thought that his public denouncement would intimidate me into giving her money.

It didn't.

Someone contacted one of those grocery store tabloids around 1986, and the result was a story about the uncaring Ronnie Milsap and the dire straits of his precious mother. The headlines screamed that my mother was starving while I lived like a king inside a mansion a block away from the estate of the Governor of Tennessee.

The story was wrong, and it hurt me deeply. It humiliated my friends and family, including my wife, Joyce.

Do I ever plan to see my mother? I'll answer that question with a question: Why would I want to see her? Motherhood means more than just giving birth. Yet that was the extent of her involvement with me. In her womb, she carried me for nine months. In her house, she kept me for a year. She spelled out the rules of our relationship when I was a child. I learned to live with them. Now she has to do the same.

I'm not bitter about my mother or my blindness or anything else. I believe my circumstances have given me an inner strength, and I thank God for my many blessings. The person who wrote that I hate my mother wrote a lie. I don't hate her. I don't even know the woman. To hate her would mean that I have feelings for her, even if they're negative. But, really, I have no feelings for her at all.

And as for giving her money? Well, I guess she forgot that I gave her my last dollar when I was six years old.

2

A common link among country music entertainers is their shared background of poverty. I am no exception, but I believe there is a difference. I was poor and didn't know it.

We had no modern conveniences, but neither did our neighbors. The nearest one lived at least a half mile from us, and without telephones, there was a sense of isolation that bred fierce instincts of survival among the mountaineers. No one had much more than anyone else, so how could we know we were poor? Most had not been off those mountain slopes their entire lives.

I was born on January 16, 1943, about seven years before television would make the mountains' inhabitants aware of another world. They were independent people who were pretty set in their ways, and I think a lot of them wouldn't have traded their country lives for the uptown things they saw on those new–fangled electronic boxes in their living rooms.

One time I remember asking my Grandpa Homer if we were poor? I had overheard somebody say that we were, and it upset me a lot. He said, "Lawd no, son, we're not poor."

At first, he told me about us having our health and each other and love and the things that really do matter, no matter how much or how little money one has. But then his real wisdom showed through when he brought it down to a kid's level. He took my hand and put it on a pocket full of change he was carrying.

"Feel all this money, boy," he said. "Now, does that feel like we're poor? Poor people don't have money like that. Poor people have holes in their clothes."

A few days later, Homer was working in the fields and wearing old clothes. I ran out to him and somehow my hand touched a hole in his bib overalls.

I felt that hole, and felt my heart break at the same time.

"Oh no, Homer, you got holes in your pants," I yelled. "I just knew it; we *are* poor!"

I must have cried for an hour.

My Grandpa Homer and Grandma Phenia went to bed around sundown and got up before sunrise. The schedule was partly due to their work load, but the early-to-bed, early-to-rise routine was also because darkness came quickly in the thick woods where we lived. Insects and wild animals sounding off in the mountains were nature's lullabies. I heard old-timers describe the faint glow of kerosene lamps making lazy shadows on the board walls of those mountain homes. My childhood imagination saw a chorus line of dancing silhouettes.

The sounds I could hear, the sights I could see in my mind, the warmth and shelter I could feel inside our little Appalachian dwelling, created a totally restful mood, making sleepiness and sundown synonymous. It was all against the scented backdrop of burning wood in the winter, and the aroma of mountain laurel in the summer.

In a curious way, I felt more security inside Homer's tiny hillside house than I do inside my Nashville mansion on seven manicured acres today.

In the mid-1970s, I heard Dolly Parton sing "Tennessee Mountain Home" about her own Smoky Mountain upbringing. I thought she captured in one line the temperament of life in the rural mountains. Life there, wrote Dolly, "is as peaceful as a baby's sigh."

That was the serenity of my grandparents' house, nestled in an unincorporated community called Meadow Branch near the western North Carolina–east Tennessee border towns of Tapoco and Fontana Village, North Carolina.

I want to stress how those little dwellings had their own brand of charm, no matter how humble. After I was grown and out on my own, I went with friends to big-city ghettos. My friends described for me the dirt, the torn-down houses, and the sense of desperation of ghetto people.

They aren't the kind of poor people you find in the mountains. The mountain folks are as proud as they are poor. There is as much appreciation for life in the mountains as there is desperation about life in the ghettos. If beauty is in the eyes of the beholder, so is poverty, and a lot of mountain people I know see themselves rich in peace and pride. They're not ashamed or embarrassed about their worldly possessions, or the lack of them. I respect and love them for that.

Homer and I drank from ice-blue streams so cold it hurt our teeth. We fished clear mountain lakes for feisty bream that fought a cane pole as if each half-pound swimmer weighed a ton. At least that's how it seemed to a five-year-old whaler. In the fall, Homer and I would go hunting for rabbit, quail, and squirrel. I loved to feel the fur and feathers, but even more I loved the deep quiet of the woods. Then Homer's .12-gauge shotgun would blast away, and the contrast of that boom against what had been a hush was breathtaking. Homer just never thought of my being blind but he was always thinking about me. That old gentleman had never been an athlete and yet he somehow came up with a ball and bat, and taught me how to play baseball during summers in the Smokies. He'd pitch, and when he thought the ball was within reach, he'd yell "swing." I'd feel the bat hit it, then hear him chase it. He had that much patience and energy for a surrogate grandchild who was his friend. And loved one.

A little thing like that can be such a big deal to a little kid growing up in the country. But perhaps the most exciting moment of all was the first time I heard recorded music. It came, with a lot of static, through our battery radio. We couldn't get many stations. Tuning the dial made a deep whine that was usually louder than the stations themselves.

But that old radio was our window to the world.

The first song I remember was Roy Acuff's "Great Speckled Bird." The second was Ernest Tubb's "Walking the Floor over You."

Both songs were recorded with only electric and acoustic guitars and an upright bass. "Great Speckled Bird," as I recall, did have a dobro line. But that sparse instrumentation was more music than I'd ever heard, as my only other musical encounters had been with the pianist and singing congregation at the Meadow Branch Primitive Baptist Church.

I was hypnotized by the "full" arrangements of three or four instruments recorded so crudely, possibly through one microphone. To
me, then, the sounds were in a way as lush as an eighty-piece symphony.

My Grandmother Phenia was the first to notice how quickly I
memorized the words to the old songs, and how I could sing their
melodies on key. Unofficially, she could be credited with spotting my
musical talent, although I wouldn't receive formal instruction until the
age of seven when I was given violin lessons in school.

My Uncle J.C. had an old guitar on which he played and sang Tubb's
"Rainbow at Midnight." When J.C. wasn't around, I'd pick up the instrument, but I had no idea how to play it. My fingers weren't long
enough to make chords, even if I'd known how. But after my first
"mental arrest" by recorded music, I never escaped its magnetic appeal.

And if intrigue with the radio's sound wasn't enough, I was consumed with its touch. I loved to feel the internal workings. I disassembled our home theater, that radio, because my curiosity wasn't
satisfied until I held each part in my hands.

My grandpa was not overjoyed when he came home to find the
radio's tubes in one room, and its dials in another. He and my Uncle
J.C. worked hard to put the thing back together each time I took it
apart. Sometimes they were able to reassemble the parts. Once they
had to buy a new radio. But always, I got a spanking, which, back then,
was called a "whipping," and appropriately so—I was swatted with a
twenty-inch razor strap that probably weighed three pounds.

The punishment was repeated each time I took apart the wind-up
alarm clocks. I just had to feel what there was inside those ticking
machines that would make them ring like magic at certain times. My
passion to take things apart forced my grandparents to put every clock
in the house out of my reach.

I don't know why I was so interested in the workings of the only
two mechanical devices we had on the place. Maybe my curiosity was
heightened because I could only hear, and not see, the sources of
sound in my home.

We laughed a lot back then. Laughter was the best way to ease
what otherwise could have been a hard life. I've never seen a Norman
Rockwell painting, but I've been told Rockwell's work candidly portrays

common people in common situations in a way that is heartwarming. I think my boyhood home in the Smokies must have been a Rockwell painting come to life.

And of course there was that instant frolic afforded through the radio. We sat spellbound around its sound as though it were a battery-powered Pied Piper.

My daddy loved music, especially bluegrass. He'd listen to Bill Monroe and other bluegrass acts on one of the only two big stations we received: WNOX from Knoxville and WSM from Nashville, Tennessee. On Saturday nights, Daddy would fall asleep to the sounds of the *Grand Ole Opry*. I'd find him there on Sundays, still asleep, snoring to the amplified fuzz on the radio, whose programs had been off for hours.

Through that old radio, I got an introduction to what would become for me a multimillion-dollar career—and all from a $30 contraption.

But don't be misled by memories of a storybook life. A person needed each of his five senses just to stay alive in that land's rugged splendor. A child missing one sense could find serious injury or death hiding beneath the mountains' natural beauty. The setting was heaven on earth, but it was a hazardous heaven.

I was frequently a victim of my own curiosity. I had all the questions that live in a boy's mind. I remember early wonder at the feel of glass, so smooth and cool to my touch. I was once feeling a mason jar when I knocked it off the shelf. Jagged pieces of shattered glass splattered around my bare feet (I hardly ever wore shoes in the summertime), and no matter where I stepped, my naked soles were cut.

It's hard enough to live without being able to see the world's beauty. It's even harder not to see its traps.

Another time when I was barefooted, I stepped directly on a rusty nail that was about three inches long. That nail went right between the tendons, and nearly broke the skin on the top of my instep.

I should have had a tetanus shot and the wound checked by a doctor, but medical treatment was about as likely as getting the money to pay for it, or the transportation to get to it. There was just no way.

So I hobbled to the home that was my hospital, my grandparents' cabin. Phenia coated my feet with something that burned all the way to my scalp. I don't know if it was iodine, mercurochrome, or what, but the way it burned, it could have been kerosene. I wondered why no one had told this blind boy that fire was a liquid.

Then there was the time I could have lost an eye thanks to a mean Rhode Island Red rooster. That bird was so cranky, it attacked anything it disliked, and it disliked everything. It even killed the laying hens that it was supposed to romance. Now that's a violent lover!

The thing charged me and went straight for my face, pecking with enough force to take out an eye if I hadn't kept batting it away. The noise got Homer's attention, and he sprinted to my rescue. He kicked that rooster like it was the first play of the Super Bowl. He told me it was dead before it hit the ground. My enemy became my dinner.

Another time I asked Homer what it was in the box that made such a neat sounding rattle when I shook it. Between gasps, he shouted for me to put down the dynamite caps.

Then there was the time I heard a rattlesnake near me. Thank God it wasn't a copperhead, or some other kind of poisonous snake that wouldn't have given a warning. I stood there, frozen with fear, screaming for Homer to come to my rescue. I thought that at any second I'd feel that serpent's fangs, but Homer got there in time, and killed it.

My loving grandparents were always on the lookout for my well-being, steering me around the pitfalls that would have been threats even to people who could see in the wilderness. You would think that two elderly people struggling to scratch a living from that mountain soil wouldn't have had time to properly watch a blind baby, but they took the time.

Another dangerous incident I recall was an attack by yellow jackets. Homer and Phenia had taken me along fishing. I was about four. Concerned that I not fall into the deep mountain lake, Homer built a playpen from tree branches on the ground. He put me inside not knowing that he had stirred up a yellow jacket's nest. I was trapped inside and couldn't get away from all the swarming bugs that attacked me as soon as Homer walked off. As usual, my screaming brought Homer to the rescue.

Homer and I have laughed many times about my merely surviving my childhood.

Through the years, when I've told friends about some of my early mishaps, they always ask the same question. "Weren't you scared to death?"

The answer is simple. I always felt safe in the presence of Homer or my daddy. And I was always in their presence. No matter what happened, I knew they would come to my rescue, and that they would make things all right.

It was the kind of old-fashioned, secure trust and bond between a child and his parents you don't often see today.

There is another, less emotional reason I wasn't overly terrified of the mountains' dangers. They were simply unavoidable. Even if you were sighted, you never took safety for granted in the Appalachian Mountains.

People expected to see scorpions inside their loosely built log homes. They weren't surprised if a snake slithered from under a rug. No one thought it was unusual to hear panthers screaming in the night. Danger was always present. It was something with which we lived the way urban people today live with crime.

So from the time I was taken to live with my grandparents, to when I went to school five years later, I was always getting hurt. That's how it seemed. I didn't know it then, but my leaving for school meant that I would be going far away from my family before some kids even started kindergarten. At the age of six, leaving my mountain home and the grandparents who loved me hurt like nothing I'd ever felt—not even rusty nails or broken glass.

3

I never cease to be amazed at how one overlooks the obvious in life especially as a child. That's what I did, at age six, when thoroughly accustomed to the benevolent love of my Grandmother Phenia. She did everything for me.

So I've often wondered why I didn't suspect something unusual when, on the day I embarked on what was then the biggest adventure of my life, Phenia chose not to accompany me.

For weeks, Phenia and Homer had been building up in my impressionable mind the fun we'd have on a journey to faraway Raleigh North Carolina. We would travel 400 miles, the farthest we'd ever been from home. We would stay in a hotel; we would eat in restaurants—and when we were finished, Phenia wouldn't have to make the beds or do the dishes!

The departure day finally arrived, and Phenia, who had been so "excited" about our going, suddenly announced that she wasn't coming along.

Instead, she cried a lot. I remember thinking how curious it was for her to be so sad on the brink of something so thrilling. And there was something else mysterious to me. There were four people in the Raleigh-bound delegation, but I was the only one for whom Phenia packed a lot of clothes.

A man named Arnold Hyde, who I later learned was my welfare caseworker, came to Homer's mountain cottage. Homer had no car so Mr. Hyde drove Homer, my uncle J.C. and his wife Dorothy, and me to Raleigh.

That night in Asheville, we stayed in a hotel, where I heard water splash from faucets onto porcelain, slick to my touch. The toilet had a plastic seat, and it made a gurgling noise after you used it and pushed a handle. I would have walked quite a way then to see something like that. But with these toilets, you didn't even have to walk outside.

It was all so neat, I wished that I had to go to the bathroom more often.

In Asheville and in Raleigh, Homer did not understand the traffic signals. I heard the wh-o-o-s-h sound of passing cars as we unknowingly jaywalked into speeding traffic, a little boy who couldn't see and a fifty-three-year-old man who'd never seen anything like bumper-to-bumper congestion. Unaware of the danger, I was enthralled by the noise and smells of the city.

In Raleigh, we stayed at the Sir Walter Raleigh Hotel and, early the next morning, drove to the North Carolina State School for the Blind. (The school is now known as the Governor Morehead School for the Blind, but the name was not changed until 1963, one year after I had graduated.)

The journey would change my life more than anything to this day.

I was so happy, and naive, as we were led around the fifteen buildings on eighty acres by Mrs. Maude Haroldson, a housemother for small boys. I didn't know the meaning of the word "stately." I realize now that that's how the place and its design felt. There were towering white columns on the fronts of red brick buildings. There were colonial shutters surrounding double windows. When I returned to the campus in 1980 for the first time since graduating in 1962, I relished the south's regal answer to ivy league architecture, fanned by ancient oak and magnolia trees.

Except for a one-room church house, I'd never been inside a structure whose rooms I couldn't cross in a few steps. In those massive buildings at Governor Morehead, the rooms were so spacious you could hear the echo of your footsteps.

The school spread across a rolling lawn of mown grass sliced into sections by sidewalks. Homer cut our grass at home with a hand sickle, so it was never short and uniform like the machine-mowed grass at the school for the blind. I had only recently, at the hotel, walked on carpets. Mowed grass felt similar.

I was enraptured with the tour of the facilities, tailor-made for unsighted people like me. Then Homer said it was time to go home. And he said I would not be going with him.

As best he could, with a heart more broken than his English, the grandfather who had hand-led me through life told me he was going to leave me at that foreign place. At an early age, I was already sensitive to sincerity in the sound of a human voice, and I knew Homer meant what he said.

But I still couldn't believe he was saying it.

Hadn't my own mother abandoned me? Hadn't I been born with virtually no sight? Didn't God know I was just a little kid?

Now, I was going to be left alone, not knowing one person, by the man whom I loved and trusted more than any other in this whole world—the world that insisted on handing me slam after slam.

And then they were gone. The cavernous rooms that earlier had echoed with my excited footsteps now rang with my crying.

I must have prayed that this wasn't happening, because my thoughts turned to the Bible.

Unfortunately, the Bible story I remembered best was the story of Joseph, who was sold into slavery as a youth. I was sure that I was a little boy who had been taken far away and sold into servitude.

And so I cried more. I lay on a plastic floor mat inside the hall and wept bitterly, not knowing I was homesick for a place where I would never live permanently again.

The new address would be mine for the next thirteen years. And I had been taken there and left by my own people. I don't know which I felt more—broken or betrayed.

I was hysterical for hours. Some people say you can't remember things that happened to you when you were only six. Nonsense. There is no time frame for trauma.

Being left at that unfamiliar school that day was my closest brush ever with self-pity, but soon, through the incredible instruction at the school, I would learn to abandon forever feeling sorry for myself.

My crying that day was soon overpowered by someone else's crying. There are nine concrete steps in front of the former Cottage Braille dormitory. Larry Atwell and I probably sat on every one of them trying to get comfortable as we wept. He was the first student I met at Governor Morehead. In the space of minutes, I made a friend for years. That same day, I met Walter Lackey. Today, Walter has a doctorate and is a political science teacher at Frostburg State College in Maryland, where he lives with his wife, Charlie. In years to come, Larry, Walter, and I were affectionately known by students and faculty as the "three fat boys." We were the best of friends.

Ten years later, Larry would play trumpet and bass with me in my first band, the Apparitions. When we got to know each other better, I accompanied Larry home on weekends and summer vacations. It was too far to Homer's, and there was no car. Larry's parents, Boyce and Mona Atwell, treated me like family. So did his brother and sister, Ed and Wanda. Whenever Mrs. Atwell bought a present for her children, she bought the same thing for me. She pretended not to notice when Larry and I huddled late at night under the covers listening to *The Shadow, The Lone Ranger,* and other faraway radio programs.

The Atwells, in fact, introduced me to television. They had a wooden console model. I remember Larry and I pressing our faces close to the new screen. We thought its brightness would enable us to see its images. He didn't see much and I didn't see anything, but we sat with the family and they told us what they were watching in sort of a play-by-play fashion. It was magical to us.

There was a lot more local programming back then, and we took in the studio productions on WBTV on Channel 3 in Charlotte. Since television was so new, watching it was a family affair, the way listening to the radio had been. Those times with the Atwell family were wonderful breaks from the discipline and structure of Governor Morehead.

Eventually, Larry, Walter, and I would share our first encounters with girls, cigarettes, algebra, masturbation, pimples, and all the rest of that terrific and terrible transition period from child's play to adulthood. We would form the kind of friendship that youngsters in public schools do not. We wouldn't merely study together; we would eat, sleep, and breathe almost as one. But we would have traded anything our futures held for a mere trip back home on that first day at Governor Morehead. Homesickness is painful at any age. When you're six, it's almost terminal.

My first days at school could not have been stranger if I had gone to Mars. For example, here was a place that expected you to eat in group dining rooms, and I had never been taught how to hold a fork properly, although I had used one. It was a place that ran on schedule, and I was accustomed to rising and retiring in nature's way, when I woke and when I was weary. It was a place that put sleeping strangers in dormitories. I had never been under a roof with more than four people, and all of those were family.

And it was a place that ran on regimentation, while I was accustomed to a home fueled by feelings.

The Governor Morehead School for the Blind has been a large part of my life. I was fed and educated, grew to maturity, and fell in and out of love there for one-and-one-third decades of my life, and memories of that place will fill much of my story.

But for now, let me say two things:

At that school, I learned I was not totally blind. After talking with other blind children, I learned I had the light vision I mentioned earlier. I could not "see" anything: I couldn't have seen something held three inches from my face.

But sometimes, in just the right situations, I could detect light. If, for example, the sky was clear and the sun was directly above, I could vaguely sense changes in the light.

I attended Lion's Club meetings and would hear talk of corneal transplants. I totally overreacted to such discussions. I just knew in my heart that someday medicine and science would put sight into my eyes.

People live by faith. They also live for it. More than I realized at the time, I was possessed by the conviction that I was going to see. I had no idea then how much that conviction was motivating me.

The other thing I want to say up front about Governor Morehead is that academic standards there were second to none. I have heard frequently that Morehead was among the nation's top three schools for the blind, including Perkins Institute, near Boston, and Overbrook School for the Blind in Philadelphia.

If there is one thing above all else that accounts for my success, it's the classroom and attitude training I received.

I was taught not to feel sorry for myself because I was blind, or for any other reason. I could read and write braille, and perform addition and subtraction by the time I left kindergarten. I was a serious violin student at the age of seven.

There was a woman who taught there who was herself a Morehead alumnus. I had been at that school for six years before I discovered she was blind. She was that victorious over her handicap because that's the way she was taught.

Were it not for that school, and the exceptional education it provided, I probably would have spent my entire life in rural western North Carolina, where there are few vocational opportunites even today. There were practically none when I was growing up.

But there was another side to the school. A dark side. And that side regrettably influenced my personality as much as the superb academics did my mind.

To put it kindly, the school had an exaggerated emphasis on discipline. And the people who administered it, who were not members of the faculty, were minimum-wage earners, unprofessional, and perhaps even semiliterate. In a word, they were mean. They didn't levy punishment to instruct; they levied it to control through fear. Or should I say terror?

Six-year-olds, myself included, were whipped merely for crying for their parents. Today, if a child twice that age, at summer camp with his friends, is lonely, it's understood. We were little more than babies who didn't know each other, the place, or what was going to happen to us. Yet our bottoms were whipped, and our heads were pounded against walls by some of the housemothers if we expressed a natural desire to go home.

You think they weren't tough? A girl, Myra D'Bruel, who graduated from Morehead High School with honors, once had a dormitory supervisor with a deep and raspy voice whom Myra called "sir." That went on for two weeks, until Myra learned that her housefather was in fact a housemother.

We were taught on the first day how to make our beds and where to position our shoes and other personal property relative to the mattress. Because we couldn't see, we might leave a shoe an inch out of place. The housemother wouldn't say where the shoe was; instead, she'd make us get on our hands and knees and feel for it. Then we'd stand up to feel the sting of an unseen slap across a teary face.

Even sighted boys don't always get all the dirt off their hands when washing before a meal. That's as much a part of a boy's childhood as measles. But if we left even a speck of soil on our knuckles, the backs of our hands were beaten repeatedly with steel rulers.

My housemother was a hefty and stout woman, Mrs. Maude Haroldson. We nicknamed her "Old Lady Haroldson." She had been so charming to all our parents and grandparents.

When the families left us at the school, she underwent an immediate transition that was straight out of Snow White. Instantly, she was a wicked witch.

It should be stressed that my resentment toward the school's disciplinary practices isn't rooted in a child's normal dislike for authority. Most of us were from working-class backgrounds, where we had been taught to mind adults. We would have had no trouble taking orders, even if we disagreed with them. But all of us had trouble with the scathing assaults on our bodies and the reign of terror under which we lived as children.

One day in kindergarten, I was told to report to Old Lady Haroldson. At that school, they could call you out of class for punishment, no matter how insignificant the offense. The housemother-dictator walked into the dormitory room I shared with five boys. She grabbed my hand and placed it heavily on the wall.

"What's this?" she demanded.

Back in the country, I had often put my chewing gum on the wall at day's end. It was an unsanitary habit, but I had never been taught differently.

"What is this?" she roared.

"It's chewing gum," I whimpered.

"Don't you know you're not supposed to put chewing gum on the walls?" she bellowed.

"Huh," I said.

"Don't you say 'huh' to me. You say, 'ma'am.'"

Then ma'am slapped me across the face.

All that for chewing gum? No telling what she'd have done if I'd spilled a glass of water or burped during church.

"You're going to whip me," I began to blubber.

"I sure am," she affirmed, and began beating me with a perforated paddle.

The weapon had been drilled full of holes. The holes lessened the wind resistance, so she could swing with maximum force.

A sixth sense told me that she wanted me to cry, and I complied. She quit soon afterwards. I quickly developed the ability to cry loudly whenever that monster accosted me.

There was one guy in our dormitory who was tough and unafraid. He refused to cry. She could have worn herself into a heart attack many times trying to prompt his tears. I think secretly we all hoped she'd do just that.

So what is the upshot to this story? Obviously, it is not that youngsters should be allowed to stick their gum to walls. I'm merely saying that someone should tell them not to do that the first time, reprimand them the second time, and beat them like a dog at no time.

I often heard that spiteful woman bound into our quarters after it was time to be asleep. Boys might be whispering from bunk to bunk, and she'd surprise them and jerk them from their beds, holding their ears in her hands. Then she'd bounce their heads off those plaster walls, and the dizzy children would be left with splitting headaches and bleeding ears. She gripped the ears so firmly, her fingernails sliced into the cartilage. For days, a lad would wear the scabs, and these would reopen and bleed again if he were slapped.

Listen, I'm not soliciting sympathy with these stories. It's just part of telling my life story truthfully. I don't want and, more importantly, don't need sympathy, particularly forty years after the fact. All I want is to tell the ups and downs of my life.

Governor Morehead was segregated. Black students attended another state school for the blind twenty miles away. It wasn't until 1965, around the time of the federal Civil Rights Act during Lyndon Johnson's administration, that the school finally received black students. Previously, the only blacks on campus were the cooks and maids.

The school was segregated sexually, too. There was a sidewalk across the middle of the campus. One side was for the boys, the other for the girls. Boys and girls were not permitted bodily contact. Even teenagers were forbidden to hold hands.

Holding hands was as much grounds for expulsion as was something truly serious, such as delinquency or academic failure. This was a very important point. Expulsion from Governor Morehead was a guarantee of personal and career failure for blind students in North Carolina. If you were evicted, there was no place else to go.

The public schools back then wouldn't accept blind students, and neither would the private schools (assuming you had the money). No matter how bad things got, there was always one fate that was worse—expulsion.

The students and their parents knew it. I think that frightful knowledge, more than anything else, ensured our acquiescence to the denial of the most basic civil rights. And that fear kept alive the climate of quiet hysteria that prevailed in Morehead's prisonlike environment.

Ironically, the lawn of the North Carolina State Penitentiary actually joined our campus. It was so close, we could lie in bed and hear the barking of search dogs when a convict escaped.

The prisoners rose and retired to the sounds of whistles. Some of the students timed their own schedules with the prison whistles. Somehow, that doesn't seem so surprising.

Most of the administrators, I'm sure, would have been outraged at what passed for punishment at the hands of the dormitory personnel. But none of the kids tattled. We were all too afraid.

We instead responded in a more traditional manner. We rebelled.

The protests, when we were young, were simply in the form of individual misbehavior. My own unruliness peaked a few years after I arrived, on a Saturday, which was good timing for Old Lady Haroldson. She needed Sunday to rest from the whippings she gave me. I got three in the space of eight hours.

Her first assault came because we were making wooden spears and seeing how far they would sail. Well, there is a little more to it. She was actually upset because I sailed mine into some kid's back. But I'll bet his back wasn't as sore as my butt after Mrs. King Kong got through with me.

I was sent to my room, where I nursed my bruised pride and backside, but I soon became bored. I wanted to go outside, but I was afraid of running into the warden. So instead, I persuaded poor Jackie Cobb to go—out the window. The only problem was we were three stories up. I solved this by weaving a rope from a bed sheet and promised I'd lower Jackie to the ground.

He actually went for it!

I held Jackie at bay, between the second and third stories, of Cox dormitory. He must have looked unusual bouncing off the building's exterior. I knew I was convincing when I threatened to drop him. I could tell by his screaming. It even overpowered the yelling of Old Lady Haroldson.

But not for long. She burst into our room, ordering me to pull the screaming and squirming boy back into the building. She didn't laugh when I asked her to please let me drop him. I even called her "ma'am."

It was no use. Jackie climbed back safely inside, and I got my butt, still sore from the last pummeling, pounded again.

I figured, after dangling twenty-five feet above ground, Jackie Cobb could use some serenity, so I persuaded him to go inside my closet to look for my Sunday school suit.

Even after all I had done to him, he actually went inside the closet. You can believe I locked him in there. The locks on our closets were on the outside of the doors. Once again, Jackie showed that while his sight was impaired, his lungs were not. He began to bellow.

He did that for two hours. And I don't know why. I mean, I know it was dark in there, but he was blind anyhow. That seemed like obvious logic to me, but not to Old Lady Haroldson, who gave me my third and final beating for the day.

My overriding childhood prayer was to get away from that hateful old wheeze bag. And the prayer seemed answered, at the end of second grade, when I graduated out of her jurisdiction. But when I returned to school in the fall, I discovered that Governor Morehead's answer to Nurse Rachett had been transferred to another dormitory—mine. Old Lady Haroldson would be my housemother for two more years.

I've recently been assured that the outlandish disciplinary tactics at Governor Morehead are a thing of the past, and that students today are punished by a reduction of privileges, not by beatings.

Four months after I arrived at the school, I went home to Homer and Phenia for Christmas vacation. I made two trips there each academic year, including one for summer vacation.

Homer would send me a bus ticket, and the school gave me 25 cents and two sandwiches. The food, and money to buy more, were gone on the first of what was a two-day trip. A few other Governor Morehead students began the trip with me, but as we proceeded, they got off, one by one, and eventually my predicament became one I always dreaded. Because I had the farthest to go, I would be left riding with strangers, alone, except for an occasional kind driver who might give me a snack or make small talk.

Sometimes, a driver would take me to a bathroom on a stop. There were no restrooms on the coaches, and I'd try to limit my liquids before taking off.

I went down the road reciting the names of the fifteen towns on my first day's travel. I had to be sure to get off in Asheville. There, I'd enter a station where I'd be left by myself in the middle of the night—in the middle of a towering and hollow stopover. The later it became, the more quiet it became.

Then I heard noises.

The station was so large, and the late crowd so small, conversation seemed like a muffled undertone. It was an auditory paradox—I wanted people to speak up, as long as they didn't speak to me. I was afraid to sit there, but more afraid to move. I'd grow weary, but that too produced fear. I couldn't go to sleep. I might miss my morning call for the next bus home. So I took a place by the ticket counter, thinking that the amplified announcement to board would awaken me if I dozed off.

I was alone in a strange place. Talk about loneliness. I felt it then in a way I can't even explain today.

At times, my sense of isolation and dislocation was so pronounced, I even longed for the familiarity of Governor Morehead.

Occasionally, someone would play a jukebox. Sometimes the familiar tunes were consoling, giving me a sense of place, as they were songs I had heard on the radio at school. But the foremost sound overnight at the Asheville station, to me, was the sound of silence.

I was six years old the first time I sat by myself from 11:30 p.m. until 7:30 a.m. on layover. I was motionless, talking quietly to myself and to God, only sure that one of us was listening. Controlling my imagination in the terminal's stale hollowness was difficult. I felt swallowed by that awesome spaciousness. I dislike giant rooms to this day.

That night, a stranger ran his hands up and down my limbs, feeling my pockets for valuables. When you can't see, something like that is terrifying at any age. On a later trip, a man mugged me for my tiny portable radio.

There were six cities on the second day's route. On that trip, I often fell asleep, losing the battle I'd fought for almost twenty-four hours. By then, I was safe on the correct coach. I could rely on the driver to awaken me.

I resumed my task of reciting the names of the towns. I can still call them in order, those twenty-one milestones between Raleigh and Topton, North Carolina, where Homer would be waiting to take me home.

Those journeys were another part of my education, nights alone in a smelly old bus terminal with transient people who asked me for money and companionship. Many had time on their hands and whiskey on their breaths. Today, parents wouldn't let a small child ride across town on a city bus. But I was a solitary six-year-old traveler on a 400-mile journey too young for the adult world he was thrown into.

But I told myself it was all right. In three days, it would be Christmas. And in three weeks, I would be seven.

4

There is another cliché about country entertainers. Besides their backgrounds of poverty, many have roots in fundamentalist religion. I am no exception.

Religion has been as much or more of an influence on me than music. Because I combined the two, my thoughts were as often ruled by the Baptist church's teachings as they were expressed through songs.

No concert I've ever witnessed (including the Beatles'), no matter how many thousands of people have attended, has held the pulsating excitement I felt as a child in tent revivals and church house meetings.

There aren't many places left where people get as passionate about their faith as they did in the rural Smokies forty years ago. The mountain churches were called "shoutin' churches." Today, it's hard to get people to tell you their religious beliefs. Back then, it was impossible to keep people quiet, as they cheer-led the preacher through his sermons with shouted encouragement.

No Hollywood director or Broadway producer has ever harnessed the drama that came from God's Bible-thumping ambassadors in yesterday's south. No disrespect is intended when I say those men were one-man revues.

They had a charisma unmatched by modern politicians. Whether or not you believed them, it was impossible to ignore them. You didn't listen to a charged-up, country Baptist preacher passively. The preacher arrested your attention and emotions with little more than the power of vocal inflections. His voice would fall to a whisper, then explode to a bellow, and all with audio punctuation worthy of an actor.

Whether or not it was good teaching, there is no disputing it was high drama.

Neil Diamond had a hit record titled, "Brother Love's Traveling Salvation Show." There is a line in that song, referring to the type of thunderous speaker I'm describing, that says, "and when he spoke, the whole valley shook."

That isn't much of an exaggeration.

I'd listen to those men rail their sermons, stomping back and forth across the platform. They'd scream warnings about hell so convincingly, you could almost feel the heat. About every ten minutes, the preacher would scoop a dipper of water from a bucket and gulp it down with such force, it's a wonder he didn't strangle. He'd be in such a hurry to get that water down so he could get right back to preaching.

He'd shout out his sentences with little time for inhaling. When he finally took a breath, he was nearly suffocating on his feet, and his desperate intake of air sounded like a tornado bolting into his lungs. Each breath was gasped as if it were his last. Then he'd go right back into another thirty-second sentence that would deplete him of oxygen. His shirt would be wet with sweat, tears, and the drinking water he had excitedly sloshed all over himself. He'd jump from the platform and land two or three rows into the aisle. The congregation would heat up to a fevered pitch, and people leaped from their pews and ran and danced and collided.

Those people didn't just *go* to church. They *had* church.

It was a social as well as a spiritual center for the poor mountain people. After all, there was no admission fee. People put what they felt they could afford into the offering plate. No one tried to extract a pledge from them, as they do now in modern churches. All the members knew each other, and their kids. They knew who had a mare about to foal, and who needed help painting his barn. And they responded. Church was a place to open your soul and take off your shoes.

In fact, about every two months at my church, there were "foot washing" services. The members removed each others' shoes and socks. They literally washed their neighbors' bunion- and corn-covered feet. They did that because Jesus had washed the feet of His disciples. Can you imagine people in today's sophisticated cathedrals being so humble they would remove each others' Gucci shoes and Dior socks to bathe each others' pedicured feet?

Those mountain folks took their religion seriously. Very seriously. At a time when 10,000 American soldiers were fighting the communist encroachment in Korea, one churchgoer cut off the little news we received about the war by demolishing a neighbor's new television with a hammer. His reason was that God didn't mean for man to have something so mysterious as moving pictures inside a cabinet. The television was worldly and, therefore, sinful.

I can't remember when I didn't attend the Meadow Branch Primitive Baptist Church. It was a pine-framed, rectangular structure heated by a wood stove with a solitary vent pipe through the roof. Meadow Branch is a valley community in the middle of the mountains and the church rests at about the lowest point in the valley, making the white, simple, sun-bleached building the community centerpiece.

During summertime, when mountain air was heavy and unstirring, the one-room sanctuary was cooled by the breeze that came off hand-held fans, donated by the Townson-Smith Funeral Home. The soft sighs from the paper fans stirred the aromas that were as much a part of the church house as the hymns.

There was the sweet-sour smell of varnish. It had been spread layer after layer, year after year, on wooden pews where rowdy farm boys carved their initials with pocket knives. There was the scent of dime store after-shave that failed to cover body odor among the hard-working members. And there was the scent of spearmint gum. Where was it ever written that country Baptists must chew spearmint? I smelled so much spearmint in my young life that I can't stand it today.

The church didn't really have a *pastor*. "Pastor" implies someone on full-time salary, whose main task is calling on people in the membership. We had *preachers*. Many had no ordination from any denomination. Many had no formal biblical training. They instead occupied the pulpit because they said God told them to do it; they said they were "called to preach."

And during sermons, they'd tell you what God had told them to tell you—and sometimes it was about you and your wicked ways. They didn't pull any punches. Those preachers preached what big-city churches later would call a "negative Gospel." Their message was built on fear. If you feared God enough, you'd repent of your sins, which otherwise were going to send you to live in a lake of fire for the rest of eternity.

"And eternity," whispered the preachers, "is like a circle. It never ends."

Talk about terrifying! Was all that the real Gospel, or just scare tactics equivalent to God's ghost stories? I've since wondered many times what that preaching and teaching did to my fragile self-esteem. My mother had told me, just a few years earlier, that I was responsible for my blindness, and for the shame she felt because of it. Now, the preacher, an early role model in my life, was regularly telling me that I was vile and evil, and so much so that I was going to go to hell!

I suspect I didn't have a very good impression of myself by the age of seven.

If your only exposure to fundamentalist preachers has been the smooth guys on cable television, you have no idea what a fire-eating evangelist is really like.

And to a small boy, it was fearful but fascinating.

I had a trait then which I retain today. I wanted to do what I enjoyed seeing others do. So I became a preacher.

Not to people—but to roosters. I'd stand on a tree stump and tell the roosters and chickens in our yard that they were going to hell if they didn't change their bad ways. Look where that rooster that attacked me ended up. He'd been warned.

I'd shake and shout and really get into it, just like the loud and angry preachers in church. Stuck on that stump, I didn't have enough room to run around the way the real preachers did. So I just jumped up and down. At real church, the believers would shout "Amen" and run about in the aisles. In the barnyard, the chickens would squawk and run. At church, the sweat would fly. In my open-air meetings, feathers flew.

My preaching probably was my first performance. Only for me, it wasn't performing, because I believed entirely in the things I had been taught in church; the doctrine might not have always been sound, but it was always intense. There is no denying its heavy appeal to emotion.

If I had raised then the religious questions I would have later in life, I would have been scolded by church leaders for letting the devil get into my head.

If I so thoroughly believed the *fearful* teachings of the church, imagine how much I believed the *positive* teachings. For me, the teaching was the most positive and optimistic that any could be. It told me I was going to see. It said God was going to heal my blindness, just as He healed in the New Testament. Now, as then, I'm ready for it.

At a time when television was still relatively foreign, when the only mass communication was static-ripe AM radio, as many as 10,000 mountain people got the notice of a revival under way, and turned out to congregate inside the tent tabernacles. Today, that's a sizable crowd under a roof. Under a canvass, it was a mob.

And so they came, distant relatives, or pious parishioners from the church, to take me far away to the electrifying tent revivals. I'd get up early, happily squirming as Phenia dressed me in my best, preparing me for the motor trip I wouldn't see, and the return trip I expected I would. I truly believed I was off to be healed of the one impairment that kept me from being like everybody else.

Even before we got out of Meadow Branch, the journey became an event. All the way to the tent meeting the adults would tell me what a glorious day this was. There were drivers from Robbinsville, Murphy, Meadow Branch and towns and hamlets throughout the county, and they all wanted to chauffeur me to the receiving of my sight. Most often, we'd stop for hot dogs and then maybe ice cream. Those people knew how to give a poor child from the Appalachians high hopes. En route to each service, my eyes might not have worked, but my smile was just fine.

Trips to those services were enthralling: glorious days of picnics, parties, and prayer, with sight itself as the promised climax!

Emotions ran as high as the temperature inside those congested tents. The dancing feet of believers stirred the sawdust, spread as a makeshift floor over dirt.

There were no windows. When the tent flaps were down, no air circulated and the sawdust seemed to hang in the steamy summer air. You can imagine how the collective body heat of thousands dancing and clapping to the music in front of their folding chairs turned the tent into a sprawling sauna.

There were the crippled on crutches, and sick folks on cots.

People pointed the way for the deaf, and the healing line was formed. All around me the confusion of blaring music and crying believers swirled. The preacher screamed above it all, asking, *ordering*, the devil to leave the afflicted alone and let them be healed. "BE HEALED!" the evangelist commanded. Some of those he prayed for fell at his touch. One preacher gripped my head and pressed his fingers hard into my eyeballs. He shook my head so hard, it was like having prayer from Old Lady Haroldson.

My fantasy was that I would step over the fallen, inching closer and closer to my turn at the front of the line, where I awaited Jesus to heal me too. When He did, I would help up some of the people who fell. I'd see my way back to them.

But to this day, I haven't seen a thing. There were others at those meetings who claimed deliverance from infirmities. There were reports of the lame being "made" to walk. There were accounts of crippled limbs straightening before people's eyes. But it was always other people's eyes.

If you're among the millions of people in the free world who were never taught that Jesus Christ, in this century, can heal miraculously, you might wonder how a reasonably intelligent person could honestly expect some kind of heavenly magic would make his body whole.

But if you're among the millions who grew up in a fundamentalist Christian church, you know that my expectations for healing were not unusual. We were taught that God could heal, just as surely as we were taught that Jesus Christ died for our sins. How many of us question what we're taught when we're young, especially if we're also taught that the questioning is sinful?

I couldn't have been more sincere in my expectations, but sincerity wasn't enough for some of the good people who took me to the meetings. The same folks who drove me to healing crusades in a mood of celebration drove me home in anger. They said it was my fault God hadn't healed me. And they didn't appreciate it.

"If you had enough faith," they said, "you'd have been healed. God doesn't like little boys who don't believe in Him. It's your fault you weren't healed."

Eyes that couldn't make sight could make tears. I felt once again that it was my fault that I couldn't see. I experienced once again some of the most hardened cruelty of my life in the name of Christianity.

I can remember riding for hours in the backseat of some old car after those services. Mile after mile passed without a word. The silence was as thick as my spirits were low. Finally, I'd muster my courage and ask to stop for hot dogs or ice cream, as we'd done en route to the healing service.

Each time, the answer was the same.

"You don't deserve a hot dog, 'cause you didn't get healed," the driver would snap. "God didn't make ice cream for children who don't believe He can heal."

Not everyone in Graham County who took me to healing crusades, and certainly not everyone in my church, would have agreed with that condemnation. But undergo it I did, and eventually, my self-hatred compounded. I hated my blindness. I hated me for being blind.

Through the years, I came to reconcile my blindness, and the spiritual attention it got me, by coming to an understanding of the people who took me to healing meetings. They didn't take me so I'd be able to see the world. They took me hoping the world would see them as noble people. Maybe they did want God to get the glory for my healing. But they wanted the credit for arranging the glory. Then they'd really look like good Christian people for taking little Ronnie Milsap, whose grandparents had no car, all the way across the state to be healed. They wanted me to have sight. And they wanted my sight to make them look good.

I'm not going to say that I don't believe in divine healing. I think I do. Perhaps it's because I believe in much of the Bible and the reports of dramatic healings. And there are childhood teachings that I, like most people, will never entirely outgrow.

While I believe in some healings, I also believe they've been few and far between. Most of the healings with which I've had personal encounters are probably more in the person's mind than they are in the affected part of the body.

So each healing service ended the same way: with the "well-meaning" people taking me back to the unconditional love of Homer and Phenia. God bless them, their hearts were unaffected by my eyes.

And I always went back to church services, twice on Sundays, and on some weeknights, and every night, during summer revivals. I didn't leave the church until I left home permanently.

Once I was threatened with excommunication, but I was allowed to remain in church because I was blind, and because the church "utilized" my blindness.

The preacher made a big deal out of my blindness when he pitched Heaven as an eternal home. He needed me as a sales tool for a spiel that went something like this:

"Friends, we're going to call him up here to play and sing for you now."

His words, in a voice dripping with compassion, were my cue to head for my guitar.

"And friends ... he can't ... he can't see like you ... like you and me," he'd continue, his emotion still heavy, his volume building.

"But one of these days," he'd promise, his voice now nearly a shout, "one of these days, he'll walk those golden streets of glory with you and me! ..."

By now the churchgoers were shouting, themselves. The preacher really had to scream, just to be heard above the scores of other screamers.

"And when he walks those golden streets ... I said, when he walks those golden streets! he'll see just like you and me!" Then in a deafening blast, the preacher promised the nearly hysterical gathering "... He'll see, 'cause someday he'll have ... don't you know he'll have ... *eyes!*"

The place, by then, was total bedlam, screaming for Jesus and my eyes. You could have hollered, "Let's hear it for eyes ... anybody's eyes," and kept the ovation going.

When he bellowed "*eyes!*," it was like shouting "FIRE!" in a crowded theater. The response was no less enthusiastic.

This spoken routine became a ceremony. Each time the people heard it, they responded with all the excitement of the first time. The crowd threw their emotions and sometimes even a few of those funeral-home fans.

Years later, I realized that they wouldn't have put me out of that church, despite the threats. I was too necessary for the theatrics of the services.

Bible scholars agree that when Jesus Christ was twelve it was His "year of decision." Mine too.

It was at the end of a church service like any other. I had sung my song after the preacher had given his supercharged routine about me being blind but someday seeing the streets of gold. The preacher was pleading as he always did for people to accept Jesus into their hearts.

Suddenly, I felt compelled to walk to the altar where I'd sung hundreds of times. The persuasion that had made little sense to my mind suddenly was pulling my heartstrings. I approached that old wooden prayer rail while the congregation quietly sang "Softly and Tenderly, Jesus is Calling," an altar-call standard. And as surely as I did it, I'll tell you it was the most pleasurable thing I've ever done.

I've felt the excitement of having recorded more number-one records for RCA than any artist in history, and I thank God for that. I've felt the satisfaction of rising from poverty to prosperity through a life-wrecking climb. But I made it. I've won more Grammy awards than any other male country singer, and I thank Heaven humbly for that too. I could go on here indefinitely about all the colossal things which have moved me to soul-jarring emotions, but none would compare with the indescribable joy I felt the night I asked Jesus Christ to become my personal savior.

People ask me today if I believe in God. The answer is yes. Do I talk to Him? Definitely. Do I ask His help? I sure do. Do I still go to church? Rarely.

Instead, I make too many excuses about not attending. I once went to a Nashville church and because I'm a supposed star, a word I hate, I wound up getting as much or more attention than the minister. My presence was disruptive and I left. So, there's an excuse. Another time, I visited a church on a Sunday and by Wednesday someone from that organization came by to ask me for a $50,000 donation. There's an excuse. When I travel to do weekend concerts, I don't get up in time to attend, and I use the excuse that my bus driver is weary. He needs his rest to drive us to the concert safely. I have no shortage of excuses for not going to church.

So I remind myself that the "church" is the body of Christ. That's not the same as the church house, a place I don't really have to attend in order to worship, or to maintain my relationship with Jesus Christ.

That explanation appeases me. But it doesn't satisfy me. There is, at times in my soul, a void that knows no schedule. I've felt it in front of 10,000 people. I've felt it in the wee hours, lying fitfully in the back of my touring bus with no idea in what state of the union I'm traveling through. But that feeling finds me.

And when that subtle, gnawing presence comes, with its mixture of loneliness and guilt and sadness, I sometimes think about the Gospel that still goes forth, long after Herod tried to kill the baby Jesus 2,000 years ago, and after the sexual scandals rocked the Christian community in 1988.

There has to be something to a belief that can survive such assaults for twenty centuries. I only have to think back thirty-four years to my own conversion to know that it's real. And I tell myself that any peace I miss on earth will be made up for, if there is a heaven.

Because if there is a heaven, I'm going. And if the streets really are paved with gold, I'll see them, because of what I learned in a little country church.

On June 8, 1988, I re-entered the Meadow Branch Primitive Baptist Church for the first time in twenty-nine years. I had to send for someone to unlock the door that was always open in my youth. Forty-eight hours earlier, there had been thirty-five people at a Sunday service, where they contributed $108.00. It's safe to assume that there is still no full-time, paid pastor overseeing the largest building and its people in Meadow Branch, North Carolina.

The day I returned to the little church, I walked, as I had almost three decades earlier, across the platform. It had been remodeled like most everything else in the sanctuary. The wood floor had been covered with carpet.

The pocketknife initials now lay beneath upholstery on the pews. The windows that once were open to the sounds of insects buzzing and cows mooing along with the song service had been closed.

The building now has central air conditioning. The place smelled new and tidy and modern.

For an instant, I found myself wishing for the aroma of sweat and spearmint.

5

I think the biggest difference between city life and rural life is that the latter is more personal. A country resident feels an involvement with neighbors that breeds a sense of "family."

Urban life certainly has numerous advantages, but, in the city, people belong to organizations. In the country, people belong to each other.

Recently I returned to western North Carolina and was driven, for the first time in eight years, through the mountains by Robbinsville grocery store owner Ray Green. He drove along winding blacktop roads past the mountain homes I knew as a child, and he'd say, "Now here is where old so and so lives. Course he died in '79."

A few yards farther he'd say, "Now we're passing old so and so's place; course he's dead, too."

It seemed like the majority of houses "belonged" to people who had died. But in the loyal mind of Ray Green, as well as in the minds of most rural Smoky Mountain inhabitants, one is dead only in the sense that he's in his grave. In memory, he remains alive. Since memories never die in the mountains, the people, in a figurative way, live forever.

In the minds of the people from my childhood, my boyhood home will always be the Homer Frisby place, no matter how many times the house changes ownership. If John Doe bought it and moved in, the area folks would say, "Have you met John Doe yet? He lives in Homer Frisby's house."

Maybe that clinging to the past is unwise. But in a day when disloyalty is too common too often, I find it somehow refreshing.

The last time I visited, in June 1988, they told me that roses and cherry trees had overtaken Homer's old place. Inside, there was a baseball cap whose logo read, "Ronnie Milsap." I'll never know who put that there. Homer had been gone from that cabin a long time before my name was a souvenir to anybody.

Someone handed me the cap, I held it, and left it for the next person who might visit a house that was once a warm and loving home that's now a falling down shanty.

"Then the cap will be here for you the next time you come," joked Tom Corley, my publicist.

"No it won't," I said. "Because I'll never be back here in *my* life."

Months later, when that was read to me, my own words were somehow haunting.

As a lad, I loved to hear Homer and other old timers spin stories about the goings on in those mountains.

Storytelling is an unaccredited art in the backwoods of the Smokies. The old men told yarns in a hypnotic way that bred a magic modern youngsters will never know. There is nothing more vivid than the human imagination. Those wise and seasoned storytellers knew how to tap it.

At day's end, the old men sat on a front porch, waiting for dark. Then their voices would fall to a whisper. Their tones implied they were letting you in on something. It was intimate. Chirping crickets and katydids became background to the spoken soliloquies.

They'd tell of laying the railroad through the Smokies fifty years earlier, of mysterious ordeals that defied logic or natural law. I hung on every word when they spun plots about the most feared and murky subject of all to a small child—death.

My grandmother Phenia told a story about the death of one of her own children, and how the child reappeared to her as an apparition. It seems Phenia was down at the springhouse (a shelter built over the place where one takes water from a mountain spring). As she filled the five-gallon buckets, she heard the deafening sound of rushing wind. She raised her eyes to the heavens where she saw June, her four-year-old boy. He had been dead for five years. Phenia had that experience twice.

If Phenia had ever lied, or even exaggerated, I could dismiss her vision. I've tried to anyhow, surmising that on two occasions a grief-stricken mother heard a jet airplane pass overhead, looked into the sky, and was mistaken in what she saw. But how many jets were flying in the late 1940s? How many of those had a flight path over rural, western North Carolina? What's the likelihood of two jets flying over western North Carolina on two different occasions when Phenia was standing in the same spot? And how many mothers, especially those with undying devotion like Phenia's, mistake the face of their own son?

Remember, I was brought up in a traditional church that taught that Jesus Christ was the same "yesterday, today, and forever," as the Bible says. The Old and New Testaments contain stories about people who reappear from the dead, including Jesus. Why would it have seemed unusual to me, in my innocent and unquestioning mind, that something divine or miraculous was under way.

I'm not saying I believe in the supernatural. But I am saying that, to this day, despite world travel, and success, and all the rest, I can't say that I disbelieve some of these things either. I just don't know.

I hated it when the storytellers stopped toying with my imagination and, one by one, walked into the night to their own cabins. I was usually so spooked by the time they left, I wouldn't have gone any-where without my grandparents. I hoped that something or somebody wouldn't "get" one of the old-timers as he walked through the black woods. I thought my grandparents and those old men must be the bravest souls in the world to leave our kerosene lamps and let darkness devour them.

Given the absence of basic hygiene in those mountains, there was a high infant mortality rate. No doubt some children caught simple colds, then got pneumonia and died when a penicillin shot would have saved a life.

There was a healthy belief in things spiritual and unexplainable back in those hills, whose people were uneducated and superstitious. The poor mountaineers had no opportunities for expanding their horizons. But being uneducated did not mean they were unwise, in-sensitive, or untalented. The older ones, especially the men, had a

captivating talent for telling spellbinding stories about anything unseen, from God to ghosts.

Homer was no exception. I had a hit song in 1983 titled "Stranger
in My House." Whenever I sing it, I think of the summer when I was
eight. For reasons I can't recall, Homer and I spent a night in what
was known around Meadow Branch to be a haunted house.

Now if Homer had simply told me that the place had ghosts, and
if he had laughed when he said it, I would have just thought it was
his own mountain mischief. But you must realize that mountain folks
had a very real belief in "haints."

There was a hit song of the 1960s, "Haunted House," and a line
that goes "ain't no haint gonna run me off."

A *ghost* was thought to be fictitious, something you talked about
but didn't believe in, like spooks or goblins. But a *haint* was a very
real but invisible thing, a spirit, a force whose intention was harm to
any mortal who intruded on its space.

Homer and I lay on the floor of that creaky and dusty old dump. I
thought I heard noises. I was sure of it when Homer said he heard
them too.

Seeing is believing, and blind people see with their ears, so I
believed what I was hearing. I believed I heard footsteps. I believed
I heard a door slam. Then I knew I heard an echo, and I did . . . the
echo of Homer's snoring.

I was certain my grandfather was going to wake up dead. How
could he sleep when I was so terrified?

I last saw Homer in the summer of 1988 shortly before his ninety-
third birthday. "Homer," I said, "I want you to meet Tom Carter; he's
helping me write my story, and he lives in New York City."

"Well why don't he move?" Homer said, without missing a beat.

It was 100 degrees outdoors that day, and Homer wore the thick,
mountain-cloth work uniform; I could feel that it was buttoned to his
wrists and neck.

Carter tried to strike up a rapport with my fiesty grandfather and
asked, "Homer, how far did you go in school?"

"I went all the way through," that creaky voice responded instantly.
"I went through the front door, then through the back."

He had six kids by three wives. He never drank, but had a part-
time income from making moonshine. He did go to school through

the fourth grade. He told me that he has no regrets about not extending his education.

"As long as I can read and write, that's all the book learning I need to know."

His son Vincent said Homer would often read the same *Playboy* magazine twice, and once he caught Homer with a woman in an embarrassing situation—when Homer was eighty-nine.

I'm revealing these things about him so people will have an understanding of the dominant male influence in my life, but please realize I wouldn't embarrass Homer for anything. I've said nothing that he wouldn't tell on himself. He has said things more unsettling than I've revealed, and he's told them in front of 10,000 people at my concerts.

He is proud of his prolonged sexual activity. He daily chews a Smoky Mountain herb called "ginseng," which the folks around Homer's house believe to be an aphrodisiac. Homer had a vegetable garden nearly all his life. The last time I saw him, he said he was too old to plant crops—but he had planted a small plot of ginseng.

When I asked Homer what was the happiest time of his life, he said it was when I was a boy and would say to him, "Homer let's go somewhere. Hold my hand and let's go."

I wish that he and I could go just once more. This time, I would hold his hand.

People who haven't been around grizzled old mountain men might resent Homer's rowdy directness. They might mistake it for insensitivity, but Homer, who otherwise won't be blasted out of the mountains, has left them in recent years to come to my shows. That was the biggest gesture of love for me he could show.

At one concert, I fell through a bank of amplifiers and could have been seriously injured. There were thousands of people on hand, but the first to reach me was Homer. He made sure I was all right. Then he yelled at the younger members of my band and crew. Why, he wanted to know, had they let him beat them to my side? Homer is a walking conflict of tenderness and toughness. He was always there to help me, but he had no hesitation about telling me tall and terrifying tales that made up my boyhood entertainment. I guess Homer thought that when I grew up I'd figure out that the stories were only stories. Everything worked out fine.

Homer and other mountain folks were fascinated by things they couldn't explain with their childlike logic. If they couldn't find a valid explanation, they'd make up one.

Mountain people also had an unshakable resistance to anything new they couldn't explain. Tradition was strong. Trends were short-lived.

I learned first hand of their opposition to enlightenment when I was eight. The faculty at Governor Morehead had taught me to read and write braille. The Meadow Branch old-timers knew that Homer Frisby's grandson was going all the way over to Raleigh to get book learning. Now how could a blind boy get book learning, they wondered aloud?

"I know he goes to that special school over there in Raleigh, but I wonder are they learning him anything?" I often heard one of them ask.

With the help of several passengers on the Trailways bus I managed to bring an eighteen-volume braille version of the King James Bible home from school one year. Each book was thick and heavy, like the enormous dictionaries in the center of library reference rooms.

One summer day, Homer and I carried those eighteen books the quarter mile down our mountain, then another quarter mile up the road to the Faset Jenkins Store.

If the Meadow Branch Primitive Baptist Church was the religious and social center of the community, then the Faset Jenkins Store was the commercial and cultural hub. Almost everybody in Meadow Branch shopped and visited there. Folks sat in hardback chairs in front of a woodburning stove, or in front of a screen door in the summertime. They whittled, and spit, and made hours of small talk about things that were big deals only in Meadow Branch.

That summer day, the big deal was little Ronnie Milsap and his books. The local talk went like this: "Why, poor little blind Ronnie thinks he can read. Isn't that sad for them to do a blind boy that a way?"

Gardner Williams thought there was something fishy or evil if unsighted Ronnie had it in his head that he could read. Gardner intended to straighten out the boy as much as he could before the confused lad went back to that school.

Gardner was one of several men at the store when Homer and I lugged in that eighteen-volume Bible.

"Now, son," Gardner said to me, his voice with an authoritative ring, "We know you think you can read these here books by touching the pages, 'cause that's what they told you in that school up yonder. So, son, why don't you just show your old friends who knowed you before you went to school; why don't you just show us how good you read them there pages."

I wonder if he winked as I opened the book.

At first, he asked me to read a familiar verse, John 3:16.

I placed my hand on the tops of the pages, as I had been taught, and felt my way in braille to the famous scripture. A hush fell over the skeptical onlookers.

"For God so loved the world," I began, sliding my fingers across the coded and raised portions of the pages that spelled sentences to me, "that He gave His only begotten son . . ."

"That's enough, son," Gardner injected, "Let's turn to another verse." I could hear him flipping through his Bible.

"See here now," he said, clearing his throat. "Read for us from second Samuel chapter 12, verse 4."

I'd wager he smiled at the others surrounding me.

"And there came a traveler unto the rich man," I began reading, "and he spared to take of his own flock and of his own herd, to dress for the wayfaring man that was coming unto him . . ."

"Stop!" shouted Gardner. The frustration from seeing what he wouldn't believe was rising in his voice. "I want to try the New Testament again. Read Revelation 5:5 right quick."

I turned the pages, and I read some more from the Bible. I went through my Biblical paces that afternoon for two hours, reading scriptures here and there, and entire chapters elsewhere. Methodically, I ran my fingers over the raised pages that were bumps to the sighted, but text to me.

I enjoyed being the center of attention. It was the first time I realized how truly fascinating my blindness was to the sighted. Some of them literally put their hands on the back of my hand as I moved it over the braille.

Gardner's fascination turned to anger.

"That's enough," he pronounced to the quiet gathering.

"It's just what I thought all along, folks. This here boy has got the whole Bible memorized! That's it, he's got it all memorized!"

And he really believed I did.

"Nobody could read just from feeling them there bumps on paper," he said. "Ain't no way they could have taught that to this here boy at that there school."

My reaction, which I was wise enough not to express to the closed-minded audience, was obvious. If the school had in fact made me memorize the entire King James Bible, the teachers had performed a bigger feat than the teaching of braille.

But that point would have been interpreted as insubordination by Gardner and the mountain folks. They would have thought that school had taken away my respect for my elders.

So I said nothing. Homer and I wrestled my eighteen-volume Bible back up the mountain, and Gardner had to wrestle with the truth he had resisted for an entire afternoon. There was a second lesson for me that day. I learned that eyes are not enough to see things as they truly are.

The Faset Jenkins Store is a fifty-two-year-old fixture of Meadow Branch. Before the community had asphalt roads, it had that one-stop store. The first patrons arrived in 1937 and parked horses and wagons to a hitching post outside. At a time when retail merchandising is more specialized than ever in this era of shopping malls and mail-order television, the honest people of Meadow Branch still trust Faset Jenkins for an honest deal. With his inventory geared to mountain needs, folks in Meadow Branch probably don't see any reason to shop elsewhere, even to this day.

Each summer until I graduated from high school, I was sent $96 by the state welfare department in three installments. It was my yearly clothing budget, and I spent it at the Faset Jenkins Store. It allowed me to buy two pairs of shoes, six pairs of Dee Cee overalls, and six shirts, and that was to last until the next summer's clothing check arrived.

Someone noted years later that my photograph is missing from yearbooks published by Governor Morehead when I was a boy. That's because I was embarrassed about my wardrobe and wouldn't let them take my picture. My face didn't appear in the class photos until I was in high school and earned enough money tuning pianos to subsidize my welfare clothing allowance.

I recently returned to the Faset Jenkins Store and found Dee Cee trousers still for sale. A country store is more than a retail outlet in a rural area. It's also a museum exhibiting everyday needs for everyday people. Faset Jenkins still uses bare light bulbs, and his store still has the half-century-old original wood floor, spotted from oil drops, cigarette burns, and tobacco spit.

In one, time-worn room, you can select fishing tackle and underwear, children's toys, ax handles, hair oil, and diarrhea treatment.

There are all kinds of canned goods, which can be opened with P-38 can openers (also for sale at Faset Jenkins'). The P-38 was a government issue to American soldiers during World War II for opening C rations. Faset Jenkins still sells them today, along with scores of other useful, but historic, American aids to better living, Meadow Branch style.

And, not for sale, there are a dozen photographs of Ronnie Milsap. The little boy that once sat in his store is now a picture on the wall. Country folks really don't forget their own, in failure or fame. It's just another affectionate indication of the mountain folks' desire to cling to tradition.

It was that love for tradition, no matter how innocently rooted, that proved to be an almost impossible obstacle to me and my music. I didn't know it, but I had a wonderful future in music. If some folks had gotten their way, my future would have stayed forever in my past.

6

My childhood, unusual in many ways, was also as ordinary as any little boy's love for fishing and apple pie. For example, I had, with every other grade-school male, a crush on a schoolteacher.

In the first or second grade, a teacher represents motherhood and leadership to boys who are still more dependent on the female than their young and fragile prides will let them admit.

As grownup men recall their first schoolboy crush, it is almost always linked to the teacher who encouraged their foremost interest at the time, whether it was baseball cards or basic mathematics.

My crush was normal, innocent, and healthy. Her name was Miss Collinge. I would have liked to take an apple to her. In fact, I would have liked to take an orchard. She was my very first piano teacher. I was on the verge of developing a true passion for piano. Miss Collinge recognized that, and had the professional wisdom and personal interest to foster it. She took an individual interest in her budding student in a way not often found in public or private schools today. I think a lot of the disciplinary and drug problems that haunt contemporary education could be lessened if students felt a human touch from teachers. The best way to teach is to make the student feel you're sharing, not just supervising, his interest. Miss Collinge did exactly that.

She didn't actually introduce me to piano. I had first touched a piano two years earlier, when I was six, in Robbinsville. But she was the first to take my keyboard intuition seriously.

I have learned to play a dozen instruments in my life, including classical violin. There was no piano in Homer's house back in Meadow Branch, so I took up guitar. It was inexpensive and portable. But piano would become my instrument of choice—88 keys that were stepping stones to the world. People who knew I played guitar wondered why I didn't feature it. It was so popular in the '50s and '60s.

But for me, piano is my priority for two reasons. One was my first piano teacher, for whom I would have done anything to win acceptance. I'm glad she taught piano and not bone flute. I might have become a singer who couldn't accompany himself. I might have hyperventilated trying to please her. Two, I like the piano because it's a big instrument and easy for me to find. I joke about that in my stage show, but there is an element of truth in it. The piano's size is a landmark I can pivot from on stage when I walk or dance.

Miss Collinge lived on campus at Governor Morehead. She stayed in an apartment next door to Old Lady Haroldson. "The Beauty and the Beast" side by side.

Day and night, whenever she had her chance, Old Lady Haroldson would maintain her declared war against males between infancy and puberty. She should have abandoned education. She would have had a stellar career as a bounty hunter.

But in the evening, for perhaps an hour, my world couldn't be penetrated by Attila the Hun's sister. I was safe in the group tutelage of my piano teacher. Every word of wrath I heard from Haroldson was overshadowed with sentences of praise from the pianist. Miss Collinge taught piano by day and read children's stories to us at night, and every little boy in that room pretended she was reading them especially to him. Once I was so touched by her reading of the children's version of *Pilgrim's Progress,* that I shyly kissed her on the cheek at the end of the story. Old Lady Haroldson saw me and told me never to do that again, adding that such behavior "just wasn't done." For her, I'll bet it never was, and that might explain a lot.

Miss Collinge was a master of motivation. I lived to please her, and there was no better way to please her than through my piano. She taught me to read music in braille. That, however, didn't affect my "ear" for melodies. I absorbed the lovely selections she gave me. But I was determined to play for her the kind of music that had grabbed my attention through the radio long before I ever heard the word "piano." So I learned to play "Down Yonder" with two hands, and I played it for her.

It blew her away.

She had taught me, the first week in her class, to play chords with my left hand and melody with my right. That meant moving my left hand fast and moving arpeggios up and down the keyboard. A lot of piano players don't play that way today.

I'll never forget how fast I progressed after she put Robert Boone, Larry Atwell and me on a piano bench. One played the bass line, another the melody, and another the chords. I thought, "What if I could learn to do all of that myself?"

I did, and the result was the recital I would give for my one-woman audience, my piano teacher. One of the few remaining career goals I have today is to play in legendary Carnegie Hall in New York City. I will, and when I do, it surely won't be as thrilling as my debut of "Down Yonder" for Miss Collinge.

One day at school, when I was seven, a list was announced of those who were to study violin: "Nancy Sports, Larry Atwell, and Ronnie Milsap."

No one ever asked us if we wanted to study violin. We were just told to do it.

But the instruction was invaluable. The violin is a complicated instrument. To learn it is to learn skills and technique that can be applied to so many other stringed instruments.

There is an old country song, laced with a narration, entitled "Touch of the Master's Hand." The song is a corny thing about an old fiddle for sale at an auction. The auctioneer could not get a bid for the instrument. At last, an old man walked to the front of the auction. He was too poor to bid on the instrument, but he picked it up and began to play. The ancient fiddle gave off celestial music to a spellbound crowd. The moral of that fairytale is that a great difference can be made by the touch of a master on things that are otherwise imperfect.

That song could have been written about Wallace Grieves, my violin teacher at Governor Morehead. He, of course, did not play country fiddle. He played the classics, and he played them magnificently. More importantly, he inspired others to want to play the same way. I'm convinced he could have taught elsewhere, perhaps at a music college or graduate school. But, for whatever reason, he chose to teach at Governor Morehead. He, like Miss Collinge, had that indescribable technique for making students want to do their best. He knew how to extract excellence, and if I could pinpoint how he did it, I would say it was through instilling discipline.

He had a wooden board on his classroom wall. It listed three categories of performance. The worst was a silly listing called "loafing at the drugstore." If a kid hadn't been practicing, Mr. Grieves could detect it immediately and enter the student's name as one who had been "loafing at the drugstore." Something that trite wouldn't have worked on students who weren't serious about their study. But Mr. Grieves knew how to instill that kind of seriousness.

I can remember his taking my fingers and situating them on the violin's neck, which seemed strangely smooth without the frets. He had the patience of Job when he thought you were trying to learn. When he thought you weren't trying, he'd become exasperated. He'd preface his frustration with one syllable—"Aye"—and then go into whatever was on his mind.

I earned "A's" in his classes, which prepared me for the orchestra, where I earned "C's." I know that doesn't make sense, but there's an explanation. In class, with the benefit of his one-on-one instruction, I was more than serious about the music. But in orchestra rehearsal, where there were other kids, I would cut up to the point of distracting the group. I would sit in rehearsal with my violin, and later my cello, and while Mr. Grieves was giving an instruction about a classical movement, I would play "I Walk the Line" by Johnny Cash. You know the famous "boom-chicka-boom" riff Cash plays on electric guitar, his signature sound that gives his tunes the driving rhythm? You ought to hear those same licks on a cello. Shall we say the instrument and the riffs aren't made for each other?

But they did make for some real laughter among the classical music students. I got laughs, attention, and Mr. Grieves' disappointed reprimands—along with the C grades I mentioned. Later in life, I thought about the quality of instruction I was so flip about then. I regret my youthful shenanigans. I learned a lot from Mr. Grieves. But I could have learned a lot more if I hadn't been showing off in front of my peers.

I became, in fourth grade, first-chair violinist under Mr. Grieves and then similarly accomplished on cello. He was a master of the English language, and his speech went naturally with his dignified demeanor. I think his sheer "class" was commensurate with his talent.

I last saw him in October 1986, when I went to visit him and his wife, Betty. When I walked into their house, he exclaimed "Aye," and I could hear emotion grip his voice. He's in his nineties now. In that masterful English, he said he couldn't believe I had come to see him. I couldn't believe I had stayed away so long.

When I was eight, during my summer vacation, I picked up the guitar owned by my Uncle J.C. I was able to transpose the high-brow music I'd been taught by Mr. Grieves. I applied the lessons to three-chord hillbilly songs.

Boy, was that fun! Not only was I learning to play the music I liked best, but in a roundabout way, I was getting back at the school and its strictness. I wonder how my instructors would have reacted, after working to teach me Mozart and Beethoven, if they had learned I was applying their lessons to Hank Williams and Ernest Tubb songs?

With the advent of rock 'n' roll just around the corner, I'd soon be reproducing Elvis Presley, Jerry Lee Lewis, and Carl Perkins. The friction really hit the fan over that.

The first time I got into trouble for my music was with my daddy. He was a true music fan, but his tastes barely went beyond bluegrass music. He, like so many rural, white southerners at the time, just didn't know what to make of this new music called "rock 'n' roll." They didn't understand how white singers could sound so black, and didn't understand why they would want to. So the rural mountaineers did what people have done for centuries when they don't understand something. They lashed out against it.

Their spoken assaults against the chord changes and tempo were scathing. The adults called it the "devil's music," "jungle music," "sissyboy music," and more. My daddy just growled that it was "that fancy music." A lot of kids in Meadow Branch were punished just for listening to it. There was greater punishment for the one kid who played it.

My daddy had seizures when he was upset. Today, people talk about epilepsy and its treatment as commonly as they discuss heart disease. But in 1956, in the Smoky Mountains, epilepsy was a dark subject not discussed.

Daddy always gave a shrill scream before his epileptic seizures. I compared the scream to a panther's in the night.

He couldn't stand Elvis Presley's music. I was consumed with it. I'd bang away during summers at home on J.C.'s guitar. Daddy would get furious and holler, "Stop playing that fancy music!"

I'd stand there silently for a moment, then ease into "Blue Moon of Kentucky," and Daddy would be fine. But one day, I didn't ease soon enough.

This one time, it must have been about 1956, I was really getting into Presley's "Heartbreak Hotel."

I hit a big chord and let fly the song's opening line.

"Well since my baby left me . . . ," I wailed.

"Don't do that," Daddy mumbled.

"I found a new place to dwell . . . ," I kept on singing.

"Don't do that, I said . . . ," and his voice tightened.

"It's down at the end of lonely street . . . ," I sang, really into it by then.

"I said don't do that . . . ," Daddy thundered.

"At Heartbreak Hotel . . . ,"

I never got to the chorus.

There was a deafening scream, and a crash, and then I heard his convulsions. It filled me with the gut-wrenching terror one feels only when a loved one is in trouble.

I laid down the guitar immediately and fumbled for a spoon for his mouth to keep him from swallowing his tongue. Elvis's version of that song had girls fainting all over the world; mine had my daddy passing out in our living room! But I still made no connection between his seizure and the stress that he underwent from his hatred of rock 'n' roll.

He never did get all the way through that number, and neither did I the two times he was around. I'd kick off the song, he'd mutter, I'd keep playing, he'd yell, I'd keep playing, and he'd pass out.

Both times, he slept for about three hours, during which I could have performed every rock song I knew, without interruption. But I was too upset and too mystified to do so. When I finally put together the correlation of rock 'n' roll with my daddy's epilepsy, I never sang the new music around him again.

*   *   *

The only piano I had access to in the summertime was inside the Meadow Branch Primitive Baptist Church. Well, rock 'n' roll wasn't entirely welcome there either.

It was a Tuesday afternoon. I was inside the church. It was never locked. A number of children and adults were there, and I was entertaining.

The songs were Bobby Darin's "Splish Splash" and Jerry Lee Lewis's "Whole Lotta Shakin'." The kids were clapping along, and I was really laying down that pumping piano style Lewis made famous.

There was a girl in the gathering, and her father was a deacon in the church. I don't know if someone asked her to dance, or didn't ask when she wanted them to, but she got mad, and then she went to get her daddy.

He burst through the church house door like the Schlitz Malt Liquor bull.

"What's going on in here?" he bellowed. "You ought to be ashamed! You play the Lord's music in this church on Sundays, then you play the devil's music today! I can tell you right now you're going to hell, and I won't allow you to play this music!

"How do you expect us to get these drunks to come to church to hear the Lord's music when you're playing the devil's music?" he went on.

Years later, I wondered if that was the problem: that I was outdrawing on Tuesdays the number of folks in church on Sundays? That's no swipe at religion, but he might have interpreted it that way. He was so devoted to his beliefs, he might have been threatened by the new music which he thought was a contradiction. Who knows? But I shouldn't have been in there playing secular music. He was a figure of authority, a man I'd known all my life. It upset me to upset him, and I ask, several decades later, that he accept my apology for being so inconsiderate about something that was so personal to him.

The outraged deacon put me out of the church that day and told me I would never play again at the Meadow Branch Primitive Baptist Church. But that punishment didn't hold.

I cannot stress too much that there were some wonderful people in Meadow Branch and in my church. Those folks are the salt of the earth. The country is full of kind folks who are nice just because it's their nature. I think immediately of Delmus McCray, a guy who un-expectedly climbed our mountain one day with a gift.

"I've been watching you sing and play at the church, and you play the guitar so good," he said. He handed me a new Gibson guitar that seemed big as an icebox. It was one of those jumbo guitars with a big hole in the middle. I was fourteen. I suspect that even back then it cost $200.

I remember hitting the first chord, an "A," and singing "Am I Losing You," the first line to a Jim Reeves classic. A quarter century later, I recorded that song as part of an album that was a tribute to Jim Reeves, and it originated with the first guitar I could call mine, given to me by a member of the Meadow Branch Primitive Baptist Church. Delmus never told anybody he gave me the guitar, and he asked me not to tell either. I guess it's all right to reveal it now.

My childhood was essentially a series of alternations. I spent three months during summer with well-meaning religious zealots. There were wonderful nights fishing and camping with Homer, and listening to the stories of the old men. Then there were nine months in that education heaven and disciplinary hell called the Governor Morehead School for the Blind.

This year-in, year-out routine lead to the independence of a mo-tivated child whose drive had probably already made him older than his years. By the time I was twelve, an age when kids are in sixth grade, I took off—intending never to return.

7

I remember the first time I smoked a cigarette. I was twelve. I was caught and threatened with expulsion from my school home. The administrators at the enlightened gestapo headquarters were going to withdraw forever my opportunity for an academic education. All my lifetime aspirations were going to go up in smoke because I had taken a puff.

Cigarette experimentation was as much a part of a 1950s boy's life as Western movies. I mentioned earlier that expulsion was a fate slightly less severe than death to a blind child in North Carolina. Being expelled literally meant the end of classroom education. No other school in the state would accept blind students.

I paced and worried for days about what I would do for a living, at twelve, after I was kicked out of school. A letter was sent to my daddy from the school officials. I'm sure he was panic-stricken too. He was often gone from home, searching for temporary work that always expired as fast as the salary it provided. If I had been sent back home, he wouldn't have been there to tend to me. And I dreaded the thought of disappointing Homer and Phenia.

For a few month-long days, I felt like a boy without a country. But I was given a second chance. I promised not to smoke again, and the administration promised to put me out for good if I did.

Smoking became legal at school when I turned fifteen, with parental permission. My daddy gave it, but smoking wasn't as much fun when I didn't have to sneak.

The year of my almost-capital smoking offense, the school gave us off-campus privileges. That represented my first venture into the world of the sighted (except back home in Meadow Branch). It was the first time for my friends and me to be in a minority. I remember the whispers as we walked into movie theaters, and I remember being seated in a special section at church.

It wasn't much longer after that that the school arranged for a man to come Thursday nights to cut our hair. Each student had a bowl placed on his head. Whatever hair protruded was sheered off.

We felt a little freakish. It was exactly the kind of assault on their appearance that kids, on the brink of becoming fashion-conscious teenagers, don't need.

The school often asked me to greet tourists who came through our tax-supported school (I was in eleventh grade by then). Many of the tourists, if not the majority, were public school students who wanted to observe the goings on at Governor Morehead.

Morehead students were regularly reminded that the state paid $1,400 a year to feed, house, and educate each of us. We were ordered to be grateful.

I was often selected to mingle with school visitors because my grades were good. I was well thought of by the faculty, which felt I'd be a good representative of Governor Morehead. I frequently was asked to field visitors' questions. I always accepted because I enjoyed being in the clique of students with good grades whose work was acknowledged by instructors.

I remember my astonishment at a few questions asked by curious tourists. One wanted to know how blind people kiss?

"Kiss?" I said. "Why, blind people don't."

I never cracked a smile, using my driest delivery. I wonder if she believed me.

Another asked how blind people eat? That one really primed me for some creative discourse.

I said the state supplied each of us a special plate with a thumb tack in its center. I said we tied a string to the tack and tied the other end to our front tooth, and then we sat upright, to tighten the string.

"Then we use our hand to guide our fork from the plate, along the string, to our mouth," I said. "When we're all finished, we wash our hands, and we never leave the string dangling from our front tooth."

That response brought laughter and put everyone at ease. Some of the questions may sound dumb, but many were tendered by sincere students from the outside who simply never had been around blind youngsters. I think a lot of us at Morehead were actually glad to mix with them, and to respond to their interest in us. My answers were not always sanctioned by the administration. But it was all in fun.

About this time, I found another place to apply my creativity. I meticulously, elaborately planned my departure from Governor Morehead. I'm not talking about commencement. My young mind was electrified at the thought of running away. So I began planning secretly, seven years before I would graduate. I must be honest and say that my running away was not entirely rooted in unhappiness with the school. The yearning to leave was based largely in the sheer fascination of doing so. It was an idea which had been growing for years, ever since Dean and Gene McGuire had unsuccessfully tried it when I was in third grade.

The McGuire twins were the "Little Rascals" of Governor Morehead. They were blood brothers (identical twins) who must have wanted proof because they tried to beat that blood out of each other almost nightly. They would wake up most of the dormitory with the crashing and screaming from their violent attacks on each other.

Each Morehead student owned a solid steel stylus similar to the scratch awls used by sheet metal workers. The stylus looked like an ice pick and was used to write braille.

The McGuire twins used them to stab each other. These sharp instruments could have easily poked out an eye, and if they had punctured a jugular vein, or maybe a temple, they would have been fatal. The twins' bodies often bore long scabs from ripping those sharp implements through each others' flesh.

Sometimes they laid down their hardware and picked up pillows, which they used to try to smother each other. When their fighting at last grew quiet, we wondered if one had killed the other.

There might have been a lot more bed-wetting at Governor Morehead were it not for the McGuires. Their wars awoke everybody, who then used the restroom. It was amazing how Old Lady Haroldson could hear me breathe, but never awakened to the floor-shaking free-for-alls of Dean and Gene McGuire.

The McGuires were the lads I selected as astute advisors for my great escape from Governor Morehead. I had heard them talk about sleeping under a bridge, and about hitchhiking during their foiled runaway. If they could do it, I surely could too.

To a kid whose whole world was an 80-acre campus, the thought of freely wandering the land was indescribably alluring.

So the planning began. Soon, I would be living off the land and loving it—Tom Sawyer minus the Mississippi River.

I huddled with co-conspirators Larry McCreary and Rex Spears. There was a fourth boy whose name I can't remember. We agreed to save our money. We made all kinds of secret plans about sleeping in barns. We'd ride our thumbs as far as they would take us. The whole thing was so exotic, we never concerned ourselves with spoilsport notions such as what we'd do when we ran out of money. We weren't thinking about minor things such as eating and lodging.

We also didn't give remote consideration to the fact that we might be conspicuous—four unescorted blind boys in the middle of rural North Carolina. The school had tried to make us independent. It had succeeded.

The excitement of figuring out the neat parts, and ignoring the practical parts of our trip, was more fun than the trip itself.

So on a Sunday afternoon in the spring, we calmly ate lunch, routinely strolled the campus, and casually walked away. I felt my feet leave the campus and touch the blacktop. I felt my heart enter my mouth.

We hadn't been gone five minutes when we were sure we were gone forever. This was literally a case of the blind leading the blind. And it was a blast!

We were so confident, that almost instantly we changed our master plan. Why hitchhike? The sun was shining. The birds were singing. The air was fresh. It was a beautiful day for running away. Who wanted to be cooped inside a stuffy old car?

So we walked, with no plans to continue, with no plans not to. I guess you could say this life-changing trip was casually planned.

Down the road we went, talking and laughing. We made fun of Old Lady Haroldson, and laughed about the time we stole her underwear, and we bragged about what we would say to old teacher so and so if she were here right now. After years of confinement, we became confident men of the world in minutes.

We walked twelve miles, all the way to Apex, North Carolina. Looking back, I can't believe that someone didn't stop to ask that quartet of young fugitives who they were. Instead, people just uncaringly passed us by. That was pleasing, until we wanted them to stop.

We must have been getting hungry, because I remember agreeing that it was close to suppertime, and that it was time to start hitchhiking. It was so cool to stand defiantly beside the highway with my thumb in the air. I got to enjoy the feeling a lot that day. Drivers kept passing me by.

Larry McCreary was the first to brush shoulders with reality.

"If nobody stops, and we're out here on this highway after dark, and we don't have food or a place to stay, what are we going to do?" he asked.

His question was answered only by the scraping of our soles against the blacktop. No one wanted to speak the truth we didn't want to hear. By then, some in the party were thinking it might have been a good idea to bring along a sandwich.

Yet, we continued. If there were thoughts of turning back, they remained thoughts, and never became words.

And then we heard it. The unmistakable sound of a motor vehicle slowing down as it approached our waving thumbs. A ride at last!

The screeching tires, in the space of an instant, erased the few hours' worth of fear. Suddenly, we knew that running away had been the right thing to do all along.

It seemed like a year before that vehicle actually pulled to a halt. I was listening so intensely, I heard the scraping of metal against metal when the driver applied his brakes. The vehicle stopped right in front of us. I pressed my face close to the idling machine. With my light vision, I could tell it was a car, and not a truck. I don't know why that made it more exciting.

We began to cheer out loud!

It was a car and it was going west—away from Raleigh! One of the most suspenseful moments of my life passed as I waited for the driver to invite us inside.

Instead, he got out.

His engine was running as we heard his car door slam. His footsteps were deliberate, and even on that open highway they seemed to echo. Their approach was like something out of an Alfred Hitchcock movie. They gradually came closer, closer to the stranded and helpless party of runaways.

What was happening? Who was this person? Why didn't he speak?

The next sound turned my blood to ice water. "Tsk, tsk, tsk." It was that disapproving sound parents make to naughty children.

Still, the stranger didn't speak. He could have been armed. Who was this person and what was he going to do? I felt my heart beating faster.

"Where do you boys think you're going?" came the voice at last.

Now, my heart almost stopped.

The voice belonged to Ted Stough, the principal at the Governor Morehead School for the Blind. We were caught! Busted! Just a few hours away from the school that we intended to leave for a lifetime.

Like the escapees we were, each of us was loaded into the idling car. With the dry wit of a warden, Stough broke the silence.

"Well, I guess you boys just ate lunch and then ran away, didn't you?" he said.

"No, we ate lunch and we walked," fired back Larry McCreary.

What a time to sass.

"Don't you get smart with me," Stough retorted.

Back at the school, virtually every privilege we had was revoked. We were forbidden from going to the school's modest student store called the "Nickel Nack." To the students, it was the equivalent of Macy's department store. I won't itemize all the punishments. Their longevity was more harsh than their nature.

Punishment was imposed for the rest of that school year and into the next.

Who knows what would have happened if Ted Stough, who later became one of my most respected teachers, had not found us aimlessly walking the highway that evening? Perhaps he saved us from being hit by a car. Perhaps he prevented our abduction in that isolated country, as rough as some of the people who inhabited it. But whatever Stough might have done, he certainly ended a flight of fancy we intended to take to the end of the earth.

Ted Stough was genuinely perplexed when he asked me why I did it. I was an honor student with training in music and industrial arts. He thought the whole thing was out of character for a model student.

I could never make him understand that model students like excitement too.

Looking back, I'm of course glad that Ted Stough found us. We were too strong-willed to ever have turned back by ourselves. The attempted escape was the biggest event of my twelfth year, and one of the most thrilling of my childhood. My only disappointment was that it was cut so short.

The next time I tried to leave that school permanently, I would be armed with a diploma.

8

By the time I was fourteen, I had developed a tremendous sense of family with Governor Morehead students. They were my brothers and sisters with whom, I felt, I'd been in bondage of sorts for eight years. Nothing brings people together like oppression, real or imagined.

My most life-altering incident resulted from my loyalty to friends and loved ones. It was March 1957, near the end of the school day. We were in study hall where some students were giggling and talking.

I was seated at a typewriter when a house father told Mack Grindstaff to be quiet. Mack talked back, and that was unusual for any student.

The house father, who also taught mattress making, was outraged. Mack's words were barely out of his mouth when the man slapped him. Mack was partially sighted, and the blow knocked off his glasses.

I heard them shatter on the floor.

You have to understand the significance to a blind person of hearing the sound of someone's glasses being broken. Sight is what any one of us in that school wanted more than anything. There were people who would have signed years off their lives, just for a few years with sight. Secondly, we shared the eyes of the partially sighted. When we couldn't detect something through feel or smell or whatever, we would ask someone like Mack who could see forms to tell us what it was.

The shattering of Mack's glasses on the floor by a temper-triggered slap was sickening to me. I didn't think before I spoke. If I had, I would have spoken anyhow. I was furious.

From my chair, I looked upward, squarely into the house father's face.

"You didn't have to slap him!" I said.

Bam!

I took the hardest blow to the face I've ever taken. My head hit the floor a split second after the strike. I was about 6 foot 2, and weighed 177 pounds. I was sitting firmly in a chair with both feet squarely on the floor, yet with one blow, the house father knocked me flat.

My face seemed to vibrate. My ears rang so loudly I couldn't "see" with them to know if a second hit or kick was coming. My light-vision eye throbbed.

If you've ever had an injury that instantly hurts tremendously, and then, second by second, keeps getting worse, you know it makes you panic. You are terrified, wondering when the pain is going to peak.

I didn't know it then, but I had been hit so hard that my eye was almost knocked out of my head; it had been loosened in its socket. The vein that was the organ's life support had been torn. From that moment, my only "good" eye began disintegrating.

The next morning, I could "see" a sea of red. The light vision that enabled me to tell day from night was gone. I scurried to a lamp my partially sighted roommate, Larry Kendrick, had. I placed my face almost against the bulb. I could feel the lamp's heat, but I couldn't see its glow.

Panic-stricken, I ran down the hall to the room of the house father and charged into his quarters, madly wanting him to undo whatever damage his slap of the previous night had done.

Breathless, I blurted his name.

"I can't ... I can't see anything!" I shouted. "Everything is red! I woke up this way and it's because you hit me!"

There was a long pause. I could hear him stirring in the room. In layman's fashion, he examined the damaged eye.

"I can't see," I continued, almost hysterical. "You shouldn't have hit me!"

"Well now," he said slowly. "We can't cry over spilled milk, can we?"

That was the long and short of his statement. It was both his reaction and his advice. I will remember forever his chilly delivery of that sentence.

Whether I stared into sunshine, or into a dark closet, the sight was the same: a glowing sea of crimson.

I went to the infirmary where I was told there was a blood clot behind my eye. A very basic explanation for the red was this: My eyes didn't work, but part of the equipment behind them did. That equipment, behind my left eye, was bathed in blood. Hence I "saw" red.

The pain was indescribable.

I began that day what were to become countless visits to eye doctors around Raleigh. They stuck needles into my injured eye and filled it with fluids they hoped would dissolve the blood clot. This went on for months, but it never dissolved.

Instead, the eyeball continued to deteriorate. It was falling apart gradually inside my skull.

Nothing took away that sky of red which I saw day and night, with my eyes opened or closed. And nothing took away the tremendous hurt of that blood clot, growing daily inside the tight pocket behind my eyeball. To ease the pain, the school infirmary gave me codeine. It was the first time I had ever taken a controlled substance, much less a narcotic. I took it as innocently as I would have taken cough drops during a cold. And in a short time, before I was old enough to shave, I developed a dependency on pain-killers. It would last almost a year.

I took the prescription each morning, then routinely threw up. I preferred the codeine and its inherent nausea over the dizzying alternative, a hammering pain behind my eye. The pain was so heavy it became a heartbeat across my face.

The cycle of pain and drugs continued for 10 months. The beginning of its end came when doctors began saying out loud what I'd refused to say to myself—that my eye, my only good eye—would have to be removed.

I could go on forever about the depression I felt, but still couldn't express how low I was. All my life I had lived with the notion that someday, someway, there would be a miracle. Maybe it would be medical, maybe it would be Heaven-sent, but I believed in, and lived for, the hope that the tiny bit of light vision I had in my left eye would be improved enough to let me see.

Way back in my Meadow Branch childhood, I was taken regularly to Lion's Club meetings, where I was asked to use a typewriter to show what blind people can do. The Lions were interested in aiding the blind, and they brought in doctors, whom I heard discuss corneal transplants of the day and the possibility of entire eye transplants in the future. I was still an impressionable and highly optimistic boy.

There were those church services, where preachers promised me and scores of others that someday I would see. These hopes, and others, and an overflow of personal fortitude, never let me question that I would eventually have sight. I never wondered *if* I would see; I only wondered *when*.

Now, doctors wanted to take away forever my chance to see. They wanted to cut out my eye!

They said there was no other way they could remove that blood clot. They said otherwise it would keep growing. They said the pain would grow unbearably worse. They said they could not safely increase dosages of codeine.

I said "No."

I was going to keep my shattered eye, and thereby keep the chance for sight, no matter how remote.

Resisting the doctors while enduring the pain was too much. I fell into a deeper depression. I couldn't eat or sleep or concentrate in school. My life was sheer suffering in mind and body, and I don't know which hurt the most. What was a reduced appetite became no appetite at all. I stopped eating. I stopped because I was too depressed and in too much pain. Then there was a physiological factor of which I was unaware. Codeine, I've since been told, is a hunger suppressor.

I dragged myself from bed and reluctantly went to class. Many times, teachers forced me to go to the dining hall. But they couldn't force me to eat. And I couldn't force myself, except for an infrequent bite or two of bread.

I lost twenty pounds in two months. The thought of food sickened me—like the thought of a future without sight. I had been a solid 177 pounds the day that man struck me. Eventually I would fall to 120. I wished I was small enough to crawl inside a hole, where no one could ever find me.

For ten months, I couldn't tell days from the nights because of the darkness that never left, and now, never would. There was night after night of fitful sleep, as I tossed on a sheet saturated with sweat and tears. I felt so alone. Everyone in the dormitory was asleep except me, and I was begging God not to let them take my eye.

I had been through things in my life that left me not caring if I lived or died. Now, I cared—I wanted to die.

I was sustained largely by the many good teachers who encouraged me. My seventh-grade teacher, Gene Nelson, was the most consoling and inspirational of all.

But I was suffering mental and physical depletion. I was taking codeine now more than ever. Then came summer vacation. The last word in that sentence is misleading, because those three months were spent with Homer and Phenia taking me to doctors. There were four in all. My grandparents couldn't believe this had happened to me. The physicians struggled in vain to freeze the eye, then they tried lancing it to break up the clot.

I should answer a question you're probably asking. What about filing a lawsuit against the school and the person who inflicted the injury? What about trying to have the man fired?

No such steps were taken.

The legal steps would have been complicated. And the reason they never were taken is simple. Mountain folks just didn't think in terms of courtrooms, or of having someone fired. And Homer and Phenia had no funds to travel to Raleigh and to stay there long enough to rectify the situation.

Years later, in a talk with a former school counselor, I was told that shortly after my assault, there was a meeting of the Governor Morehead board of directors. They were more aware than I realized of what I was undergoing. At that heated board meeting, a motion was introduced to fire the man who had attacked me. The motion failed by one vote. I was told that the deciding vote was cast by school principal Ted Stough. His vote, reportedly, had to do with a long-standing friendship he had with the man who battered me.

I went back to school in the fall. There were no changes. I couldn't concentrate in class. The nights were still sleepless; the pain was still there. Christmas came, and I went home again to my one secure hiding place. By then, Homer and Phenia were speechless at what they saw. My uninjured eye sat deep in my head because of emaciation. My injured eye sat perilously in the socket and it felt as though it was about to disintegrate. Still, I wouldn't relent and consent to the removal of my one chance for sight.

I needed nothing less than a miracle. I was holding out.

But on a frigid February morning in 1958, I surrendered my lifelong dream. The few minutes of surgery changed my life forever. The procedure was performed inside the school infirmary, otherwise routinely used to treat hangnails and skinned knees. The most plentiful medicine in the place was probably aspirin.

That's where I left my eye.

I was incredibly nervous. I had never even had a tooth filled.

I wasn't given a general anesthetic. Instead, they gave me a local, which consisted of poking needles into my useless eye, after first deadening my face with a shot into my temple. Then the light-vision eye was removed and thrown into the sanitary waste of Raleigh. I stayed in the infirmary for five days.

For a month afterwards, I wore a patch over the hole that was left in my head. That did wonders to lift my spirits.

Eventually, I obtained a glass eye. I remember that it cost $15. One day while I was cleaning it, it fell from my hands and exploded. It sounded like a shotgun going off inside the old high-ceilinged rest room. Glass shrapnel went everywhere. I wondered what would have happened if that thing had exploded inside my head?

One punch from a McGuire twin, I thought, and this thing goes off!

So I had it replaced with a plastic eye, similar to the one I wear today.

I've wondered many times through the years whether I would have ever seen, had I kept my light-vision eye. But with surgery as unrefined as it was thirty-two years ago, in an infirmary that wouldn't even qualify as a minor emergency clinic by today's standards, I'm glad they got it out without my bleeding to death.

If I had that light-vision eye today, with all the advances that have been made in optical science, who knows, perhaps doctors could alter the eye enough to make it function. The situation for me now is eternally hypothetical.

Almost as much as I've thought about sight, I've thought about the man whose physical violence took mine away. I've wondered if he thinks of me, and what he thinks when he does? For he knows what he did to a defenseless boy, decades ago, in a study hall on the third floor of a dormitory. He's had ample opportunity to remember.

Until 1987, when he retired, he reportedly was still teaching and disciplining students, at taxpayer's expense, at the Governor Morehead School for the Blind.

9

I concentrated on my music more than ever after the loss of my eye. By the time I was a teenager, music was not just a passion, it was a companion. My playing was improving and there were accolades from teachers. That part of my life, which eventually would become the biggest part of my life, was fine.

Yet there was a paradox. I didn't understand why *my* musical talent had to be applied exclusively to *their* songs. I loved the classics, which were the mainstay of the music department's curriculum, but I liked other types of music too. If I played well the kind of music the school wanted me to play, why couldn't I play some of the contemporary sound I liked too? Governor Morehead had given me a genuine appreciation of music. But it seemed to me that true appreciation should encompass a spectrum of music, not just the classics.

While some people had many categories of music, I had one— good music. I didn't care if it was classical, popular, country, gospel, or rock 'n' roll. My enjoyment of almost any kind of good music remains today. I love country's George Jones, but I love Beethoven as well.

At fifteen, I was hardly in a minority in my excitement over that fusion of country music, gospel, and rhythm and blues to make the hot hybrid called rock 'n' roll.

Elvis had started it all for me a few years earlier when my daddy got upset because I emulated Presley's songs with my guitar. By 1959, I was sixteen and pretty salty on piano. Rock 'n' roll had been the rage of the airwaves for four years. There were already probably more

AM radio stations programming rock 'n' roll than any other kind of music.

Naturally, those of us enrolled in the music school wanted to play this new thunderbolt sound. I mean, much of American music of the time was bland. It was an era when one of the biggest hits of the decade was Prez Prado's "Cherry Pink and Apple Blossom White." The void in American music was filled by rock 'n' roll, up-tempo tunes with a blistering beat, sung recklessly from the gut. As teenage players, we made heroes out of the young rock 'n' rollers.

A teenager who sang show tunes or Tin Pan Alley songs in the 1940s would have idolized Frank Sinatra, the Tommy Dorsey Band, Glen Miller, and a handful of others. I don't know why Governor Morehead music teachers thought we were unusual for wanting to reproduce the sounds of Jerry Lee Lewis and Ricky Nelson.

Music students were forbidden from playing the modern sounds. We sneaked and played it anyhow, and were caught, and were punished. Then whenever we got the chance, we played it again.

Every generation has its own music and you can imagine, then, how heartbroken I was on February 3, 1959, to hear of the airplane crash that claimed the lives of Buddy Holly, the Big Bopper, and Richie Valens. Those guys planted musical roots for me. I still draw on them. In 1985, I had a huge-selling record entitled "Lost in the Fifties To-night." I play that song now in my live shows as a prelude to a 1950s medley that includes Buddy Holly's "Everyday," the Del Vikings' "Come Go with Me," and Little Richard's "Lucille."

I'll never forget the first time I heard Buddy Holly on the radio. I thought he sounded so sincere. And he wasn't that much older than I was!

It was like being hit with a tow sack full of wet cement the day they told me that Holly and the others had died. It was like losing a member of the family; I think there *is* a family of sorts among all musicians, especially those who want to play one type of music and are persecuted for it.

By the time of Buddy's death, I had heard many news accounts of how his music, and that of other pioneer rock 'n' rollers, had unleashed the anger of America's parents. I thought that Buddy must have undergone harassment similar to what I received from the Morehead music teachers. So I felt close to him, although we would never meet.

Minutes after we learned of the rock 'n' roll trio's fiery deaths, Jay Spell and I, heavy in heart, walked to the basement of the music building. We didn't say much; we could say best through song what we were feeling. We couldn't go to their funerals, but we could do their songs.

We were teenagers who were going to honor a timeless tradition of the bereaved. We were going to hold a wake for our fallen heroes. Jay and I did it of our own will, on our own time.

The ceremony was filled with respect and admiration. Our throats choked with emotion as our voices raised high with Holly's, Valens's, and the Big Bopper's songs.

Then someone charged through the door.

It was Miss Mary Davis, head of the music department. She was the woman who had repeatedly declined to give me voice lessons because she said I sang well enough. None of the students could figure out Mary Davis's criteria for giving voice lessons. She refused to give them to many students who asked, and yet she gave them to one student who sang flat for twelve years. I guess that it was just a matter of personalities, and that she liked some students more than others. Today, she didn't want me singing at all; not if I was going to sing rock 'n' roll.

She told me to get out. I tried in vain to explain that we were holding a wake, and that she had actually walked into a service.

She wouldn't listen to Jay or me.

And she didn't just want us out of the room, she wanted us out of the music department. She probably wanted us out of the school altogether, but she didn't have the power to levy that punishment.

But she could and she did expel us from any and all music programs at school. And all because we had eulogized some teenage musicians, who died in an airplane's twisted wreckage, on a snow-covered farm field in Iowa.

We had practiced all winter for the spring music competition just around the corner. But we were omitted from the festival at the Overbrook School in Philadelphia, and all the other competitions that spring.

Mary Davis wouldn't listen to our appeals to get back into the music programs, or to those of faculty members who said her harsh punishment didn't fit the crime.

Summer passed, and when Jay and I returned to school in the fall of 1959, Miss Davis invited us to return to the music department. At the time of my expulsion, I had been first-chair cellist, and I think I might have been invited back because the department was facing a big competitive recital.

I returned to the department to pursue musical studies, but I refused to play cello. '

My old violin teacher and object of admiration, Wallace Grieves, joined Miss Davis in asking me to return to the orchestra and continue playing cello. But I turned him down as well. I had been hurt and offended when Mr. Grieves did not back me up when Miss Davis expelled me seven months earlier. He was astonished, I think, at how adamant I was about something I believed to be right.

I reminded Mr. Grieves that when I was kicked out, I was holding a sincere wake, and holding it on my own time, not during the school's music practice time. When Mr. Grieves saw how sincere I was, he said, "Well, just what *are* you going to do?"

My response was completely spontaneous, and surprised even me. "I'm going to play clarinet!" I blurted.

I said that because I was trying to think of an instrument that he and the other teachers, especially Miss Davis, would least expect me to select.

I didn't know a thing about clarinet (my first woodwind instrument), but I knew it was taught by Delton Creech. He earlier had taught me how to tune pianos; he was a nice guy, and he understood my fascination with rock 'n' roll.

I practiced really, really hard, largely out of defiance. And it paid off. In only four months, I was invited again into the orchestra as a clarinetist. In two more, I was moved to first chair. Attaining the premiere seat in half a year I hoped showed the faculty that I was sincere about music, and so much so, that I was justified that day I performed my wake for my fallen heroes.

Mr. Grieves was his typically gallant self when I returned to the orchestra. Until then, the orchestra had never performed selections featuring a clarinet solo. Mr. Grieves wrote two such selections, just so my playing might be highlighted. It was a fine gesture to heal the wounds over what had been a hurtful situation.

*   *   *

One of my fondest memories of high school is the student construction and operation of a campus radio station. There's no telling how many federal laws we violated with that thing.

The administration did not know that we were broadcasting from right under their noses over what became an underground station. We had two sets of call letters. No one bothered to check with the Federal Communications Commission to see if those letters were already assigned to a licensed station. Did I say license? We didn't bother with a little thing like that either. Official FCC applicants waited for years for a license, then paid a fortune to get it.

But Danny Hampton, Jay Spell, and I built our station from Army surplus stuff. Gene Nelson, my house father and former seventh-grade teacher, loaned us a turntable and a Wollensak tape recorder. Then we began invading the airwaves. It never dawned on us that violating federally licensed air space was a federal offense.

Danny was a bright guy who built the transmitter. Jay and I did the programming. And what programming it was!

We'd go on the air in the afternoons and evenings, and maybe for an hour in the mornings before school. That's another FCC requirement we conveniently overlooked, the establishment of regular broadcast hours.

The broadcast "staff" was Larry Atwell, Jay Spell, Chuck Langley, and me. They were my roommates. They later made up my first band ever, the Apparitions. We'd play music, deliver messages to our girlfriends, and make public service announcements. We were the hit of the campus.

We also took telephone requests. Since there were no telephones in the rooms, the kids would call from the pay telephones for ten cents. One would put in a dime, he'd talk for a while, then he'd pass the receiver to someone else standing in line. We'd do that when calling our girlfriends in the dormitories too. Ten guys would get four hours of conversation out of one dime.

Jay, Danny, and I also shared an amateur radio hobby that continues to the present. People have always been fascinated by my aptitude for electronics. It was enhanced by my work at that makeshift radio station. Today, I can repair some parts of small appliances with tubes or transistors. I'm really pretty good with things with parts, including pianos. I've taken them apart and put them back together ever since Delton Creech taught me how to do it when I was fourteen.

We spoke with deep voices over the radio waves and pretended we were big stars. Our radio hero and mentor was a disc jockey named Charlie Hicks at WSHE in Raleigh. We thought he had a really cool voice, and we tried to emulate him. We even made our own commercials for campus enjoyment, and cut them in the boy's bathroom where there was an enormous echo. I wonder what passing motorists thought, picking up our signal on the AM dial?

The radio has always been an enormous part of my life. For one thing, I can't see the sources of sound, and neither can anyone else who listens. I'm an equal in the radio audience. Radio just leaves more to the imagination than television.

There was a time when I almost gave up being an entertainer to become a radio broadcaster. That interest in broadcasting was accelerated by our high school radio station.

My fascination for radio began in my childhood and continues today. I'm basically a night person, and sometimes I'll spend the entire night just turning the radio dial, entertaining myself with faraway signals and the magic that broadcast airwaves carry. I do the same thing in a car.

I grew up listening to what's become a dying breed ... the old-fashioned radio personality: Lowell Blanchard on WNOX in Knoxville, Tennessee; Cas Walker on WIVK in Knoxville; and the late Archie Campbell, when he was on WNOX, before he went on to become a touring entertainer and one of the stars on television's *Hee-Haw*. There was Wayne Rainey at WCKY in Cincinnati, Ohio, and those wonderful R & B deejays on WLAC in Nashville: John R. (John Richbourg), Gene Nobles, Hoss Allen, Hugh "Baby" Jarrett, and Herman Grizzard.

I really enjoyed listening to Ralph Emery, the dean of country music broadcasters when he had his all-night show on "clear channel 650," WSM in Nashville. I stayed up late with Charlie Douglas when he was on WWL, in New Orleans and WSM. Charlie surprised me one night when he said the only one who didn't know Ronnie Milsap was blind was Ronnie Milsap.

I'm a fan of Billy Parker at KVOO in Tulsa, Oklahoma; John McCormick, the "man who walks and talks at midnight," on KMOX in St.

Louis; "The Truckin' Bozo" (Dale Sommers) on WLW in Cincinnati; "Big" John Trimble on WRVA in Richmond, Virginia; and the voice of Bill Mack at WBAP in Ft. Worth, Texas . . . he's so smooth. I carved my name on his desk during one of many nights I was a guest on his show.

Those veteran disc jockeys, and modern keepers of the flame, are to radio what Johnny Carson is to television. They're hosts, not merely announcers. You tune in to hear what they have to say as much as what they have to play.

They were my secret companions in Homer's tiny mountain cabin and inside the cavernous dormitories at Governor Morehead, and they still are, wherever I happen to be today. It's great how radio can reach the masses, yet seem like it's being programmed only for you.

There is one personality from my childhood who is still on the air, forty years behind a microphone. Whenever I'm in his signal range from Knoxville I still tune into the Reverend J. Basil Mull. He is a radio institution, who plays traditional gospel music with his wife, Miss Mull. They dedicate songs to ailing listeners, who they still call "shut-ins." They keep listeners abreast of all the "doings" in their area, and they do their own commercials.

The Reverend Mull, who may or may not be ordained, has a speaking voice as rough as the late Louis Armstrong's. Miss Mull's is high and fragile.

Whatever he talks about on the air, she agrees with. This woman has missed the feminist movement. He'll talk for a while in that sandpaper, throaty voice until you wonder if he is ever going to play another song. Then he'll say, "ain't that right, Miss Mull?"

She, on cue, will always come in with a delicate "That's right, Reverend Mull."

I mentioned that the Reverend Mull does his own commercials. There's a famous story, whether fact or fiction, that's been circulating for years. The story goes that one day near Christmastime the Reverend Mull was at full tilt doing a commercial for a grocery store owned by Cas Walker.

Imagine that deep growl, as the Reverend Mull proclaimed, "Do your Christmas buying at Cas Walker's grocery. He's got the sweetest candy . . . he's got the prettiest apples . . . he's got the best oranges . . .

and this Christmas season, he's got the biggest nuts in town ... ain't that right, Miss Mull?"

"That's right, Reverend Mull," came her agreement, on cue.

"Now here's a song by the Chuck Wagon Gang," she said, and pressed right on into the program.

I wondered if the good reverend and his wife were even aware of their innocent humor, but it wouldn't have mattered. They were, and are, unshakable pillars of the airwaves in rural east Tennessee and western North Carolina.

One of those radio personalities was sued for slander by a woman. She alleged he had called her a prostitute. The radio star, who by then had a television program, went on live. There was no opportunity to edit anything. He shocked his director and viewers by bringing up the incident. Before anyone could stop him, he said he had not called so-and-so a prostitute.

"I called her a damn whore!" he thundered.

He was known to throw people off live television if he thought they were playing too loudly, and one time he got angry at a female guest and beat her up with the cameras rolling!

Our shows at Governor Morehead on our campus radio station were not as, shall we say, "controversial" as the shows of my radio heroes. But I'll bet we had as much or more fun doing them. I often fantasized that I would someday sit at an enormous control board for a giant 100,000-watt AM radio station, the likes of which aren't even licensed in the United States, but sprang up just across the border in Mexico.

But for all the joy I got from radio, my greatest thrill was when I formed the Apparitions my junior year in high school.

I had already been playing in bands with older guys. When I was twelve, I played in a band with Don Ange, one of my all-time favorite people at school. Don was about four years older than I, and very musical. He eventually played keyboards with Arthur "Guitar Boogie" Smith and George Hamilton, IV. Ange was someone I tried to emulate. He always wore nice clothes. He wore unusual colognes. Fragrances always got my attention and still do.

He and the guys already had the band formed when I went to Don and asked him if I could play.

He said, "We need somebody to play bass, but you can't play bass, can you?"

I had been playing cello in the school orchestra. Once you play cello, it's easy to play upright bass. You just transpose what you know on cello to bass. Well, that's what I did, and Don let me join his band.

I was twelve, and the other members were from sixteen to eighteen years old. When you're twelve, the only thing you want more than the acceptance of your peers is the acceptance of the older guys. I had it.

There were other little bands I joined as well. In 1957, when I was fourteen, I played for the school assembly. We did Jerry Lee Lewis's "Whole Lotta Shakin'" and Bobby Helms's "Fraulein." Two people in that band stand out in my mind. There was a fiddle player named Wallace Brame, who was great, and there was Bill Massey. At that time, Bill was the best electric guitarist that I'd ever heard live.

In the Apparitions, I played electric guitar, and Larry Atwell played upright bass. Chuck Langley was the drummer, and Jay Spell was on piano. Today, Jay Spell lives in Nashville. He is a consummate studio musician who has played with numerous entertainers. I use Jay on my recordings whenever possible.

The fact that I was able to form a rock 'n' roll band at a school that had evicted me from its classical music curriculum just twenty months earlier proves that almost every adversity carries an equal blessing. A lot of the teachers were not pleased that Jay Spell and I were booted out. If we had not known our assigned music lessons, it would have been different. But we were fine classical musicians who wanted to play rock 'n' roll for our own enjoyment.

Because we were kicked out for so long, and because the school's representation at music competition suffered, the administration softened by the time I wanted to form my own band.

We played off campus for various groups, including college fraternity parties. Ralph Thompson was our unofficial manager-booking agent. Imagine being a high school junior and entertaining young adults who applauded and congratulated your work. It did wonders for my self-confidence.

And our band wasn't bad. We did several return engagements at Meredith College and North Carolina State College, both in Raleigh. A few times we earned as much as $15 per night per player.

We won a talent contest at WRAL-TV, Raleigh, and received $250.

We played local Saturday television many times thereafter, and developed a genuine following, along with another local group, the Embers, who still play around there today.

The Apparitions will always hold a spot in my heart. It was that group that gave me my first exposure.

In my senior year I was enjoying many of the benefits of adult life, and little of the responsibilities. I was popular on campus, and was already dreading leaving the close friends of my most formative years.

My high school education, like most people's, is filled with happy memories. For example, there was a tunnel system that crisscrossed underground at Governor Morehead.

I spent many a secretive and gleeful hour down there with my buddies, smoking, telling stories, cussing, and buying and trading for records, clothes, and black market condoms.

Today, Governor Morehead is an overall facility for the multihandicapped, not just for the blind. In 1970, the state of North Carolina started "mainstreaming" blind students, incorporating them into its public school population. I gave an interview, at the time, with a Charlotte newspaper applauding the overdue wisdom of putting blind students in with sighted children.

My opinion was sincere, thought-out, and wrong. I've since decided that public school teachers cannot teach the blind, unless the blind first have had special training at a resident school, such as the Governor Morehead School. Teachers in public schools, no matter how well-intentioned, just aren't trained to teach the blind. Consequently, the blind student winds up doing little more than going to class. He may get by. He may even get a diploma.

But he doesn't get a full education. Too often, the blind are promoted from class to class without really deserving to be.

The main incentive for mainstreaming the blind is social. The thinking is that a blind child will fit into modern society well, if he is an integrated member from childhood. There is merit to that theory, but most mainstreaming will make a child socially normal, but academically deficient.

I believe in mainstreaming after a blind child has acquired his basic skills in a residential school equipped especially for him. Teach a blind child how to type, to read and write in braille, and teach him how to be personally independent. Then move him into the public schools, where he can compete with and keep up with sighted students. Don't just throw him into a sighted world where he spends most of his energy playing catch-up.

A lot of parents who don't want to send their blind children to a residential school are going to disagree with me. I understand their wanting to keep their blind child near home, in a public school. But they are indulging their feelings, to their child's disadvantage. I suggest they are guilty of having their own heartstrings, not their child's education, ultimately in mind. Those parents say, "I want my child to be able to come home at night." Fine. Do they also want him someday to enter the work force?

Sixty-five percent of blind adults are out of work. That's because the majority have never been properly trained to do a job. Give most people the skills to work, and the self-esteem to want to work, and they will work.

I have been back to Governor Morehead several times since leaving in 1962. The name of Cottage Braille dormitory, where I lived from age six through nine, has been changed. It's now the Ronnie Milsap dormitory. I stood on those steps where, at age six, I had wept bitterly because Homer had left me at that foreign place. Above the concrete once moistened with my tears hung a sign bearing my name. I can't tell you about the whirlwind of thoughts that rushed through my mind. The scene of so many mixed memories was now a scene of celebration. The school that played such an important role in my development was now heralding me as a famous alumnus. The word "appreciate" is so inadequate to convey my gratitude.

I left that school able to type 120 words per minute on a manual typewriter. My grades were such that I would have no trouble getting into college, and later, the state of North Carolina offered to pay my way through law school.

At my high school graduation, I was given a diploma, a braille watch, and a good citizenship award, which was really nothing more than the result of a popularity contest. I treasure those mementos, and still have them.

On graduation night, I had my first swallow of alcohol. I was nineteen. The boys and I went out to celebrate. We all bought something to drink. Walter Lackey told me about beer and how it tasted. He said it was awful! But I thought I'd try it anyway. I bought a six-pack and drank the entire thing, got sick, and didn't eat for two days. That was the first of only two times in my life that I became "bombed." I hate the taste of Schlitz to this day because of it.

Before I leave the topic of the Governor Morehead School, I want to mention some of the other teachers there and what enormous value they were to me.

I could not have had better teachers to start me on the educational path than my kindergarten teachers, Ms. Christine Benton and Mrs. Ethel Lewis. I had Mrs. Lewis again for a teacher, in third and sixth grades. In third grade, the three fat boys were consumed with baseball. The most popular baseball personality in America then probably was not even a player. The honor, instead, belonged to retired St. Louis Cardinal pitcher Dizzy Dean who, with Pee Wee Reese, was an announcer on NBC television's *Game of the Week*. Mrs. Lewis helped us write a letter to Dizzy Dean. The thrill could only have been surpassed if Dean had answered the letter—and he did! Helping us with that letter was beyond the bounds of her vocational assignment. None of the other boys or I ever forgot it.

Mrs. Polly Grimes, my fifth-grade teacher, was another whose patience and training stand out in my memory. She was one of the few who actually invited us into her home. Having someone into your home is, to me, the supreme testament of friendship, even to this day.

Gene Nelson was my wrestling coach and bowling instructor. He taught me how to use a cane. I didn't use it much, but he took the time to get the instruction himself so that he might teach some of the students. He was partially sighted. I've heard that it's hard for someone who is your boss to be your friend. I think it's harder for someone who is your teacher and authority figure to be your friend. Yet Mr. Nelson pulled it off for all his students.

Thurman Perkins, an eighth-grade teacher, was overflowing with positive attitudes. This guy could have given a boost to Dale Carnegie! He was walking optimism, and his attitude was wonderfully contagious to some students at their impressionable ages.

Ted Stough, the school principal, taught me that first impressions, no matter how lasting, can nonetheless be wrong. I thought that discipline was the extent of Mr. Stough's abilities. I was mistaken. In ninth grade, I had him as an algebra teacher. He was patient and sensitive, and one of the most effective teachers I've ever had.

Miss Lucy Gilmore, my tenth-grade teacher, taught me American history, civics, and two years of French. She was firm, and as demanding as she was instructional. Unlike most teachers, she was void of pretenses and made it apparent she had two favorite students, Ralph Thompson and me.

Gene Anthony taught industrial arts, including ceramics and woodworking. I could sand wood as smooth as polished glass. Mr. Anthony was so effective as a teacher, I built an entire desk by myself and sold it to the school for fifty dollars.

Mrs. Elizabeth Ashcraft was my high school piano teacher. She was as effective with my advanced studies as Miss Collinge was with my early ones. Sometimes, it's more of a challenge to hold the interest of a student who knows a field than it is to interest a student just learning.

Mrs. Frances Morrison, my twelfth-grade teacher and English teacher all the way through high school, was another who was so skilled, she taught me a field that otherwise wouldn't have held my interest. English was not my favorite subject, but I enjoyed studying with her. She gave me an appreciation for the literary classics including the works of Hawthorne and Shakespeare.

And there was Miss Rachael Rawls, a school counselor who empathized with students to the point of almost being able to think like them. Her empathy gave her credibility as a counselor. Her words implied that she knew what we were feeling. We were therefore always ready to take her wise and seasoned advice seriously.

In 1962, I had graduation and Governor Morehead behind me. Manhood waited in the wings. There would be college and more. Adulthood would be as victorious as parts of childhood were traumatic. What a life was waiting for me!

10

Homer and Phenia moved from my boyhood cabin in the fall of 1959. They wanted to live near relatives and were weary of the isolation of that craggy slope. So they settled in Hayesville, North Carolina, a tiny town not far from the Georgia–North Carolina line where Phenia's two brothers, Grady and Wayne Colvin, lived.

Two days after Christmas, Phenia, Grady, and I visited my daddy who still lived in Meadow Branch with his second wife. He'd been married for six years to a woman who had a flashing temper. Phenia was worried about Daddy because he had been injured. He had had a quarrel with his wife, and she had busted him over the head with an iron skillet. He was addled for days, and his behavior was different. He might have suffered a mild concussion.

He was reluctant to seek medical help. Mountain men thought it wasn't manly to see a doctor about an injury caused by the "weaker" sex.

After Phenia was satisfied that Daddy was going to be all right, we started back to Hayesville.

We stopped in Robbinsville to visit friends, maintaining the holiday spirit. But the mood was marred when Phenia became sick.

She complained of chest pains. For her to complain told me she hurt a lot, because that rugged farm woman never complained about life's infirmities.

Grady insisted that she go about twenty miles to the nearest hospital in Andrews, North Carolina. All the way there, she kept saying how bad she felt.

I was scared.

We arrived at the emergency room, and I stayed in the car. There was a scurry to get Phenia inside, and I didn't want anyone to waste time helping me inside too. Phenia could tell that I was hurting with worry about her. I heard her approach, then I felt her arms ease tenderly around my neck.

"Don't worry, son," she said, "I'll be all right."

They were the last words I ever heard her speak.

After my grandmother was admitted to the hospital, someone drove me to my Uncle Grady's house where I spent the night. I was awakened about eight o'clock the next morning by my daddy, who had come down from Meadow Branch. The fact that he was here, so soon after we had just visited him, told me instantly that something was wrong.

Phenia Frisby was dead at fifty-six. It was now about ninety minutes after daylight, and the dawn of life for me without the woman who had been, in effect, my mother.

There is no way to describe my grief. I enjoyed being an independent person except when I was around her. She was the only person I would let "wait" on me, because she enjoyed it so much. I enjoyed letting her.

Imagine, the biggest thing I could do for her was to let her serve me. Her love was that pure and unselfish. The things she did for me were wonderful. But I most enjoyed the love that motivated the deeds.

I didn't sleep for four days after she died. My head never touched a pillow. For the first time since those months I had struggled to keep my eye, I lost my appetite. People brought food to my Uncle Grady's house, the way folks do in the South when there's been a death in the family. I never touched a plate.

In the country, they still bring the body of the deceased to the house. It lies in state, and friends and relatives visit, and talk, and stay up all night, just sitting by the body. Folks who aren't from the rural South may think that's eerie. But it's a time-honored tradition, founded in respect for the dead and concern for the survivors. They did that with Phenia. Her open coffin sat in Grady's front room for two days. I remember how upset I was at how cold she felt to my touch. She didn't feel like flesh after the embalming.

Phenia had been the first to recognize my musical skills, and the one who always supported my endeavors. There was nothing in the world she enjoyed more, I think, than hearing me sing. She could sit in a rocking chair and listen for hours.

So I was asked to sing at her funeral. It was the hardest thing I've ever had to do. I played guitar and sang "Give Me the Flowers While I'm Living," a mountain Gospel song she loved, and "Peace in the Valley."

We buried her in her beloved Smoky Mountains. Not even death could take her from those pine-covered slopes. She rests beneath a hillside, about 100 yards from a blacktop road, where the loudest noise is the occasional acceleration of a pickup truck.

I'm glad she didn't suffer long. I know she thought she would be up and out of that hospital the day after she was admitted. If it hadn't been for Grady's insistence, she wouldn't have even gone to see the doctors, and perhaps would have died at home.

Her funeral was held the day before New Year's Eve. For me, there was no holiday celebration. Instead, my Uncle J.C. and Aunt Dorothy drove me back to Governor Morehead before the dirt was dry on Phenia's grave. I was hurting, and I wanted to go home. And with Phenia gone, Governor Morehead was my reluctant home more than ever. The dormitory was largely empty, because kids were still on Christmas vacation.

I didn't care. I wanted to be by myself.

Not long before her death, my grandmother had visited her brother, Wayne Colvin, in Sawyers Cove, North Carolina, not far from Hayesville. Uncle Wayne introduced Phenia to Rena and George Bristol. George was a public school teacher. Unknown to me, Phenia later asked Rena if she would look after me if Phenia passed away. So Phenia knew exactly what she was doing when she encouraged my fondness for the Bristol family. And after she died, I lived with them for most of the time during my final two years at Governor Morehead, when school wasn't in session.

The Bristols had a son, Jennings, a couple of years older than me who preceded me at Young Harris Junior College. I went there to be near Homer, the Bristols, and the rest of my relatives. The State Commission for the Blind wanted me to go to a big university, but I refused because of my need for the sense of family.

I remember when Phenia and I first went to the Bristols' home.

They had a piano, and I played Hank Williams's "You Win Again," only I played it the way Jerry Lee Lewis had recorded it. The Bristol kids stood around and clapped in time. Their enthusiasm was a jolt of excitement to me during summer vacation from school, where I was forbidden to play rock 'n' roll.

The Bristol household was filled with people, laughter, and love. And at that time, I needed to be around a lot of people. I know that my staying at their house hurt Homer, and that hurt me. But I was just too freshly wounded over Phenia's death. The Bristols intentionally gave me love, and unknowingly gave me therapy. I was never a guest; I instantly became family. The Bristol ranks swelled to eight with the arrival in the summer of 1960 of seventeen-year-old Ronnie Milsap.

The students at Governor Morehead never made a big deal out of my blindness, because they were blind too. But the Bristols were probably the first "civilians" not to be uneasy around me because I couldn't see. They even had a healthy sense of humor about it. Instead of feeling sorry for me, they laughed with me.

For example, George came home one day and nearly became a cardiac patient after he saw I had disassembled the family piano. I had parts and wires all over the house. He forced a chuckle when I told him I could put it all back together. He laughed out loud when I did.

We played tag in a deep mountain lake where I could catch and dunk everyone in the family after it turned dark. They couldn't see, but I was in my element.

One time Rena and I were watching television. A giant spider ran out and stopped in the middle of the floor. She jumped up on a table and kept screaming for me to kill it. I began stomping up and down, while she hollered "left, right, more this way, he's getting away," and the like. The spider did get away, but not before I had done an impromptu square dance. She told everybody who came by what a sight I was, a 175-pound teenager doing the Virginia Reel across her living room to the cadence of her bellowing.

The Bristols had a three-bedroom house that sat right on the highway outside Hayesville about two miles from the state line. The road had a big bump in front of their driveway. I'd direct drivers to that house, including taxi drivers, by waiting for the feel of the bump in the road. I never once missed the turn.

In 1988, when I last visited them, the road had been fixed and the bump removed. I let my driver go all the way to Georgia waiting for the jolt that never came. We had to call George Bristol from a pay telephone to come get us.

Mountain youngsters, without the stimulus of city modernization, cling to tradition longer than urban kids, and country children are more easily amused and entertained, particularly by simple things. So even as a teenager, I played hide and seek with the Bristol kids. They weren't used to relying on sound as much as I was. I amazed them by always finding them in the thicket of rose bushes and other foliage on their six-acre lawn. It was easy for me; I could hear them breathe because my sense of hearing is overdeveloped.

I, like so many other blind folks, have "shadow vision." I get my bearings and evaluate the closeness of my surroundings by snapping my fingers. I listen for the slightest air current, vibration, or echo to determine how close I am to an object. It's particularly useful after arising in a strange motel. So I've daily, sometimes hourly, snapped my fingers over the years.

One day Rena overheard me explain the process of shadow vision to a visitor. She said she never knew I snapped my fingers to find my way around. She said she thought I was just a happy person.

The summer of 1960 was a happy time. Jennings and I worked up several duets, with me on piano, him on guitar. We'd harmonize vocally. We didn't have a drum, but with people always around, we often let whoever wanted pound out the tempo on a cardboard box.

I connected a microphone to speakers, which I attached to the outside of the house. The house sat at the top of a valley. In the stillness of a mountain sundown, my voice would carry from those speakers and float across the valley. Scores of mountain folks sat on their front porches in the evenings and listened to my sunset concerts as I sang and played piano.

Many of the folks who listened at day's end dropped by the Bristols' house. They'd give me song requests, then ask me to wait until they had time to get home, eat supper, and get settled on their front porches. Sometimes, when the air was still, I could hear the faint sound of someone's distant applause.

There were two Mormon missionaries staying with the Bristols, during the time I was there. They were Elder Robert Laudy and Elder

Roy Mouritsen. They introduced me to the Mormon faith, and I was baptized into it. That was a marked departure from my Baptist up-bringing.

Although my Mormon affiliation ended in just a couple of years, I was quite sincere about it at the time. I have a deep respect for the personal discipline of Mormons, who don't believe in consuming tea, coffee, or alcohol, or in using tobacco.

After graduation, I went on a trip with the Bristols out west. We all packed into their station wagon.

The trip became a wonderful adventure. Six kids with the windows down, the wind in our hair, the east to our backs, and the west in our windshield.

I was old enough to understand the geography, and young enough to feel the excitement. Mass transit and rapid travel will never offer the magic of a motor trip when one has the time to enjoy it. Merle Haggard, when he has the time, still likes to ride Amtrak trains instead of flying across the country. There is a special closeness to the soil when the only thing separating a man from it is inches of spinning steel.

The Bristols told me about the ocean of wheat, waving as far as they could see on the Kansas prairie. They told me about the Northwest and the big sky so sprawling it seemed both above and around us.

They told me there were no billboards or utility poles, just land. I came to realize that there were still places in this nation man hadn't settled, and the idea of a surviving frontier excited me.

We had a snowball fight in the Colorado Rockies in June.

We stayed at the home of Rena's sister, Grace Ericksen, near Sher-idan, Wyoming. It was my first chance to ride a horse—Old Morgan. I had visited Custer's battleground, and I was on a working ranch, so the impulse to be a cowboy came easily. Old Morgan and I were going to ride the high country. Apparently, Old Morgan had a different itin-erary.

They assured me that horse was slow and gentle—and he was. He slowly and gently walked under every low-hanging branch he could find, and ever so lazily tried to knock me off his back. When I came in from my first ride, my clothes were torn off me and I was a bloody wreck.

Ronnie at about five or six.

A young Ronnie playing his Uncle J. C.'s guitar.

Ronnie at about eight.

Ronnie's father, James Millsaps, leaning against a Model-A Ford in 1946.

Ronnie (*far left*) at age eleven in 1954, sitting in with a square dance band in Fontana Village, North Carolina.

Ronnie in June 1955, standing with his Uncle J. C. Frisby and J. C.'s two daughters, Carol Ann (*standing*) and Cheryl Jean.

Ronnie in July 1959, with his beloved grandmother, Phenia, five months before her death. This is his only photograph of the two of them together.

Ronnie's picture as it appeared in his senior high school annual.

Ronnie at his high school graduation with some of his classmates. *Left to right:* Larry Atwell, Ronnie, Stella Hall, and Walter Lackey.

The Apparitions in 1962. *Left to right:* J. A. Spell (piano); Ralph Thompson (manager); Ronnie (guitar and vocals); Larry Atwell (bass); and Chuck Langley (drums).

Ronnie and Jennings Bristol in July 1962 during the trip out West, playing at the Five Sisters Lounge near Sheridan, Wyoming.

Ronnie in his first publicity photo for Scepter Records in November 1965. (*Scepter Records*)

Ronnie with his band at the Whiskey-A-Go-Go in Atlanta, Georgia, in February, 1966. *Left to right:* Skippy Robertson (drums); Stan Reece (guitar); Johnny Christopher (bass); and Ronnie (organ).

Ronnie in a 1968 publicity photograph. (The sideburns are real.)

Ronnie on *The Mike Douglas Show*, performing a skit with (*left to right*) Mike Douglas, Arsenio Hall, and Ron Howard. (*The Mike Douglas Show*)

Ronnie does his thing in Las Vegas with former background singers (*left to right*) Suzy Storm, Barbara Wyrick, and Marie Tomlinson.

Ronnie accepts his first CMA award in 1974. *Left to right:* Lynn Anderson, Anne Murray, Ronnie, Jack Johnson, and Tom Collins. (*CMA*)

The first Nashville band and crew on the road. *Seated, from left:* Steve "Hawk" Holt, Jack Watkins, Todd Milsap, and Dicky Overbey. *Standing, from left:* Johnny Cobb, Billy Coren, Ronnie, Sherry Cobb, and Phil Jones. (*Ramond O. Borea*)

The triple crown winner at the CMA Awards in 1977.
(*Dean Dixon*)

The CMA Awards in 1978. *Left to right:* Johnny Cash, Dolly Parton, and Ronnie. (*Hope Powell, Dean Dixon, Bill Welch*)

Ronnie, Joyce, and Todd backstage at the CMA Awards in 1978. (*Don Putnam*)

Ronnie, Todd, and friends outside Todd's tree house. (*Jim McGuire*)

Joyce gives Ronnie a good-luck
kiss before a show.

Ronnie in concert in 1981.

Ronnie receives his first gold album for "Ronnie Milsap Live." *Left to right:* Dave Wheeler, Jerry Bradley, Donald Reeves, Ronnie, Tom Collins, and Joe Galante.

I didn't care, I was having too much fun.

One day, Jennings and I went to a cowboy bar in Grable, Wyoming, where I got drunk for the second and final time of my life.

I threw two drunken sprees in one month, and the last one was so disastrous, it cured me forever of any compulsion for intoxication.

I had just graduated from high school, finally had gotten out of state at age nineteen, and had traveled nearly the length of the country. Each of my senses was on fire. I figured celebration was in order.

I swaggered to my seat at the bar with the confidence of an old west gunslinger. All around me were the heavy footsteps of western boots. The choking thickness of cigarette smoke contrasted sharply with the purity of the Rocky Mountain air outside.

I felt conspicuous and not because I was 6 feet 2 inches tall, feeling my way through an unfamiliar place. It was because I had no cowboy hat!

The waitress asked in the best western movie tradition, "What'll it be, boys?"

Talk about a he-man feeling. John Wayne was a wimp compared with me right then. I shifted in the wooden chair, put my elbows on the table, and in the lowest, most masculine voice I could affect, started to order.

Then it hit me.

I'd never had a drink of whiskey in my life. I didn't know the first thing about what to ask for. How could I come off like John Wayne if my knowledge of alcohol was like Captain Kangaroo's?

They say musicians have music as their first instinct.

There was a popular song at the time by the Kingston Trio called "Scotch and Soda."

That title unexplainably popped into my mind. "I'll have a scotch and soda," I said, as if I knew what I was doing. I didn't know that scotch and soda is a popular cocktail among the upper class. I'll bet that was the first time a white-collar drink had been ordered inside that cowboy bar.

She brought it, and I drank it down like Kool-Ade. It burned, and I nearly choked, gulping a concoction I was supposed to sip. I was trying to be cool, so I forced myself not to cough as my throat contracted.

I also didn't know that real drinkers usually drink the same kind of drink in one drinking session. I thought I was supposed to change with every order, and that would show I knew my way around the boozing world.

"What'll it be?" the waitress asked again. Again, I was stumped. Again, I thought of that song. There is a line that says, ". . . jigger of gin." "Bring me a jigger of gin," I ordered.

She probably left the table scratching her head. Can you imagine chasing a bolted scotch and soda with a straight jigger of liquid fire gin?

I inhaled that, and the effect of ingesting two ounces of alcohol in two minutes reduced my inhibition. More and more, I began to care less and less about letting my newness to drinking show.

"How about a dry martini?" I asked.

"OK," she said.

"Bring it," I snapped.

We sat there all afternoon, two boys trying to show off a manhood that wasn't quite ready. I went through the drinking lyrics of that entire song, thinking them, then drinking them, just as the words said. I stood up to leave, and the room spun. The young drinker, who strutted in with cocksure arrogance, was physically assisted out. I became sick, and this time, the hangover was worse than the second day of the flu, while riding the down side of a roller coaster.

That was my last drunk. A lot of people are going to be suspicious of a musician who claims not to drink, but it's true. I don't like the way alcohol makes me feel during and after excessive consumption.

Don't get me wrong, I occasionally have a drink when I fly. But I haven't been bombed since I was nineteen. I'm not on a soapbox about alcohol. I just don't like it, so I don't drink often. I think that actually disappoints some people, who think musicians and other artists must be self-indulgent, as a requirement for good work.

A lot of creative people rationalize. They say they have to have a liquid or chemical crutch because they're sensitive. Their sensitivity, they say, makes them feel more emotion than the average guy.

That's nonsense. They're either weak, or they have a bona fide sickness. I believe there is medical evidence to support the theory that alcoholism is a disease, not always a moral failure. Often, it's attributable to heredity. If I thought I had the disease, and I couldn't whip it myself, I'd get professional help.

Later that summer, Jennings and I wound up playing as a guitar-piano duet at a bar called the Five Sisters Lounge, near Sheridan, Wyoming. They paid us each $15 a night and fed us one meal a day. We took the job for a couple of nights and were held over for two weeks.

George, Rena, and the rest of the family returned to North Carolina. A week later, Jennings and I started back to North Carolina in a 1950 Ford he borrowed from his cousin.

We spent the first night in the car when it broke down in Casper, Wyoming. Jennings somehow got it running. We parked the second night just outside Kansas City, and the third night we parked in a cornfield in Kentucky. The fourth night we parked next to a railroad track in Nashville.

Did I say "next to?" I could almost say "on top of."

It was late at night when we prowled Nashville looking for a place to park and sleep. Jennings backed into a field, so his headlights were facing away from the tracks, and he didn't see them. We immediately fell into a sound sleep.

The train's engineer must have thought we were on the track and, no doubt, couldn't stop his speeding locomotive. He blasted his air horn and that bolted us up from sleep. We could hear that massive engine bearing down on us, and we began to scream. Jennings wanted to run, but he was too disoriented. He said all he could see was that train's front light in the car's back window. The engineer laid on his horn until the engine was even with our car. I felt the earth shake when that thing passed. I think if our car had worn another coat of paint, the additional thickness would have been enough to make us train bait.

We drove through Nashville on our trip home because we wanted to pitch the music we'd been making all summer. Our idea was to pick up a recording contract. Youth is so wonderfully optimistic.

On August 10, 1962, I made my first Nashville recording. Jennings and I did record a monaural demonstration tape at Globe Studios. A demonstration tape is not made for broadcast. It is merely intended to give a recording company a rough sketch of your skills or ideas. Then you hope the listener has enough imagination to realize how good the artist would sound with full recording benefits.

We spent what little money we had saved from our Five Sisters gig to record Johnny Tillitson's "Keeps Right on a Hurtin'," Bobby Darin's "Things," and "Pocket Full of Rainbows" from Elvis Presley's *G.I. Blues* motion picture.

Then we began pounding the sidewalks to show our demonstration tapes to major recording companies in Nashville, to see which one would give us the highest offer. There was no highest offer. There was no lowest offer. There was no offer.

We went without appointments, and needless to say, we weren't even seen, let alone heard.

Except by one man. His name was Mr. Silverstein. He is deceased, but in 1962, he was with the now-defunct Decca Records. At the time, another blind singer-pianist, Ray Charles, had the biggest record in the nation called "I Can't Stop Loving You." That song was from an album titled "Modern Sounds in Country and Western Music." I think it sold about fifteen million copies. Mr. Silverstein was nice. He said he knew it was hard for someone who can't see to try to make it in music. But our music, he said, just wasn't as good as we thought it was.

He told us to go home and work on it for about a year. He told us not to get discouraged.

Mr. Silverstein took great pains to let us down gently. But I'm sure we thought his courtesy exceeded his recognition of quality music. I took his advice and returned to Nashville—but not for eleven years. After my arrival that time, a few million people would hear I'd come to town.

I had not spent much time with Homer since Phenia's death, so for the remainder of August 1962, in the wake of Mr. Silverstein's pronouncement that our music wasn't as good as we thought, I went to visit Homer for a month. He had moved off the mountain in Meadow Branch. His "new" place was also a cabin, embedded deep in a woods, invisible from the nearest road, a quarter mile away. He had electricity and, by then, owned a television. But there was no running water. My acquaintance with bathrooms was interrupted, once more, for the month I stayed with Homer.

Homer cooked and read for me. It was a fitting reunion with the man who had raised me, and as I look back, I'm glad I went to live with him until school started.

George Bristol drove me the nine miles into Towns County in northeastern Georgia to Young Harris Junior College for enrollment. The State Commission for the Blind would have subsidized my tuition at any of the big, state universities, but it was enough of an adjustment to be with sighted students for the first time in my life. I didn't want the added adjustment of living on a rolling campus that was far from Homer and the Bristols. Young Harris was close enough for them to come see me, and vice versa, frequently.

The State of North Carolina financed my tuition, books, and dormitory at an out-of-state school the members of the State Commission for the Blind had never even heard of. They even paid someone to read my lessons into a tape recorder for me. I'll always be grateful for that. Their generosity was partly due to my grade-point average at Governor Morehead.

It was at Morehead that the wonderful spirit of independence was instilled in me. As part of our instruction, we were taken to downtown Raleigh, about five miles from campus. We were not told where we were, or how to get home, and we were left there.

It was our responsibility to ask for directions, then successfully negotiate traffic and traffic lights as we walked with a cane, by ourselves, back to campus.

I completed that exercise many times, but I was nonetheless anxious about the Young Harris campus. I was the first blind student to go there. As I look back, I don't know if I even wanted to go to college. I wanted a career in music. But everybody told me I had no chance, because the music industry was high-risk for anybody, sighted or blind. I was accused of being impractical and of "having foolish dreams" by folks who cared about me. I had vowed long ago not to be a financial burden on society, so I thought college might be the only route to vocational independence for me. I guess I looked at college as a meal ticket.

But college wound up doing more for my self-image and personal esteem than anything else. It gave me social confidence I never would have had otherwise. My academic training at Young Harris was sufficient to earn me a full scholarship to law school at Emory University in Atlanta. Nonetheless, the most valuable part of my junior college education was social.

I used a cane for about a week at Young Harris. I didn't want to be led by classmates. But that was the last time I used it. I tired very quickly of shoving it under tables and accidentally poking people and things. I was always around people, so I didn't need a guide dog. After I was shown around campus a few times, I had no trouble making my way by myself.

I was assigned a room with Ed McDaniel and Dwight Rayburn. They'd never been around a blind person; they were uncomfortable and told me.

"What do we have to do for you?" they asked. "Do we brush your teeth, do we comb your hair?" They were not being malicious; they were honestly seeking information, and sincerely trying to help.

But given the nervousness I felt anyhow from being with sighted strangers, their questions did not make me feel especially welcome. They told me the first day they really didn't want a blind roommate. They had a friend who was rooming with someone else. They asked if I would trade places with their friend.

Well, I wanted to be liked. But I didn't want to start my college career by going against the assignments and rules, and I had been assigned to live with Ed and Dwight. So I told them I would not move, I would remain their roommate.

I wound up having some classes with both Ed and Dwight, and they were very helpful in showing me the way. But I think they viewed me as an albatross, restricting their activities.

That all changed one day when, after a week on campus, Ed and I visited a new dormitory, Winship Hall, because it had washers and dryers. Ed was going to do his laundry.

En route, we passed a room, and I asked him what went on in there.

"This is a recreation room," Ed said.

I asked him about the furnishings, and he mentioned a ping pong table, a dance floor, and a juke box.

And then he said the magic words—"and a piano."

The news of the piano did more to make me feel at home in this home away from home than anything else ever would.

"Listen," I said, "you go on ahead and do your laundry, and I'll just stay here with this piano."

"You play?" he asked.

I merely said again that I would stay there, and Ed went off to do laundry.

I sat down alone in the empty room where my voice was an echo and did some "cooking." The sound escaped through open doors as I played and sang "Lonely Teardrops," "Stand by Me," "I Couldn't Sleep at All Last Night," "Sherry," and others.

In about an hour, McDaniel returned for the roommate he had left alone with a piano. By then, the place was packed. There was a party going on, with lots of cheering, dancing college students. That might have been the first real party of the new academic session. The event was a smash. I never heard talk again about my becoming someone else's roommate. I was a hit with Ed and Dwight. On the rare occasions when I see Ed today, he always scolds me kiddingly for telling people that he didn't want me as his roommate.

After my spontaneous concert on the way to the laundry, the majority of students wanted to be my friend. I had several invitations to become a roommate. I don't resent that. If I have anything that makes people accept me, I thank God for it. It so happens I have music as my medium for acceptance: It's up to me to break the ice, to make people feel comfortable around me. It was my attitude then; it's my attitude today.

Blind people, I've noticed all my life, are the targets of unfair stereotyping. People seem to have a preconception that blind folks have to be small in stature and without skills.

I'm neither. I participate in sports (I bowled a 160 average at Governor Morehead), I read regularly, I'm an avid ham radio operator, and I can build or repair some electronic things.

I love to drive the "bumper cars" on carnival midways, whenever I play state fairs or big theme parks. I've even been stopped by the authorities for driving a real car.

I know there are blind folks who want to be dependent. I'm not among them. Since leaving Young Harris at twenty-one, I've always been a taxpayer, not a tax burden.

Ed McDaniel became my best friend at Young Harris. Eventually, it was just the two of us, rooming together, and he'd read my lessons aloud to me. We had a lot of the same classes, and we shared study time.

I loved many of the classes. I had some wonderful instructors. My favorite was Zel Miller, a political science teacher, who went on to become the lieutenant governor of Georgia. His classes were an event because of his electrifying lectures. His presentations were as entertaining as they were informative. I looked forward every school day to his charismatic delivery. He and I are still friends, and I intend to endorse his campaign for governor.

My only failing grade at Young Harris was in music appreciation. If you think that's ironic, think about this: I loved the course and passed the tests, but failed anyhow. It was my first course of the day on Mondays. At that time I had begun spending weekends on Atlanta's Auburn Avenue, a rough neighborhood, where I occasionally sat in at the Royal Peacock. I loved to go there for the sheer entertainment. It was virtually an all-black club whose members were very warm toward me.

I love rhythm and blues music. I heard some of the biggest names in black music there, including the Ike and Tina Turner Revue, Diana Ross and the Supremes when they were just called the Supremes, Sam and Dave, Jackie Wilson, Stevie Wonder (when he was known as "Little Stevie Wonder"), and others.

The people in that club loved me. They'd jump up on the tables, or else pound the tables with the wood swizzle sticks that came with their drinks. One end of each stick had a wooden ball. Whenever the audience got pumped up over an entertainer, they would beat those balls on the tables. It sounded like a deafening orchestra composed entirely of revved up drummers. Whenever I went there, I'd be called up to sing.

That was a lot more fun than the school's music appreciation, which I nonetheless studied. But I missed a lot of classes because I overslept on Mondays after too much weekend at the Royal Peacock. Missing classes was interpreted by the instructor as insubordination. He told me he failed me because I thought I was too "cool" for his class. In fact, I didn't. I wish he had been content to instruct me, and not second-guess me.

The college dean and I also had our differences. Once I was standing with a group of boys and asked, "What do you think about the dean?" I didn't pose the question politely. My tone was a cue for them to say he was a creep. But no one responded. I later learned that he was standing there when I asked the question. O-o-o-p-s!

The dean heard that I was playing and hanging out in what he thought was an unfit environment. He'd heard that there was suspicious behavior at the Royal Peacock. There was nothing suspicious about it. There was wide-open drunkenness, brawling, fornicating, and an occasional stabbing. I'd hear customers beating each other, bellowing painfully to sounds of shattering beer and whiskey bottles, which they broke over each other's heads. The dean thought it wasn't exactly the conservative concert hall one might select for someone with my background in classical music.

He thought my playing the club in Atlanta cast a negative light on

Young Harris. I couldn't ask him to come see the place for himself. I was afraid someone would knock him out. I'll admit I was running with a hell-raising crowd at school. I just enjoyed a good time when I was younger. My circle of partying friends and musicians were more fun than the button-down brains at the school. I guess because my grades were good, and because I was blind, people expected my personal life to be more subdued.

There was a guy named Earl McClain who lived in the Young Harris dormitory next door to Ed and me. He played drums with a band in Gainesville, Georgia. Earl persuaded me to meet the guy who ran the band and subsidized it financially. His name was Joe Lothridge. (Joe was the guy who first took me to the Royal Peacock.) The following Friday, Earl and I went to Gainesville, and I spent the weekend at his house. That night, I sat in with the band, called the Dimensions. We played the Gainesville Civic Center. I sang, "You Don't Know Me," "Lonely Teardrops," and "Crying," among other songs. The people went crazy, so Joe invited me back the following weekend and asked me to stay at his house.

Next week, I returned and stayed with Joe and his parents, Fred and Inez. They were the first wealthy people I ever knew. Fred owned, with his brothers, a construction business that built roads and interstate highways.

I played with the Dimensions again that weekend and virtually every weekend after that for a long time, except when I went home to Hayesville.

Joe would pick me up and drive me to Gainesville or Atlanta or wherever he had booked the Dimensions. His family took me to the nicest store in Gainesville and bought me hundreds of dollars worth of clothes—Gant shirts and pants and loafers and wing tip shoes.

I never thought I'd ever wear clothes like that. I'd always worn those Dee-Cee jeans when I was a kid, and then I bought some nice clothes from money I earned tuning pianos, but I never bought anything that nice.

The Lothridge family took me to parties, and invited me to stay with them. Going to college and being accepted by people like the Lothridges really excited this boy from Meadow Branch. I'll always appreciate their kindness and generosity.

Joe was the catalyst for my continued interest in rhythm and blues.

He loved James Brown, and he wanted me to sing like him, but I wasn't really into James Brown's music at the time. (I was more into Ray Charles, Chuck Jackson, and Bobby "Blue" Bland.) It seemed to me that Brown screamed a lot. "U-u-h, Good God!" was one of his famous, belly-bolted yells.

Still, I was so desirous of keeping Joe's acceptance that I started listening more to James Brown's music, developed an appreciation for it, and started performing his songs during the Dimensions' shows. By then, I was an all-out member of the band.

I always loved rhythm and blues music. Joe and I shared the same love. He took me to Atlanta to meet Jackie Wilson. I got to go backstage at the Royal Peacock to meet Ben E. King. Sometimes the stars would ask me up on stage to sing with them.

And so Joe and I and the Dimensions became regular attractions at Atlanta's rough and rowdy Royal Peacock Club. Joe and I were both accepted because the crowd could sense our genuine love for their music.

We became a band of white boys playing the blues. We performed for the crowd during shows, and had late-night dinners with them afterwards. We'd go into cafes that were just as rough as the night-clubs, or even more so, because by the time the crowd got there after closing a bar, they were really drunk. Years later, people asked me if I was afraid. It's a question I never thought about at the time. Our music made those of us who played it, and those who listened, color-blind.

The Civil Rights Act, activism, and scores of social programs have done wonderful things to bring the races together. We had none of that, and needed none of that, in 1963 on Atlanta's Auburn Avenue. For blacks and whites alike, music was the melting pot.

The most popular disc jockey in Atlanta at that time was Pat Hughes. He was the star of WQXI-AM, the big pop radio station. He had come to some of the Dimensions' shows, and he invited us to be his guest on the radio. He became a dear friend and booster to my career. I didn't know it at the time, but he had a reason for suggesting that we play Atlanta's Misty Waters Club.

The place was actually a roller rink, and many of the popular music giants of the day headlined there. If the Royal Peacock was the "in" place for blacks, Misty Waters was the jumping joint for whites.

And Pat insisted we play there.

"If you can make it at Misty Waters, you'll have proven yourself in this market," he said.

So Joe booked us into the roller rink, which at night was converted into a teenage dance hall. The kids were milling around as we were setting up our instruments. No one paid much attention.

Then the music kicked off and the excitement kicked in. People crowded around our bandstand. They were jumping up and down in front of the stage. They screamed and yelled, and we encored after each set. We couldn't have gone over better.

Recalling that night reminds me of a question I'm frequently asked today, now that I am a major concert act. People want to know if I'm glad that I no longer have to play dances. The answer is "no," I'm sorry I no longer get to play dances.

Playing a dance is touching fans on the front lines. They get so turned on they don't just applaud, as they do in a concert setting, but actually quit dancing. They crowd around me in an effort to touch me. Some of the girls get on their boyfriends' shoulders just to reach me. There is a kind of chain reaction in which my enthusiasm mounts as I draw off theirs. It goes back and forth, and it's a high with its own brand of ecstasy.

So why don't I still play dances? I can't afford to financially. When I began my career, and wondered if I'd ever reach the point where I'd be a concert attraction, there were four or five of us in the band who traveled in one car with our equipment. Today, my band and crew number around thirty. We travel in three customized touring buses. A semitrailer truck transports our sound equipment. I pay for the lodging, feeding, and salaries of all of those people, as well as the purchase and maintenance of the equipment. It amounts to several thousand dollars a day, and millions of dollars annually.

What dance halls in the world are large enough to house enough ticket-buying people to meet my overhead expenses? There is Billy Bob's in Texas and a handful of others, most of which are in Texas. I have to play large arenas where thousands of tickets can be sold to pay all the people and expenses I incur just to show up.

People think I earn a lot of money. It would be more accurate to say I handle a lot of money.

*   *   *

At the dance that night at Misty Waters in Atlanta, Pat Hughes was watching very closely how well the Dimensions went over with the crowd. He wanted to see if our magic worked at a white club the way it had at a black one. And I guess he figured seeing was believing, and that we in fact had mass appeal.

Pat connected me with Huey Meaux, the "Crazy Cajun" record producer from Houston, Texas. Pat even arranged for Huey to come to Atlanta to hear me. The Dimensions were still Joe's band, but by then, I was doing at least half, and often more of, the "front" work.

I sang most of the solos and played a lot of lead on piano. Huey listened with the idea of producing a record which he in turn would take to major record companies. The system then, as it is today, is largely a matter of a producer making a record by an artist, both of whom derive a commission from copies of the record sold by the record company.

Huey paid a whopping $1,500 for me to record four songs.

Today, with high album production costs, it seems as though I pay $1,500 to produce a single note!

I recorded the songs in a studio owned by the LeFevres, a southern gospel group. It was the first real studio I'd ever been in. I don't count that demonstration tape Jennings Bristol and I made the day after the train nearly killed us in Nashville. I took the Dimensions plus a twenty-piece horn section. Twenty horns! If Gabriel had signaled the call to Heaven that day, his blast would have been lost in a brass section in Atlanta.

We recorded each of the songs in one or two takes. And we did it live, that is to say, with each musician recording his part of the song at the same time the others did. We used a three-track recorder.

Today's records are often made with a thirty-two-track recorder. They are recorded instrument by instrument, one at a time, using electronics and computers, which are just as important to the modern product as the musicians' skills are.

Today, it often takes months to get a record distributed after it's recorded. Huey had the songs recorded, pressed, distributed, and for sale in two weeks.

We sold 15,000 copies in Atlanta immediately, where Pat played them on his radio show, and where I was performing at Misty Waters and the Royal Peacock.

The record was less successful outside Atlanta. I'm not sure we sold one copy beyond Atlanta's city limits.

I think the disappointing sales had to do with the assassination of President John F. Kennedy the same week my record went on sale. One side of the record was titled "Total Disaster"; the other was called "It Went to Your Head." Neither had a thing to do with the shooting, but that was so heavily in the days' news, I think a lot of folks thought the tunes were irreverent ditties about the assassination.

When the record came out, and I became known in Atlanta, I received the first significant "press" of my career. A reporter came to one of the clubs. He stayed for the entire show. He liked what he heard. He wrote a rave review. His report was distributed into newspapers throughout Georgia.

And he misspelled my name.

My name at birth was Millsaps. I went to Governor Morehead and Young Harris Junior College as Ronnie Millsaps. Now that my performance was finally reviewed, I was so excited, that I never would have complained to the editors or reporters of the *Atlanta Constitution* about the misspelling.

I changed my name instead.

Not long after the article, I went to the courthouse and had my name legally changed to Milsap. And that's how it appeared on my record for Huey Meaux on the Princess label.

I spent the spring of 1964 enjoying the success of what became only a local record. It brought me a bunch of fans, one of whom was beautiful. Her name was Joyce Reeves. That was a quarter century ago, and she is still with me. You see, she was going to change her name to Milsap too.

12

In April 1964, just one month before my graduation from Young Harris College, the scent of rain-drenched Georgia pines was everywhere. Life was coming alive. I was twenty-one years old, a milestone for an American male, and my friends and I were busting out that spring. With our junior college years almost completed, we were being courted by the four-year schools and state universities. The North Carolina State Commission for the Blind had arranged interviews for me with officials at Emory University, Atlanta. By April, I had my first record behind me, and a career as a lawyer ahead of me.

Soon, both would be forgotten.

Twenty-one is a nice age. It signals the closing months of one's free-spiritedness. You can still act crazy, and people will forgive you and say you're just an overgrown teenager. My buddies and I drew on that attitude as long as we could get away with it.

Joe Lothridge was dating a girl named Pat Haynes. Pat was hostessing a dinner party one night and invited Joe and his friends. One of the guests that night was Pat's cousin, Joyce Reeves.

All Joyce knew about me was that I was a singer and that I had a record out. Joyce's brother, Billy Reeves, liked my two-sided Georgia hit, but at that time, Joyce had not heard it.

There was another singer popular in Georgia then, Harry Aldridge. Joyce remarked to some friends, "He isn't as good as Harry Aldridge, is he?"

She had never met anyone blind before, and she really didn't know what to expect. Later she told me that she didn't expect me to be so tall, and so confident! She also said I was charismatic. That made me feel good. She's always made me feel that my blindness made no difference to her.

The night of the dinner party, Joyce and I talked with ease. I've never met anyone, to this day, whom I've been so attracted to so instantly. Something just clicked between us. Joyce is the warmest and most caring person I've ever known.

I remember we played records, and that she liked Patsy Cline, Timi Yuro, and Ray Charles. She liked country and pop, and she loved the blues. She was the first girl I'd ever met that liked the same kinds of music that I did. It was as if everyone else at that party was invisible. I was that tuned into her, and she to me. We found our own little corner of the world.

When the evening ended, I asked Joe Lothridge about Joyce. I wanted to know what she looked like. I had to know if she was as pretty outwardly as she was inwardly.

Joe said she was a doll. He said that I ought to call her, because he thought she liked me, and because I could be proud to take her anywhere.

So call her I did. About a week after the dinner party at Pat's house. I told her a group of us were going to go listen to music the following evening in Atlanta and asked her to come along. I don't suppose you could call that invitation a date. But the mass invitations were a ruse. I invited all those people to go to the nightclub just so I could be around Joyce. I had been with her just once at a dinner party, but I couldn't get her off my mind. I was afraid to call and ask her to see me one on one, for fear she would refuse. Years earlier, I was unafraid to walk five miles alone through Raleigh, North Carolina's bustling traffic. But now I was afraid to ask this new girl in my life for a date.

We went to a place called the Casanova Club in the Bel Air Hotel in Atlanta. The group included Joyce, Joe, Pat, and members of the Dimensions. There were twelve in all.

I was wishing ten would get lost.

Everybody was drinking except Joyce. I had one Singapore sling, and nothing else. Some of the people in our party were really drinking it up. Joyce never liked to drink, and we have that in common today.

There was a black, three-piece band at the Casanova Club that night, led by a guy I knew named Nat Foster. The Casanova Club was not a dive. Its audience was racially mixed, and the music was always good. Most of the time it was jazz.

Nat asked me to get up and sing, and I thought, "Oh boy, this is my chance to impress her." Since she hadn't heard my record, this would be the first time she would hear me sing. I was going to wow her with my dynamics.

I sang "Try Me," by James Brown, and a couple of Elvis tunes.

I walked off the stage to applause, and as I sat down at our table, Joyce leaned over, took my arm and said, "That was really great, Ronnie!"

She'd just made my night!

Some of the girls at our table began to giggle and whisper. It was the kind of laughter girls emit when they're up to mischief. A good-looking guy nearby had sent a note to Joyce, asking her to dance.

Now Joyce, as I've explained, was not my date. She certainly was not "with" me. But instantly, I felt jealous. But I didn't say a word. I didn't have to.

Joyce could see I was upset. She was perceptive enough to pick up on it, and kind enough to act on it. She refused to dance with a man she didn't know to spare the feelings of someone she barely knew.

That made a big impression on me then, and I never forgot. Later that night I got up enough courage to ask Joyce to dance with me. We slow-danced, as the band played "Misty." It was the first time I held her.

The band played its last set, and we paid our tabs. I told Joyce I'd walk her to the car, but once outside, she was in a playful mood and said, "Let's race to the car!"

Her mood was contagious.

"Race?" I exclaimed, "You think you can outrun me? You're on!"

We broke into a run. I assumed that if she wanted to race, it would be across a path with no obstructions. It was, until we reached the parking lot. In the heat of the race, Joyce forgot to tell me that we were getting close to the car. So I ran into it . . . at full speed!

I tore my slacks, my leg was scratched, and I was hobbling around in mock pain. I had impressed her with my music; I wondered how I was doing with my athletic skills.

She knew I wasn't really hurt, but I still braced myself for the sympathy people sometimes naturally showed to me when they thought I was injured.

Instead I heard laughter.

Joyce was laughing at the sight of me dancing on one foot and holding the other, while occasionally bouncing off the car. My antics entertained her like nothing I had planned.

I loved it.

I was determined long ago not to let any person, place, or thing stand in the way of what I truly wanted to do. My life is a nonstop quest for independence and individuality. Even in 1964, when I was an obscure entertainer, I wouldn't allow people to treat me with pity, but occasionally a few would.

Not Joyce.

She figuratively knocked me to my knees by being able to laugh with me that night, and there was nothing malicious or unfeeling about it. She would have laughed if a sighted person had made such a blunder. And she laughed because I had too. The absence of well-meaning discrimination toward me was wonderful.

About two weeks later, Joyce came up to Young Harris for my graduation. My zoology teacher said, "Is that the girl you've been dating? You'd better hold on to *her;* she's beautiful!"

I loved it.

Neither of us dated anyone else after that first night.

When I met Joyce I fell in love with her instantly.

It was love at first sound!

It was the most wonderful thing that ever happened to me! I was so shy. Despite all the social progress I had made at Young Harris, I was still personally insecure.

When we performed around Atlanta and the crowds were so tremendous, I couldn't help but think that the people were coming because of Joe Lothridge.

"If it weren't for his money and power and my being in his clique, I wouldn't be anything," I thought. "I'm something, but only because I'm in with the in crowd."

Later that summer, in a painful effort to establish my own identity, I broke off from the Dimensions. I toured North Carolina with my own band. I returned to Atlanta in the fall and by then the Dimensions had dissolved forever.

To move to another state for three months just to test myself on my own should demonstrate how insecure I was at twenty-one. My insecurity and the fact that I'd known her only two weeks prevented me from expressing my feelings to Joyce. But it took tragedy to put me in touch with my true feelings.

One of my best friends in the Dimensions was Larry Dixon, a horn player who attended the University of Georgia. He was a likable, outgoing guy, an electric personality, whose festive spirit made every minute a miniature Mardi Gras.

After the Dimensions' shows, I'd often go to Larry's home in Athens and spend the night. On this particular night, he again invited me to go home with him. We had played a show near Atlanta, and I would have gone with him, but Joyce came to the show, and I wanted to be with her after the nightclub closed.

It was a Saturday night, and I told Larry to go on home. I said I'd see him at our next show. I saw him, but not at the show. I helped carry his body at his funeral.

Larry had almost reached his house that night when he apparently fell asleep at the wheel. Investigators said he drove off the road and was thrown from his car, which rolled over on him. If I had been with him, I no doubt would have sat in the front seat, where I would have played the radio, talked, and kept him awake.

For two weeks after Larry's death, I could feel his presence. He was there in spirit, but invisible. He was as strongly apparent as if he were breathing.

That might sound spooky, but there was a lesson in it for me. The more I felt Larry, the more I missed him, and the more I wished I had told him how much I cared for him when he was alive. It hit me like a thunderbolt.

I vowed I would never again refrain from telling those I loved just how I felt. The next time I was with Joyce, I told her that I was in love with her, and I've told her every day since for twenty-five years. We celebrated our twenty-fourth wedding anniversary on October 30, 1989.

People may expect me to reveal more about my relationship with

Joyce, but I'm very much a private person. Consequently, I can't talk or write comfortably about my love, respect, and deep feelings for my wife. But let me say, she has been more responsible for all the good things that have happened in my personal and professional life than anybody. We are very lucky to have each other; she is the light of my life.

13

When I broke away from the Dimensions in the summer of 1964 and took a new five-piece band of musicians with me to North Carolina, our first job was in Asheville, at a little place called "The Pump Room."

We stayed in Asheville for about a month before moving on to Charlotte and Fort Bragg.

One evening while I was working at the Sky Club in Asheville, I got a phone call from Joyce back in Georgia. Someone trying to reach me had given her a phone number for me to call. A friend of mine had died.

I recognized the number immediately, and it broke my heart. I knew it had to be Larry Atwell, my best friend throughout my student days at Morehead.

I spoke with Larry's father, and he confirmed what I dreaded to hear—Larry had died five days earlier. The cause of death was kidney failure.

I couldn't believe he was dead. He was just my age, twenty-one years old. When I went away to college, in another state, it was harder for Larry and me to keep in touch.

I'd been close to the Atwell family since I was six. I still love them, and I thought of all the pain they were going through. I wanted to help in some way, because Larry was like a brother to me. I told Mr. Atwell that I would be there as soon as I could get a ride. After the show that night, the band and I packed up and drove to Charlotte.

One of the guys in my band arranged for an audition at Winston's, a local nightclub there. I stayed at the Atwell house during that three-week engagement.

We had plenty of time to talk about old times: the first day of school when Larry and I met while crying on the steps of the dormitory; when Larry, his sister Wanda, and I played Monopoly all night; about all the fun trips I had coming home with Larry; about the time Larry and I played records on his brother Ed's record player ... without Ed's permission! And when Larry and I would stay up all night at school getting way behind on our homework, talking about our girlfriends.

I told them about Joyce, the wonderful girl I had recently met and fallen in love with. I told them we planned to get married soon. I only wish Larry could have met her.

In the fall of 1964, I moved into a tiny studio apartment at 247 Eleventh Street in Atlanta. I had enjoyed limited success playing during the summer in North Carolina, but the success I had was mine. The people who came to see me did not come to see the Dimensions. I now had the professional reassurance I needed.

When I moved back to Atlanta that fall, Joyce was living with a roommate two miles away. She worked days as a secretary and drove me and the equipment to engagements around Atlanta in her Volkswagen at night.

I felt like an important person and had carved out my own identity, more than I ever had up to that time. I was living by myself in the middle of a big city. I had paying jobs; I wasn't earning the kind of money I had earned with Joe and the Dimensions, but I could support myself. And I was in love.

It was decision time.

I had gone to junior college for two years studying prelaw. I had done so as part of a master plan to go on to Emory University where the State of North Carolina had arranged for my financial subsidy in law school.

Now, with the start of the fall semester just days away, I was having serious doubts about wanting to become a lawyer. The pull toward a career in music was forever on my mind. Over the summer, I had wrestled with the idea of going to a new college in the fall. I had sought the advice of friends and loved ones, probably looking for somebody, anybody, to talk me out of becoming a lawyer.

But everyone's advice was the same. "Go on to law school," they said. "Don't neglect an opportunity like this. Music is too risky. Get into something with a solid future."

I came close to getting the advice I wanted from a few people who said to get the law degree, then if I still wanted to pursue music, I at least would have a sheepskin.

I told the North Carolina officials about my possible change of mind. I told them I had been sincere when I planned to go to law school; otherwise, I would not have spent two years in prelaw at Young Harris. I explained, though, that music remained my first love, and that I had always wanted it to be my career.

They told me I had a moral obligation. I was reminded of how the state had put a lot of money into my junior college education. They reminded me that two years of undergraduate study had been financed contingent upon my promise to finish college—in law. They reminded me of the red tape they had cut arranging for the State of North Carolina to subsidize me at an obscure junior college in Georgia.

They reminded me I was breaking that promise if I didn't go to law school, and said I should forget the pipe dream of becoming a professional musician.

Joyce was the only one who understood what I was going through. She said, "I'll stand by you whether you are a lawyer or a musician. You should do what *you* want to do. If your dream is music, then do it!"

So my decision was made.

A lot of fine people with the North Carolina Commission for the Blind had labored long and hard to secure my junior college education. In the fall of 1964, I let everyone down. I declined the scholarship to law school and went for the brass ring. I opted to pursue a career as a professional singer and musician.

The people who had worked for my academic future were angry, disappointed, and hurt. I'm sure they felt betrayed and taken advantage of. One of the many reasons I'm thankful for the success I've had is that it eased the pain for those good folks, and for me.

All I can say in my defense is that two wrongs don't make a right. I was mistaken when I said I wanted to be a lawyer. I would not have erased that mistake; I would have compounded it by going to law school.

So at twenty-one, while earning only $200 a weekend and not work-ing every weekend, I walked away from a full scholarship, complete with books, board, and tuition to an esteemed school in the South.

Until then, I had often wondered about my wisdom. After that, I had little doubt about my nerve.

In September, when school resumed all over America, it resumed without me. I had been going back every year without fail since I was six. I felt disoriented. I was conditioned to think academics when that first hint of fall touched the air.

Others my age, including many musician friends, went to campuses by day; I went to Atlanta's bars by night, playing and singing the rhythm and blues that was my musical signature until I signed with RCA Rec-ords as a country artist years later.

I still love rhythm and blues music, but I love it more than the majority of my fans do. They're the ones who indirectly pay the bills, and to whom I'm directly indebted for my success. I sing for me at home, but I sing for them on stage, and I sing what they've indicated they want to hear.

In the early fall of 1964, I was an indisputable item with Joyce Reeves, who back in June, had taken me to Douglas, Georgia, to meet her parents, Lewis and Pauline Reeves, and their three children who were living at home at the time, Billy, Kay, and Terry.

I've been asked through the years if Joyce's parents resented her throwing security to the wind by marrying a musician, and one who was blind.

The answer is "no."

In fact, Mr. Reeves told me right after Joyce and I were married that if the time came when I didn't have a job or a place to stay, we could live in his house. And he really meant it.

The Reeves have been supportive of Joyce and me since day one. They are my family; they have been for twenty-five years. I married one and employed two.

The foremost requirement I have for someone who works for me is integrity. I have entrusted my money to people who have squan-dered, mismanaged, embezzled, or flat-out stolen it. Joyce Reeves and her brothers have honesty in their veins. Trustworthiness is the blood of that family. That's important to me. I'm not necessarily tempted to surrender my career to someone who has an office in Burbank and can get a slightly higher performance fee.

I've tried that. Not everyone was dishonest, but too many times a person helping me to earn more money offset the increase by taking more from me, legally or illegally—but always unfairly.

I'll stay with Joyce and Donald Reeves as my cabinet of professional advisers. This is a family affair.

Donald Reeves, Joyce's brother, came into my life in 1965. Joyce spent much of that year living with Donald and his wife, Brenda. She would take them to clubs where I was singing in Atlanta.

One night, Donald came without Brenda. The three of us left the club at evening's end in Joyce's Volkswagen. Donald had had too much to drink, so I decided to accompany Joyce home and help get him into his house.

We sat him upright in the Volkswagen's back seat, but he kept falling over like a sack of potatoes. I'd feel the tiny car listing to the right, and shove my right arm quickly from the front seat just in time to keep him from toppling over. I'd get him situated, then he would lean to the left. This went on for miles.

When we got him home, he couldn't undress himself. I stood him against the wall, felt for his belt, and tried to lower his trousers. Before I could, plop, down he went. I hefted him back onto his feet, leaned him against the wall, and tried to unbutton his shirt. I got it partially undone, and he fell out of it. Thud, he hit the floor.

This went on until I finally got him down to his underwear, and in his bed. That was my initial introduction to Donald Reeves, the man who runs my conglomerate of businesses today.

I couldn't have made a better choice.

Donald enjoys telling that story on himself. He says it indicates how both of us put the past in the past, and he uses his drinking days as a testimony about his changed ways. Donald is a Christian today who is born again in the New Testament way. He doesn't go around preaching his beliefs. He just quietly lives them.

In April 1965, my disc jockey friend Pat Hughes arranged for me to sign a five-year contract with Scepter Records, a recording company in New York City. That represented my first affiliation with a national label, and the fulfillment of one of my lifetime dreams.

I was to go back to New York in November for a recording session at Scepter. I wanted Joyce to go with me, but she of course wouldn't, since we weren't married. Now, Scepter had already released my first record, entitled "Never Had It So Good." It became a top-five song around the country.

I could now provide for Joyce. I was getting some engagements around the nation as a result of the record. I needed Joyce to go with me to New York; I wanted her to become my wife.

We'd been engaged for about a year, and we had made plans to get married just after Christmas in Douglas so her folks could give us a church wedding.

I called her on October 30, 1965, on Saturday morning. I said, "Honey, let's get married today. I know your folks will be disappointed. I know they want you to have a church wedding. But if we're married now, you could go to Washington and New York with me! Let's do it now!"

She said "Yes!"

I had heard of a place in Lanet, Alabama, about a hundred miles from Atlanta, where we could get a blood test and a marriage license, and be married in an hour.

We needed a witness, so we drove to Donald Reeves' house. He was still in bed. We told him to get up, that we were off to get married, and needed a witness.

He wouldn't go.

"I've heard all of this before," he said. "You say this every Saturday. You-all aren't going to get married." And he went back to sleep.

We drove across the state line to Lanet, where we asked a total stranger in the courthouse to serve as our witness. We were married by a justice of the peace, and there were no pictures taken. Then the county gave us some "wedding cheer." It was a box of Cheer laundry detergent! We laughed and couldn't have been happier!

We stopped at a pay telephone, and Joyce called her folks and told them what we had done. She expected their disappointment, but instead received their love and best wishes. Their daughter had just eloped on Halloween eve with a blind musician whose immediate employment was playing a sock hop that night.

We stopped by to see Donald on the way back, who by then was out of bed. He didn't believe we were married. We showed him the marriage license and the Cheer. Then he got upset because we hadn't invited him to the wedding.

We reminded him that he wouldn't get out of bed for our wedding. He said we should have forced him, or gotten married when he wasn't sleepy.

There was a disc jockey in Atlanta at the time named Hugh Jarrett. He had reportedly been fired from WLAC radio in Nashville for using blue language on the air. He later sponsored sock hops, called "Hugh Baby Hops." We spent much of our wedding night in Marietta, Georgia, where I played a "Hugh Baby Hop."

After the show, we returned to Atlanta with members of my band, who took us to the Casanova Club to celebrate our marriage. Joyce and I stayed for a while, but finally, it was time to go home.

I returned to my apartment, with almost no furniture, and a new bride. Life was better that night than it had ever been.

My first record for Scepter, "Never Had It So Good," came out in September 1965. Its success had much to do with my decision to get married a month later.

That was an enormous year for me. I signed with a national label, got a top-five song, and got married.

I had heard about the record's heavy airplay, but I hadn't heard the record itself until late one night in the fall. I've always liked to turn the tuning dial on the radio. Even today, when I can't sleep nights, which frequently is the case, I lie in bed, listening to the radio. I was lying in bed, my mind drifting like the radio fuzz that filled the room. Then, on WQXI in Atlanta, there was a quarter note drumroll that jarred me from semisleep. I knew that signal to my song's introduction. Then there was my voice, pouring from the radio. My excitement was overpowering!

I leaped from bed and just walked around the room, listening to my song. I think my feet occasionally touched the ground. I struggled to keep from singing along, so I could hear the quality of the record.

I wanted to open my bedroom window and play it for the world. Soon after, I heard the song on stations in New York, Washington, D.C., and the Carolinas. My Gosh! I had a record out, played between other records by name artists! It is every singer's dream to have a recording contract. It's a bigger dream to have a hit record, and I had mine!

It didn't take long for me to get confident. I remember saying jokingly, "This thing of becoming a recording artist wasn't nearly as hard as everybody said it was going to be."

Yet, did I feel lucky? "Lucky" is understating it. I remember thinking how easy the recording industry was; how easy it had been to get a hit song. I stayed on Scepter Records from 1965 through 1969, releasing two singles a year. And I never had another significant hit on Scepter.

Furthermore, I never made any money on Scepter. No matter how many copies a record sold, I was always told that production and promotional fees had absorbed potential profits.

One day I called Scepter. I wanted to talk to Paul Cantor or Stanley Greenberg. Around Atlanta, I was getting accustomed to people knowing who I was. The Scepter receptionist wanted to know who was calling.

"This is Ronnie Milsap," I said.

"Who?" was her baffled reply.

"Hmmm," I thought, "must be a bad connection. Maybe she didn't hear me."

"This is Ronnie Milsap in Atlanta," I said again politely, waiting for her response.

She cupped her hand over the telephone's mouthpiece, but I could still hear her gum-chomping shout.

"Hey, does anybody here know a Rodney Milstone or something like that from down south?" she yelled.

No one in the office knew me, she said.

"I'm Ronnie Milsap and I'm on your label," I yelled.

She put me on hold.

Imagine: my own record company not knowing my name. This didn't reassure me regarding the company's promotional intentions. If she hasn't heard of me, how are those folks going to make anybody else aware of me, I wondered?

It was a valuable lesson in humility.

However, the two key promotion men for Scepter, Pete Garris and Steve Tyrell, later heard about the incident with the receptionist and were mad. Pete and Steve had worked hard to get me my first hit record, and during all the times I worked with them, they were always supportive.

Steve Tyrell and I became good friends, and he helped me with some recording sessions in Houston, his hometown, in the summer of 1966. I regret that I don't get to see him anymore.

That same year, the executives at Scepter expected me to "work" my hit record, and make personal appearances to promote the song.

My first major engagement was a seven-day booking at the Howard Theater in Washington, D.C., on a package show. When I say "major engagement," I mean that I was booked with artists who comprised the "Who's Who of Rhythm and Blues Entertainers" of the day. There were Little Anthony and the Imperials, Sam and Dave, Maxine Brown, among others. Not a bad booking for a guy with only one hit record. Joyce and I and my bass player were literally the only white people in the entire theater.

The instructional value was measureless to me. For example, I had no idea that as a name attraction I was expected to tip certain theater employees. Maxine Brown took me under her wing and explained that there was an unwritten rule in show business that entertainers were expected to take care of people who took care of them.

Maxine gave me a pecking order of those who were to receive gratuities, such as the stage manager, dressing room manager, and band leader. Today, wherever I play, I continue to express my appreciation to those in the service part of my industry. The difference is that on today's engagements, I don't have to wait to be paid before I can pay, as was the case at the Howard Theater in 1965.

I broke into the big league R & B circuit doing four shows a day for a solid week. That's how Joyce and I spent the first week of our marriage.

I don't know how I kept my excitement under control.

"Exciting" is the word Joyce uses most frequently too, when recalling that Howard Theater engagement.

Each day's show was not just a concert, it was an event. The entertainers began each day with a matinee performance. We'd do a couple of hours, then the theater would play a motion picture. Fans would come and go and watch and listen. It was all wonderfully informal, rehearsed but loose, and conducive to the relaxation that makes entertainment click.

A touring package show came to Washington one day during my

week-long engagement. It was called the "Motor Town Revue," and its entertainers were giants of the "Motown sound," the most popular music of that period.

The Motown performers had a day off and came unannounced to see the Howard Theater show one afternoon. Among the visitors were Martha and the Vandellas, the Temptations, and Stevie Wonder.

Stevie came backstage, and immediately, a good rapport developed between us. We talked shop and music and more. While the movie was shown out front, Stevie and I sat behind the screen at two pianos. The instruments were invisible to the crowd. Unknown to us, their sounds were not.

We were playing together, swapping licks and such, and apparently we got a little loud. Our voices behind the screen served as the unintended soundtrack for the film on it. I imagine the crowd was squirming in curiosity about the mismatch of video and audio.

Stevie and I were immune to any distraction we might have been making. Our momentum was interrupted by the theater manager. He was less than happy when he tripped through the darkened area between the back of the screen and the backstage wall.

He said he could hear us out front, and so could the audience. Stevie said to me, "The guy hasn't heard anything yet!"

Stevie was a major entertainer of the day, and somewhat independent. He told me to ignore the man. That's what Stevie did, and I followed his lead. Our playing continued. Then Stevie told me he wanted to do a song that would be his next single release. It was in that setting that I first heard Stevie Wonder do "Up Tight (Out of Sight)."

I think of that time and place each time I hear what is now a true Motown standard.

The Howard Theater gig came to a close seven days and twenty-eight performances after it began, not counting the movie reruns. Then, for Joyce and me, it was back to our home away from home: the road. The "road" is the figurative name given to the distance between engagements. It has nothing to do with concrete or asphalt. The road isn't always on the ground.

I was booked in Milwaukee where I was to be an opening act for James Brown. That was the good news—that I was going to be on a show with the hottest male singer of the day, perhaps in all of show business at that time. The bad news was that there was no way for me to make the show in time without flying to the date.

I couldn't go without Joyce, and Joyce wouldn't fly. It damaged the honeymoon mood of our marriage because I asked her to fly. She knew I knew about her fear of flying. She couldn't believe I would even ask her to board an aircraft.

I told Paul Cantor, my manager at that time, who had booked the date that I would accept no engagements requiring me to fly. He said that meant I wouldn't accept a lot of his engagements. He told me, in no uncertain terms, that if I weren't willing to fly, to find another agent, and to consider getting out of show business altogether.

I relayed that advice to Joyce, who was so upset because I was leaning toward flying that she slept that night in the bathtub.

She finally relented, and we flew to Milwaukee. We rode one of those old propeller planes which rose and fell markedly with the air pockets. It was not a very reassuring aircraft to someone afraid of flying.

My being a rhythm and blues act, with only one hit record, and getting to play a bill with James Brown is somewhat like a Baptist seminary student getting to hold a crusade with Billy Graham.

In 1965, the British invasion of rock stars was only one year old. Woodstock was still four years away. Elvis Presley's career had cooled, and the popularity of country music had not yet gone to town.

James Brown was one of the great soloists of the day. He was a showman's showman who sailed across the stage in lightning steps, faster on one foot than most entertainers were on two.

I got to the auditorium in Milwaukee and did what was supposed to be only a sound check with his band. But it turned into a two-hour, jam session. We blasted away the afternoon, singing virtually every song in my rhythm and blues repertoire. It was blistering hot—me and about fifteen pieces. I was soaring with confidence. I couldn't wait for that night and the show. I was going to knock Milwaukee on its ear.

My band consisted only of a bass player. Therefore, he and I learned the routines with James's full band, which was to accompany me in the concert.

Curtain time came and I was given a regal introduction. I hit the stage almost in a run. I was so anxious to play with James's scalding band the way we had during rehearsal that I dove head long into my first number. I heard my voice, my piano, and my bass guitarist. I heard nothing else.

What was happening, I wondered?

When the instrumental break came on my first song, I was playing piano and yelling at my bass player.

"What's going on?" I demanded. "I don't hear anybody playing."

"I don't know," he yelled. "They look like they're playing, but I don't hear them either!"

I did my entire thirty-minute set with just a voice, piano, and bass. The production would have been more complete on a demonstration tape recording.

I came off stage furious, frustrated, and mostly confused.

I went immediately to James Brown's bandleader and demanded an explanation.

"Is this the first show you've ever played with James?" he asked.

"Yes," I fired back.

"Oh, man, I thought you knew," he said. "James will let his band rehearse with you, and jam with you, but he won't let them play with you on the show. The horn players put their horns to their lips, and the guitarists hold up their guitars, but nobody plays anything. James doesn't want his players making anybody look good but him."

Had I known that I would make my debut in a major American market with such sparse instrumentation, I probably wouldn't have accepted the date. But that's the story of my thin-sounding premiere in Milwaukee with James Brown.

The B side of my first Scepter release was just beginning to get some attention when I was introduced to Ray Charles in Atlanta. It was my first encounter with him, and he was very nice to me. He congratulated me on the success of my record. Having applause from the legendary Ray Charles was a real thrill. He had long been one of my idols, and to this day, I regard him as one of the world's true recording geniuses.

So I was basking in his praise about my work when he dropped the other shoe.

"Yes sir, I really like the way you sing 'Let's Go Get Stoned'," he said. "I'm going to record the song myself."

Ouch.

I knew that if Ray cut the song, it would cripple the popularity of my version. He did, and it did. I've got to tell you that I thought my version of the song was good, but Ray's was better.

Later that year, Joyce and I went to New York, where I did my second recording session for Scepter. I saw the city as I never had before. Other folks had taken me up there and said things like "That building is seventy-five stories tall."

Joyce was more descriptive, describing a building as "so tall it goes into the clouds." She described in detail the people wearing furry hats and heavy coats in the bitter November cold. She filled me in about Christmas decorations during the festive holiday season. We were still newlyweds in Manhattan going to record for a label on which we already had a national hit—blissfully in love in the Big Apple, going for the gusto.

Life was getting sweeter!

Christmastime in New York is magical. Joyce and I still try to get up there each December to do our shopping. But the first Christmas there together will forever be special.

Scepter Records was footing the bill for our trip to New York. They had rented an inexpensive hotel room for us. The room was so tiny, you could lie in bed and turn on the television with your feet. We were on the twenty-fourth floor, and the old building would sway in the wind. The movement did little to reassure me. This was not what I'd meant when I said I wanted to make it to the top.

We ordered continental breakfasts because that was the cheapest thing on the menu. Scepter hadn't offered to pay our food. But at the time we didn't mind. We were too much in love and this was a honeymoon. If God made anything more exciting than young love, He kept it a secret.

We had ridden a train all the way from Atlanta to Manhattan. Joyce had her fear of flying, and I wasn't too crazy about it either. I still don't like to fly. You can just about gauge how many cocktails I drink annually by the number of times I fly. I'll have one before a flight to steady my nerves.

Whoever heard of a transportation service that reassures its passengers by having the stewardess put an oxygen mask over her face before takeoff? Each time I hear that preflight lecture about ". . . in the unlikely event of cabin depressurization," I want to get off.

Then they go into that rap about how your seat can be used as a flotation device in the event that the plane lands in water!

Landing and water are contradictions that mean crash! Who do they think they're kidding? Watch those flying commercials on television, and you think it's all so elegant. They don't talk about herding passengers onto aircraft like cattle, arriving late, and losing luggage. I got on an airplane once and thought it was a bigger plane than it was. During the preflight lecture from the flight attendant, I found out it was just a propeller plane, and not the bigger, safer jet I had thought. By this time, the plane was in the middle of the runway.

I made them let me off. They had to steer a flight of steel steps out to the cabin door, and I deplaned while everybody watched. I didn't care. I hate flying. Flying is at times unavoidable. It's almost never enjoyable.

That's why I mostly travel in my customized bus. I can read, get away from the telephones, and have some control over my departure and arrival times.

Joyce and I really got into that train trip on our visit to New York. We couldn't afford the sleeping car, so we slept sitting up. Joyce made roast beef sandwiches to bring along, because the dining car was financially impossible for us. Yet food and sleep were the least of our interests. When you're young and in love, none of that matters.

A month earlier, back in Atlanta, my decision to get married was also prompted by the fact that I had a job at a pretty solid nightclub.

My disc jockey friend Pat Hughes contacted me about a job at the Whiskey A-Go-Go, *the* thriving night spot in Georgia. Pat said there was a guitar player and singer there named J.J. Cale heading a three-piece group.

He was talking about the same J.J. Cale who went on to write "After Midnight" for Eric Clapton and "Magnolia" for himself, and lots of other big hits for big artists.

Pat urged me to audition to play keyboards with this Cale fellow. He said the band needed it to fill out its sound. "And," Pat said, "the job will probably pay you $500 a week."

I was astonished. A regular job that paid in three figures that were half the way to four!

"There just isn't that much money in all of the world," I told Pat.

"Yes there is," he said, "and you can get that job. You go on down there and audition!"

So I did.

Cale didn't want me. He didn't mean that personally; he just didn't want any keyboard player, and he told me so. I think his hint was something delicate like, "I don't want no God damn keyboard on my show." I played several numbers with him for several nights before he ever said anything else. Then he grew friendly. He began to mumble occasionally.

Eventually, I won his respect through my playing. The four pieces came together, the engagement ended, and I stayed on, adding three new players as part of my act. Cale and I went our separate ways with mutual respect. Once again, my skills had broken barriers. Cale is the type of guy who doesn't like you until he respects you, and among musicians, he only respects the best, he later told me.

But I nearly blew what was going to become my bread-winning job before I played the first night. I was all pumped up psychologically because I had listened too intently to Pat Hughes, who told me I was good enough for the engagement.

And Pat had insisted I could earn $500 a week at the place.

So I did my audition with Cale. Chic Hedricks, owner of the Whiskey A-Go-Go and a place called the Domino Lounge, called me into his office.

I had been my own agent before, but never for a job that was both high-paying and steady. I was trying not to let my nervousness show as I stood before him. What if he offered me more than the $500, I thought to myself? Should I act nonchalant and ask for even more?

I had barely earned any money that year, I wanted to get married, and I probably had nothing in my pocket. I can't recall if my rent was current.

"You got the job, Ronnie," Chic said, getting right to the point. He rushed along, saying when I could start, and that he'd pay me $450 a week.

"And I want you to remember . . . ," he tried to continue.

"Pardon me, sir," I interrupted. "Did you say $450?" I asked.

"Huh?" he exhaled, "yeah, four hundred fifty. Now as I was saying . . ."

"Wait a minute," I interrupted again.

I shifted from foot to foot, and put my hands nervously in my pockets—my empty pockets.

I should have explained how my diversified talent would go well in such a socially adaptable nightclub, and that such adaptability was worthy of a higher fee. I should have come with some kind of multi-syllable poppycock that sounded polite and educated during this, my first round of self-representation in employment negotiations.

But I said nothing like that.

The moment's silence grew heavy. Chic tried to go on again about what would be expected of me when I opened at the showcase room of the South.

"I'm worth $500 a week!" I blurted.

The room fell silent again. What had possessed me to say that? What had I done? How dare I? I've blown the whole thing. There won't be any job. There are plenty of other keyboard players. What had I done?

"You think you're worth five hundred a week?" Chic said at last.

More silence.

"Well, I think you are too."

I breathed a sigh of relief that was louder than anything I had said.

When I told Joyce and Donald Reeves that I had the job at the Whiskey A-Go-Go, he said I would need some sharp clothes worthy of the stage. I agreed, but said I had no money.

He said he did.

Donald was working as the manager of a finance company at the time. He took one entire paycheck and spent it on clothes for me. I remember arguing with him about how he needed his money, about how he had kids and a wife to support. He said he did need his money, but not as much as I did.

He didn't lend me the money; he gave it to me. He took me to Rich's department store in Atlanta and bought me a dinner jacket and other clothes. Because of Donald and his generosity, I opened in style.

I never forgot it.

*   *   *

There was a temporary slowdown in work in 1966. It was one of those breaks that seem to plague musicians eternally. Joyce and I went to a beach just outside of Jacksonville, Florida, for a second honeymoon. On the beach, Joyce taught me to write my name.

I was twenty-three years old, could type 120 words per minute, was self-supportive, already had played venues with national artists, but couldn't write my name. I don't know why, in light of the thorough education I received at Governor Morehead, that they didn't teach us to write our names. It was so embarrassing not to be able to sign a check, or even apply for a checking account.

Back in Atlanta, Joyce had tried to teach me the alphabet in cursive. I couldn't understand it. But the sand—ah, that was different. I could feel my work. Joyce guided my finger through the sand. I then felt the raised sand bordering my writing. The raised sand gave me a tactile picture.

That's how I learned to sign my name. In years to come, after entering into some agreements, I'd wish I had learned to erase it.

By 1966, I was becoming well known around Atlanta, and around the national rhythm and blues circuit. My first Scepter record would stand as my biggest R & B recording. I was also getting plenty of one-night show dates.

Sometimes, the shows were little more than orchestrated fights. More than once I slid under the piano for shelter from flying beer bottles during free-for-alls.

By this time, Joyce was doing a lot of the show booking. She handled all the business, a bride of one year going in and out of the knife-wielding clubs of America's roughest inner-city neighborhoods. She handled the telephone negotiations, executed the contracts, drove me in a van to the shows, set up my VOX organ faster than anyone I'd ever seen, and collected the performance money after we arrived.

And she never complained.

Around this time, Joyce and I were in Manhattan, where I was scheduled to do a recording session. A Scepter representative took us to Queens to an automobile dealership. We thought that Scepter was going to give us a van we could travel in from show to show. Instead, they gave the dealership a down payment. They gave us the payment book. Then we gave payments for thirty-six months.

After acquiring the van, Joyce drove me, in one sitting, through the fast and narrow streets of New York, to North Carolina, to our next booking in Houston. She had married me for better or worse. During the lean years, she got the worst end of trying to make my career successful.

We had our regular address in Georgia. Notice I didn't say permanent. We moved three times in three years. I can recall the addresses as vividly as I can the names of those towns I traveled through as a kid going back to Meadow Branch on a bus from Governor Morehead.

There was 5375 Roswell Road, Atlanta; 2510 Sherwood Drive, Jonesboro, an Atlanta suburb; and 2541A Shallowford Road, Atlanta.

Because we were often on the road when the utility bills came due, we'd sometimes return to find the electric and telephone service disconnected. It was no big deal. We'd simply call the utility companies and send the payments, and service would resume. It was imperative that we have a telephone, so Joyce could communicate with show promoters around the country. Many times we returned to Atlanta just in time to call the promoters to firm up arrangements for the next tour.

We were evicted from our first apartment. It was a painful experience. Joyce had decorated the place, and it was our official home away from our unofficial home—the road. It was there that we adopted the big things that make a house a home, such as glorious immersion in romance, and the nuts and bolts part of a day-to-day marriage, such as doing the laundry and paying the bills. We had the best of both under one roof—our roof—our first roof. It was our permanent address renewable every thirty days. We loved the place where we were in love.

Virtually any married couple can remember two things about their early romance. One is their first kiss. The other is their first home.

We were evicted because of a third person who existed in the landlady's imagination. Mrs. Peck managed the garden apartments. From her own apartment across the courtyard, Mrs. Peck was sure she could hear someone pounding a bass drum inside our apartment.

There was no drummer.

But Mrs. Peck could not stand the low, steady thud of the bass drum—the bass drum that just wasn't there. She came over several times during daylight to tell my guitarist and me that we could continue to rehearse. But that guy playing the bass drum would have to get out immediately.

How could I put out someone who wasn't there?

The problem was, as I tried to explain to her, that I kept time to the music with my left foot, which I stomped heavily to the beat, while playing my piano.

"Oh, no," she insisted, "what I heard wasn't somebody's foot. It was a bass drum."

Joyce and I reluctantly moved from our first apartment. The phantom drummer walked out with us.

Work was thinning out in Atlanta for me. I had simply played all the clubs there I could without wearing out my popularity completely. There was now the worry of finding another job. So I was excited when Ron Peters, a promoter for military installations, got me some engagements at Ft. Bragg, North Carolina, lasting four months. All I would have to do, I thought, was play the job, go home to the same motel every night, and play again the next night. There would be no hundred-mile trips between shows.

That's exactly what I wanted.

Joyce and I and the band stayed near Ft. Bragg at the 401 Motel. It was a run-down but clean and orderly place, but Joyce didn't like to be left alone there during shows.

I was so fatigued when I got home at night's end, I could have slept in a feather bed minus the feathers. My hunger to get work far exceeded my endurance to perform it at my outrageous and self-imposed pace. I played five nights a week from 8 p.m. until 2 a.m., six sets a night. Then I played weekends from noon until 2 a.m. We'd set up our equipment, play, tear it down, and move across base to another venue.

I was paid $157 a day, from which I paid three other musicians, bought Joyce's and my meals, and paid for everyone's rent at the motel.

I was doing forty-six shows per week. The sets were an hour each, minus a ten-minute break. That was the pace.

We played an officer's club on the main post, and they were the most subdued of our audiences. We also played the E-4 club, accommodating enlisted men of that rank and below; a club for enlisted men whose ranks were from E-4 through E-9; and a club strictly for members of the 82nd Airborne.

Ironically, the airborne soldiers were among the best-behaved. At the E-4 club, it was a repeat of what I'd seen on the R & B circuit— high times and flying furniture.

These guys would throw everything but themselves off of the balcony into the crowd and onto the stage, where I again took sanctuary under the piano.

One night, when Joyce was in the front row, a drunken soldier asked her to dance. She declined and he asked her again. When she again refused, he became aggressive. I knew something was wrong when the band stopped playing, leaving me playing an unintended solo.

The incident was also seen by Sergeant Kane, the club's master of arms, who had befriended Joyce, the band, and me.

I could hear the commotion as he pulled the drunk away from my wife. Kane took the guy to a back door and threw him down the steps. I later counted thirty solid concrete steps over which the drunk tumbled. Bloody and bruised, the drunk came back, but this time with Sgt. Kane twisting his arm. The sergeant reminded the soldier that he had left so hastily, he had forgotten to apologize to Joyce. The blubbering soldier said he was sorry. Then the sergeant escorted him out the door again.

What a joint!

It was during an engagement for the hell-raising troops at Ft. Bragg that I realized I was not a man of steel. I was singing R & B, and it was going over like electrified magic with the largely black audience. The place was jumping to twelve-bar blues. I was in special form.

Then it stopped abruptly.

In the middle of a song, in the middle of a line, my voice failed. Stopped.

There had been no hoarseness; no gradual loss of vocal power. I was singing one second, and utterly silent the next. The singing that had always been easy for me wouldn't come now, no matter how hard I struggled.

That is terrifying to anyone, but to a singer, it is a nightmare come to life.

It happened, I'll never forget, during my fifty-fourth consecutive day of the forty-six-show-a-week grind. I walked off the stage, and people instantly formed around me. It was no use. Since I couldn't make a sound, I couldn't tell them what went wrong.

The band took me to the hotel. Joyce was overcome with worry.

I was horrified that I had ruined my voice forever. I thought about the years ahead, and what they would be like if I couldn't sing.

The next day, Joyce took me to Dr. Barry, a Fayetteville physician. The doctor probed my throat and went through the routine.

He saw the signs of physical strain on my vocal cords and told Joyce about pronounced symptoms of vocal stress. Then he asked her how long I had been singing during my current run.

He couldn't believe it when Joyce said this was my fifty-fourth day. "Even God," he gasped, "takes Sundays off!"

I couldn't speak for two weeks, during which time I recovered in Douglas, Georgia, at the home of Joyce's parents.

I spent the time listening to the radio, reading, sleeping, and letting Joyce's mother take care of me. She cooked for me as if I were a visiting head of state, not a sick singer. I was her loved one, and it showed.

I have never again tried to be music's marathon man.

Such was the pace on the United States military circuit in 1966 and 1967. I had accepted those sit-down engagements to get away from doing one-night shows laced with miles of travel in between. The idea behind the military shows was that they were to be less stressful.

Other than the forty-six shows a week, a military base can be a boring place. The band was always commenting about the people and the buildings all looking alike. A military installation is such a repro-duction of itself, civilians often get lost trying to find their way around the nondescript setting. There regrettably are about as many different things to do as there are different things to see at most Army instal-lations.

The monotony was the reason behind my decision to drive my van. At first I just drove around the abandoned parking lot outside the nightclub we had closed at 2 a.m. Stan Reece, my guitar player, sug-gested that I drive where there were no obstructions. He said he would push on my left shoulder when I should go left, and my right when I should go right.

I decided to use Stan's system to drive on the street and headed for Bragg Boulevard, where I could drive all the way off base to the 401 Motel.

I didn't take to driving immediately. I oversteered, crossing the center line, weaving through the silent and late-night streets of Ft. Bragg.

When Stan told me to push the brake, I stomped it. They were power brakes. The drummer (a replacement drummer who was sitting in that night) sailed from the back seat to the console between the two front seats.

He wasn't amused. "You guys are crazy," he said, and got out of the van.

One passenger lighter, I resumed my journey.

I was driving magnificently, easing quietly through what I thought were the deserted streets of Ft. Bragg, North Carolina. Then I heard Stan gasp.

Straight ahead, there was a line of cars. At the head of the line was a military policeman. I had driven directly into a routine roadblock, where MPs question drivers and check their identification.

I was in the line before I knew it, having eased to a coordinated stop, as Stan directed. I would have immediately changed places with Stan, except that I was told we were in the direct light of the MP station. My riders were sure that I would be seen changing places, and that the move would arouse suspicion.

The roadblock was just a few yards away from Bragg Boulevard, which would take me off base and to the motel. I was that close, yet that far away, from safety. Convinced that I couldn't leave the driver's seat, I panicked.

One by one, the cars ahead of me were processed through the MP gate. I alternately inched forward and then stopped, advancing with the skill of a seasoned motorist. Within a few anxious minutes, I was at the front of the line.

It was summertime, my window was down, and I could hear the MP's regimented footsteps as he marched more than walked to the van. He put his head inside the cab.

Then he told me to get out.

"Turn around," he said, "and put your hands on the roof."

It was the first time I had ever been searched.

I don't know what he was looking for. It might have been a bottle, since he said he saw my van weaving as I approached the station. I was wearing sunglasses, and that might have. made him think I was trying to conceal bloodshot eyes that go with drinking alcohol.

I told him I hadn't been drinking.

"Let's see your driver's license and vehicle registration," he said.

I told him I didn't have them, that I'd left them at the motel, and right out there in the open air, he hit the ceiling.

"What do you mean you don't have them?" the MP yelled. I don't imagine anyone whose job was enforcing military law could imagine that anyone would so flagrantly break such a basic rule. But there I was, driving without a license and registration, not to mention a slightly more serious impairment, of which the MP was still unaware.

I was afraid. I knew he was going to detect my blindness. I didn't know what he'd do then.

"You can't drive without a license," he continued to rail.

I called him "sir," was overly polite, and told him that I had to drive.

"You see, sir," I said, "these guys have had a couple of drinks, and we wouldn't want anyone to drink and drive. So I figured it would be best if I drove. I don't drink, and we're musicians who are playing on this base, and we were just on our way home."

His anger began to subside. I had been nice, apologetic, and respectful. And it worked. He told me to go on home, and never to let him see me driving that way again.

For him, the routine incident was over. For me, the crisis was heightening. I had to open the door by feel, slide onto the driver's seat, start the engine, and pull away in front of the suspicious stares of I don't know how many MPs.

My moves were calculated. And miraculously, they were convincing. I got into the vehicle, drove away from the check station, and as soon as were out of sight, changed places with Johnny Christopher, my bass player, who could legally drive—and see. I had pulled it off, and I never saw that MP again. He never knew I never had.

16

After the grueling four months at Ft. Bragg came to an abrupt and frightening halt with the loss of my voice, I convalesced in Douglas at Joyce's parents'. I waited until my body was strong and my voice was sound before I even thought about returning to work.

They say that every cloud has a silver lining. Joyce and I left her mother's care to return to our home in Atlanta, where the lining, unknown to us, was beginning to peek through.

I had hardly been back in Atlanta any time at all when I heard from Scepter Records. It was 1967, and the company was perhaps as hungry for another top-five song as I was. They wanted me to do a recording session, and I wanted to oblige.

What's more, they wanted me to record in Memphis with Chips Moman, a producer who had a great recording studio and a hot studio band. The band consisted of Gene Christman on drums, Tommy Cogbill and, later, Mike Leach on bass, Bobby Emmons on organ, Reggie Young and Bobby Womack on guitar, and Bobby Wood on piano.

The name of Chip's studio was American Studios. It would become home of the hit makers. Elvis Presley eventually recorded at American.

In September 1967, I cut two songs at American Studios. One was "I Can't Tell a Lie," written by my bass player, Johnny Christopher. The other was a remake of the old standard, "House of the Rising Sun."

I had a foot in the door with Chips Moman at American Studios. It was a door I'd pass through many times for many big reasons in months to come.

Back in Atlanta, I was sitting at home when the telephone rang one day; it was my old buddy Pat Hughes, the WQXI disc jockey. He was calling about another nightclub he thought I should play. It was part of a national chain that was perhaps the most famous of adult playgrounds in the nation in the 1960s—the Playboy clubs. He said that the Atlanta Playboy Club's manager, John Barnes, was looking for an entertainer who could sing all kinds of music, including jazz and blues, as well as play instrumentals. Pat told Barnes about me, and asked him to audition me.

Then he even showed up at the tryout.

Barnes and I hit it off immediately. We formed a musical bond and a friendship. In late 1967, the music that had taken me from Meadow Branch through the military, by way of rhythm and blues houses everywhere, had let me off with a bouquet of beautiful "bunnies," Hugh Hefner's world-famous cocktail waitresses.

After I successfully auditioned for the job, I was given a plaque bearing a furry bunny tail. I brought it home to our apartment, where Joyce wondered aloud what in the world had gone on at the audition. I told her the main thing that transpired was that I got the job.

There was something wonderfully peculiar about those days at Atlanta's Playboy Club. I was working six hours a night, six nights a week, and the schedule was a contradiction of my vow not to return to an exhaustive pace. Yet this time, in that place, the schedule wasn't tiring, at least not unreasonably so. The job was fun, the people were nice, the place was prestigious, and it was close to home. After each show, I slept in my bed.

I look back on those days between October 1967 and September 1968 fondly. John Barnes even built a special stage for us at the club. In June 1968, he took me to Lake Geneva, Wisconsin, to work for a month at the new Playboy Club there. He was a good employer, who was definitely the boss, yet he never acted "bossy."

The customers at the clubs were polite and, often, famous. I got to know many players of the Atlanta Braves baseball team, including Hank Aaron, who would later became baseball's all-time champion home run hitter. The Braves even gave me a baseball autographed by the team.

One night Chips Moman showed up at the Playboy Club. Between sets, he and I discussed the Scepter session we had done the previous year in Memphis. Chips was pleased with it, but he thought we had touched only the tip of the iceberg of our true potential. He said that I was a tremendous talent that needed only the polish of his production to become a world shaker.

Here I was in Atlanta working a steady job for an international chain and meeting indisputably prominent people. And Chips wanted me to move to Memphis.

He wanted me to move to where I could get additional recording sessions and plenty of session work for other artists. He assured me that it would be a great way to expose my skills and meet "name" acts. He stressed that I would be in the thick of the great rhythm and blues and rock 'n' roll recording that had characterized Memphis since the days of Sun Studios in 1954.

He was echoed by Tommy Cogbill, a tremendous bass player who earlier had been a famous jazz guitarist. The two of them promised that Cogbill would be one of the session players I'd be working with in Memphis.

It was all very enticing—but there was this great job in Atlanta, paying a four-figure weekly salary split among four of us. There were no travel jumps between shows, there was no motel food, and I was working for a corporation that gave some of its employees, with time, fringe benefits. The job was too good to leave.

So Chips upped the ante. He said that besides my potential studio work, I'd meet a lot of music industry people by playing a Memphis nightclub. He said that if I moved to Memphis, he would get me a job at *the* jumping nightclub—T. J.'s.

He did, and I did.

In November 1968, Joyce and I became official residents of the State of Tennessee. The job at the Playboy Club had been one of the best regional engagements any musician could want. But I didn't want to be just a regional musician, and my sights went beyond the regional forum. From the beginnings on Auburn Avenue, all the way to the Playboy Club, I had done well in Atlanta. But I had gone as high as I could go there. If I was to take the next step on a career climb, I would have to take it in Memphis.

My work at T. J.'s was, for a while, as fun and as beneficial as Chips had said it would be. One of the first people who came to the club to see me was Rob Galbraith, a friend and former disc jockey Joyce and I had met back in 1965 in Knoxville when he was working his way through the University of Tennessee. Rob brought along a school-teacher named Tom Collins. Their arrival at T. J.'s was an example of what Chips had promised regarding my meeting folks who could help my career. Rob Galbraith oversees all my music publishing interests today, and has coproduced many of my hit records. Tom Collins later worked for Pi-Gem-Chess, Charley Pride's former publishing company, where I would record many hit songs. Collins eventually became a publishing magnate and record producer who coproduced seventeen of my twenty-one RCA albums.

All of that was in the uncertain future.

I also met Mike Post, the genius musical arranger of television theme songs for such hit shows as "Rockford Files," "Hill Street Blues," and "L.A. Law." I met him in 1971, not long after he had produced albums for Kenny Rogers and the First Edition. In 1980, I would call upon him regarding the production of my shows for presentation in Las Vegas and Lake Tahoe. Today, I consider him one of my closest friends. He contributed to the audio and visual aspects of my 1980s concerts with show-stopping dance routines.

It was at T. J.'s that I met the legendary John Fogerty, songwriter, singer, and guitarist for one of the most popular rock 'n' roll groups of all time, Creedence Clearwater Revival. They had put out a monster record called "Run through the Jungle," and I was intrigued by the layers of certain sounds on that record. I couldn't figure out how it was done, until Fogerty explained the technical process to me one night at T. J's.

And it was at T. J.'s that I first met Leon Russell, the self-proclaimed "master of time and space," who has played piano and arranged music for everybody from Frank Sinatra to George Harrison. Leon penned some valid American standard compositions for Joe Cocker, the Carpenters, himself, and others. In 1984, he was my guest on my television special, "In Celebration," which was still in rerun in giant markets, including New York City, as late as 1989.

To some that I met there, I was just that night's house entertainment. To others, I became a friend. To others, I became a lifelong associate, and to still others, I became all of the above. Nashville would eventually become my door to the entertainment world. The steps to that door were laid in Memphis.

There was one other person I met in Memphis. He had done amazing things in the entertainment industry for the fifteen years before I met him. His feats were then, and are now, unsurpassed in all of entertainment history. Before, during, and for five years after my time in Memphis, he mesmerized us as no one had before or has since.

The first time I was introduced to Elvis Presley, someone said, "This is Ronnie Milsap." He said, "Okay."

There was no "how are you?" He didn't even mumble or grunt. He just said "Okay." That was in 1968.

Elvis's records had been produced for years by Felton Jarvis for RCA in Nashville. Felton got the idea to record Elvis in Memphis, where many of his 1950s hits had been recorded on Sun Records. So Felton, Elvis, and the musicians set up at American Studios, where Chips worked with them as coproducer on a series of sessions for RCA.

Chips made good on his promise to get me work. He recommended to Felton that I play on Elvis's session. Elvis recorded two albums at American Studios, and I played and sang on some of the cuts.

The first day I went down to the studio, Elvis was working on "Kentucky Rain," which became a million-selling record. Chips suggested to Elvis that I sing harmony and play piano on the song. The next time you hear "Kentucky Rain," that's me on the high vocal harmony and piano.

In 1980, I asked Tom Collins's writers to compose a song about my part of America, the Smoky Mountains. The writers, Dennis Morgan and Kye Fleming, came back with "Smoky Mountain Rain." It reminded me, and Collins, of what Elvis and I had done on "Kentucky Rain." I decided to use the same sound of thunder that Elvis had used. The song turned out to be a big hit. I still do it in my shows, ten years later.

While I was playing at T. J.'s, Elvis flattered me by asking me to perform at a New Year's Eve party he was throwing. He figured the best way to do it was to rent the nightclub where I was performing. So he rented T. J.'s, which was closed to the public, and opened to Elvis and about 150 of his closest cronies. There was a guest list, and guards at the door who enforced it.

That night, when the band and I took a break, Elvis came over and told me how much he liked my playing and singing on "Kentucky Rain." What a compliment!

I'll tell you, visiting with Elvis Presley was a natural high. I had always thought he was larger than life. I guess I had always thought of him as a sound, as a force, as a voice coming out of my radio! Until then, I had never thought about the flesh and blood person who went with that powerful presence. Then to meet him, to work with him, and for him to have me play at his private party was overwhelming.

Being a singer who had met Elvis was the equivalent of being a painter who had met Leonardo daVinci. You may think that's crazy, but that's how I felt on New Year's Eve, 1969.

That night I made the mistake of inviting him up on stage. "Hey, Elvis, I sure would like to play for you if you'd come up and sing a song," I said to him. "We'd love to hear you sing 'All Shook Up'." The request freaked him out. He didn't want to have to perform that night; it was his private party. He just wanted to enjoy the fellowship of his friends.

Elvis wanted nothing more than simply to be normal. After getting to know him, I realized how hard it was to be Elvis. The pressure of this might have been what prompted his alleged drug use, perhaps the entertainment industry's biggest open secret, until it became publicized after his death. I'm not making excuses for the man, just citing what might have been a reason for his self-indulgence.

A lot of us coveted his role in the spotlight, but none of us ever walked in his shoes. And no matter how many millions admired him, there were always times when he was alone—like all of us. During those times, he faced the pressures that no one could face for him. Elvis, perhaps, was like a lot of creative people I've known—lonely—sometimes even in a crowded room.

The size of the load he perpetually carried was driven home to me on New Year's Eve, 1970, the second time I played a private party for him at T. J.'s. That time, I had the wisdom not to ask him to sing.

I was told that night that each time Elvis went to the men's room, he was escorted by four bodyguards—one in front, one behind, and one on each side.

I thought that was peculiar, and I mentioned it to Alan Fortas, who worked for Elvis. "We're at T. J.'s," I said. "Everybody here knows Elvis. This is a private party, and it's his. Do you think he really needs bodyguards in here to go with him to the bathroom?"

Alan's answer floored me.

"That's where he gets hit up, man," Alan replied.

Alan explained that Elvis was generous to a fault. When he'd go to the rest room, he was an involuntary captive of people who would ask him for money.

"Man, my mother is having an operation and I don't know how I'll pay for it," someone would say. Or, "My son needs braces for his teeth and I just don't have the money to pay."

Elvis just couldn't say no. Usually, he'd write them a check on the spot. That man's popularity, and character, were actually haunting him to where he couldn't even go to the men's room without being hounded.

One time in Memphis he bought twelve Mercedes for his friends. Two or three times a year, Elvis rented the *Memphian* movie theater where he screened first-run motion pictures for his friends and himself. They'd stay in there for two or three days at a time watching movies. Other times, he rented an amusement park in Memphis, and he and his friends would ride midway attractions all night. But people in his organization became concerned about the freeloaders. When they hired bodyguards for Elvis, the guards understood that part of their job was to accompany Elvis to the restroom.

That second New Year's Eve party marked the last time I saw him. He was having a real good time, but he was acting a little strange. He carried two loaded six guns inside cowboy holsters strapped around his waist. At midnight, Elvis went from table to table and gave a "Happy New Year" kiss to every woman at the party, including Joyce.

He had one of those five-cell flashlights and went around holding it in front of everyone's eyes until they were blinded. He even held it in front of my eyes.

In 1973, I was playing at Nashville's King of the Road Hotel. I was between sets, catching my breath. The waitress said, "Pardon me Ronnie, Elvis Presley is on the phone for you."

Elvis had, on occasion, invited me to his private parties. The invitations were always relayed through Alan Fortas or Red West, and unfortunately I always had to decline, because I was working.

This time, Elvis was calling me himself. And this time, like the other times, I was working and couldn't go.

I wanted to go, and I certainly didn't want to say no to the King. But I did, and he didn't argue. If he was disappointed, he wasn't nearly as disappointed as I was.

That telephone call from Elvis would stand as the last time I heard from him. Four years later, he was dead.

Today, opinions about Elvis Presley are like noses—everybody has one. Here, in part, is mine.

I've read all this junk about Elvis's alleged drug use and self-destruction. I don't know if any of that is true, and neither does anybody else who wasn't there. But the question is: Does it matter?

It doesn't matter to me, because it doesn't take away from the impact of the man's career. And that's what I look at.

Elvis never presented himself as anything more than an entertainer. He didn't ask to become the personal role model some people wanted him to be. I've know firsthand the incessant pressure of being Ronnie Milsap. What would it have been like to be Elvis Presley?

I've seen what the subtle but unending pressure of stardom has done to some of my friends. Some cope and some don't. There are enormous highs, and deep lows, that seem to characterize the moods of many people in public life, particularly in the visual and performing arts.

I'm not making excuses for those folks. I'm just talking about what I've observed.

Through no fault of his own, Elvis was economically deprived during his childhood. He quit high school to become a truck driver. Then, at an age when many young men are still trying to find themselves, Elvis's musical talent was discovered by millions. It had to be a psychological ambush for him.

I've know many formally educated people from economically and psychologically stable backgrounds who could not have carried the burden of fame that clobbered Elvis. I say give the guy a break.

This stuff about Elvis sightings everywhere in 1988 puzzled me. Were they by well-meaning fans who wanted to keep alive his memory? Or were they by people who, even in death, wanted to exploit him?

Those people who never knew the man, but who are making financial profit from him, thirteen years after his death, make me sick.

I don't mind their selling souvenirs or mementos at Graceland, his Memphis home, if the proceeds go to his family. But some of these guys who worked for him, or who only met somebody who met him, are stretching it too thin when they sell stuff using his name, and claiming some kind of attachment to him. It's a hustle.

Most of those people don't give a damn about Elvis. They'd do the same thing in connection with Keith Whitley, a fine young country singer who died in May 1989, and they'd do it in connection with the passing of Ronnie Milsap. It's just an ugly and probably unchangeable part of the free-enterprise system. But I don't have to like it. It disgusts me.

And as far as Elvis and I go, I can only report from personal recollection, based on personal experience. He was always nice to me, and I know firsthand that he was even nicer to others. He left us recorded songs that became standards; he left us a memory that became a legacy. That should be enough.

17

Memphis sits on the east bank of the Mississippi River, and the water runs through it like memories through my mind. Those memories have sometimes been clouded and at times detoured, like the waves in that mighty stream. But just as the current rolls on, so does my nostalgia for one of the happiest times of my life.

I lived a lifetime during those four years in Memphis. In Memphis I became a father and homeowner. In Memphis I received encouragement from other recording artists. In Memphis I formed lifelong friendships, some struck up in little more than an evening. In Memphis I nearly put an end to my career. I could write an entire book just about my time in Memphis. Someday I might.

Our first Memphis address was a townhouse at 2092 Vollintine Avenue; it was the biggest place we'd lived in up to that point in our married lives. We were childless for a few months after our arrival, and enjoyed all the blissful independence of a responsibility-free life. I'd play my music until closing time at T. J.'s, and then friends would join Joyce and me at our house for a party and parlor games until dawn. We'd play Yahtzee, gin, Scrabble, and the like until the paperboy arrived.

I was a happy suburbanite, a productive John Q. Citizen with a wife and a place of his own, a regular job, and a plan to keep it all and the hope of earning more.

It was the American dream rapidly coming to life. The only element missing was a child. Our family portrait was completed by the birth of Todd Milsap almost twenty years ago.

Having a child is an experience that happens to so many, but when it happens to you, it's so fulfilling, it's as if it never happened to anyone else. It has been written that no man ever stood so tall as when he stooped to help a child. I know I never stood taller than when I held my baby. I vividly recall holding his hand, as soft as it was tiny, delicately nestled between my thumb and forefinger. I remember his cottonlike face, so small that I could bury it in the hollowness of my cheek. I remember his tender breaths, which came and went so rapidly compared with my own.

Sometimes, I put my ear close to his sleeping face, listening intently to the human symphony of his breathing. I'd stand there, drawing life from the exchange of air that sustained his. Then the spell would heighten when he'd sigh or squirm.

I recorded much of Todd's childhood on audio tape. When video tape recorders became popular in the 1970s, we began preserving Christmas and other special occasions in a video library. Joyce filmed Todd and his teammates during athletic events, as I wrestled the accompanying shoulder apparatus along the sidelines.

I affectionately recall Todd "testing" a microphone I set up for him when he could barely pronounce the word "test." He had heard me say "test, test" enough to mimic the command. He once pretended to shoot me, the way he had seen grownups do it on television. I left the tape recorder running as I feigned my death.

"Da-dee, Da-dee! Wake up Da-dee," Todd cautiously pleaded, as he shook my body, sprawled on the floor.

"Da-dee, Da-dee," his pleas intensified. Then there was silence . . . and then the inevitable: "I want my Mom-mee!"

Todd had traveled more by the time he was six than most people do in a lifetime. By the age of nine, he was attending to little errands in my road show, simple but necessary details that I would later have to hire someone to do after Todd had grown up and gotten too big for the menial tasks. It's true, adults later would execute those tasks with more proficiency, but with never my son's "touch."

The arrival of Todd meant the departure from our house for another. We had two bedrooms in the townhouse, but I thought it would be more fitting in the long run, and more fun in the present, to get a real house surrounded by a fence and a mortgage.

So Joyce scanned the classified advertisements and found a place at 4790 Hornsby Drive, in Whitehaven, a suburb of Memphis. The three of us lived there for almost three years.

I played long sets at T. J.'s and was often left at the nightclub without a ride. I might have thought the band would have offered to give me a ride, because they knew that Joyce was home with a new baby. Yet the shows would stop, and I'd be stranded.

Joyce had to get out of bed, start the car, let it warm up, wrap Todd in a blanket, then drive with a baby on her shoulder while steering with one hand through the dark, frigid, and crime-ridden streets of Memphis. I'd get in the car, hold Todd, and we'd head for home.

For about three of my four years in Memphis, playing T. J.'s was like working in a home away from home. I didn't mind working there at night, even though the weekend schedule included six or seven shows a night, and weeknights, if crowds were big, five. If it hadn't been for having to leave Joyce and Todd, there were many nights I would have looked forward to going in.

There are many happy, unforgettable memories connected to that nightclub, like the waitresses and bartenders who gave Joyce a baby shower and hosted our fourth wedding anniversary.

I'll never forget a man named Campbell Kinsinger, a Vietnam veteran who had been shell-shocked in that war. Campbell was a bouncer who gave me protection beyond the call of duty.

One night, when Campbell wasn't working but happened to be inside the place, some guy pulled a gun and I got under the piano. I was in danger, and Campbell came to the rescue. He grabbed the guy, pistol and all, and threw him through a plate glass door. Another time he removed a fellow who put one foot on the stage to request a song and unwittingly touched me—a big mistake when Campbell was around.

Years after I left Memphis, they told me Campbell had been killed by a shotgun blast to the chest.

It was at T. J.'s that I met Steve "Hawk" Holt, my drummer and personal companion for almost fifteen years. Hawk was the only black musician in my band in 1975. I recall once, we were booked to play a redneck establishment in Louisiana. When the hosts of my show saw Hawk setting up his drums that afternoon, they sent someone to tell me I couldn't play with a black man on stage. I was about to leave the place, and tell the racists that some sighted folks would do better to be color-blind, but before there was time for a confrontation, Hawk's charm defused the situation and we played a smooth engagement that ended with an invitation to return.

I met businessmen in Memphis from Pepper Tanner, a radio jingle company, whose staffers came regularly to see me at T. J.'s. I wound up doing radio spots for Blue Cross/Blue Shield Insurance Company, Safeway grocery chain, and other conglomerates. I made jingles off and on for two years, and was paid a whopping $25 for each, which were probably sold for thousands of dollars apiece. But the studio and professional experience was beneficial to me then.

I remember falling off the high stage at T. J.'s one night through a bank of amplifiers while holding a glass of water and an Alka-Seltzer. It seemed as though I was falling for an hour, tumbling toward the floor. When I stood, the room was silent.

"I broke my damn Alka-Seltzer," I said, and the place erupted into applause. That taught me a lesson in how to use humor to relax a tense situation.

T. J.'s was a place where someone like Dionne Warwick might walk in unannounced to hear me, and sit with the everyday folks. Some of those customers came so faithfully to see me, I wondered if they didn't actually live in a room in the back. Although I was a long way from being a celebrity then, I appreciated them as much as I do folks today who drive hundreds of miles to see my concerts.

And there was one more event among the memorable Memphis memories. It was traumatic, to say the least. It taught me that sometimes the seemingly most insignificant thing can change your life, even if only to make you appreciate the life you already have.

It was just another night at T. J.'s. The band and I were setting up our equipment for a show. I had a problem with my amplifier, and back then, I did all my own electronic repair. I remember I had my right hand deep into the cabinet when suddenly there was a shooting pain through my little finger.

It was sharp, as though I had been bitten by something hidden inside the amplifier. I had run a metal sliver into my right little finger. The small dagger broke off inside, lodged in the bone.

I tried unsuccessfully to pull it out. Merely touching my finger sent waves of pain all the way up my arm. My finger swelled instantly. I played that night in excruciating pain. I tried to play songs that utilized my left hand more than my right. Often, I played without piano accompaniment. I just stood on stage holding the microphone with my left hand.

"I'm going to the doctor the first thing in the morning," I thought to myself. "Isn't this dumb, to have to go to the doctor over a silly thing like a splinter?"

Sleep was fitful that night. Often I rolled in my sleep onto my hand, and each time I did, I awakened in piercing pain.

I sometimes slept until noon back then, since I worked so late. But on this particular morning, I was up early. I wanted to get to the doctor's office and be done with what I was sure would be routine, in-office, light surgery. My goofy injury, I thought, would be relieved with little more than cosmetic treatment.

The sliver had been in my finger for about sixteen hours by the time I saw the doctor. My little finger had swollen to the diameter of a small pickle. The doctor held my hand steady by firmly gripping my wrist and asked me to put my open palm under a light so bright I could feel its heat. He shot novocaine into my little finger, and soon, I could no longer feel his probing.

I wondered why it was taking so long to get a mere steel shaving out of a finger. When I was a kid, I used to get splinters all the time. Phenia would take a sewing needle and pop them out in no time. Here was a medical doctor who was struggling to remove a tiny sliver.

He never did get it out.

He said that the steel had cut its way into the bone and that it was impossible to remove it. He couldn't leave the sliver inside my finger, because the pain would only intensify, and the finger would become infected. He said his only choice was to amputate my finger.

Amputate my finger? Over a splinter?

He was telling a pianist he was going to cut off his finger? Didn't he know I played for Elvis? What kind of doctor would want to alter my life over something as simple as a metal sliver?

I was angry when I left his office. If I'd had a cold would he have wanted to cut off my head? I couldn't wait to get to another doctor and get that annoying and insignificant sliver out and get on with my work. I had wasted too much time on something so insignificant.

I saw a different doctor. His diagnosis was the same. The steel was irretrievably lodged in a bone, and the finger was going to become infected. It could not be cut out, and the finger would have to be cut off, he insisted. He knew it was crazy, he said, but true.

By the time I left that doctor's office, I was beginning to be a believer.

Doing my job was contingent on my being able to do what I did best: sing and *play piano*! People lost fingers in industrial accidents or car wrecks. Nobody lost a finger because of a splinter, steel or not! But the doctors had said, sorrowfully, that I was going to lose it. And they said I shouldn't procrastinate.

But procrastinate I did. I carried the burden of that pending amputation for a week. I thought of all the crummy nightclubs I'd played grudgingly. I wished now that I could have my health guaranteed and play them forever. I thought about a lot of things that had been big problems at one time, and how all of them were suddenly unimportant when compared with my little finger.

Everybody in the band was down.

Joyce had gone with me to the doctors, and had heard their diagnosis. She worried along with me and kept reassuring me that I would not have my finger amputated.

That little finger played havoc in so many lives. It was like a candle flame growing to burn down a forest. Nobody could believe this was happening.

Chips Moman heard about the panic concerning my finger and mentioned it to his wife. She had a solution.

"If you've got something lodged in your finger," she said, "tape a piece of fatback over it. The salt in the fat will draw it out."

Fatback is fat taken from near the back bone of a hog. When I was growing up in the mountains, Phenia used to cook with it. Mrs. Moman's idea was an old country remedy for which I had little hope. But when you're sinking for the third time, you'll grab for a stone. Or fatback.

So Joyce went to the grocery store and bought some. She taped a slice of the stuff around my little finger and covered the fatback with Saran Wrap, as Mrs. Moman directed, so it would be airtight.

I wore that conspicuous concoction for two days. Needless to say, I didn't play piano during the span, but I did do a lot of explaining to people about the unusual bandage on my right hand. At the end of the second day, Joyce removed the greasy and smelly Saran Wrap from the fatback and then removed the salty fatback from my finger. And there, on the surface of the skin, was a sharp piece of splintered steel. The fatback had drawn it from the bone to the surface, just as Mrs. Moman said it would. I didn't even need a needle. I simply lifted the shiny sliver off my finger—the finger I have to this day.

Mrs. Moman's remedy was simple and brilliant. It made me wonder about doctors and scientific remedies. I take a lot of vitamins and herbs and eat a lot of natural foods today. I have seen too many "curings" and "miracles" throughout the years to ignore some of the preventative and curative medicine that comes from the provincial households of the deep South.

By my second year in Memphis, Chips Moman had started his own record label, Chips Records. We enjoyed moderate chart action with "Loving You's a Natural Thing." Earlier, we had spent a great deal of time in his American Studios, where I obtained the best technical experience I'd had up to that time. Chips seemed to work then as hard as he had said he would toward producing a hit, and I just never had any doubt that it would happen. My only question was *when* it would happen. But over the next two years it became apparent that what had been promised regarding my future was not happening in my present. I grew to understand during that period that it was time to close the book on Memphis, Tennessee.

18

We have lived in various places in Nashville, but in only one home. Joyce and I still live in the house where Todd spent most of his childhood and all of his teenage years. We bought the place in 1976, four years and scores of career breakthroughs after we moved to Nashville.

It's a turn of the century estate we bought for $300,000. It was appraised in 1987 for $3 million. It's owned by a man who was raised in a three-room shack.

That house is special to me in a way that has nothing to do with dollars and cents but everything to do with the family inside. And it is a testament to the American dream come true. Success can be had in this country, no matter how disadvantaged one is.

I think of that, and relish the thought, whenever I step onto the lawn's seven groomed acres.

Yet talking about the house presents a quandary to me. I know that some folks don't have as much materially as I do now, so I have reservations about this subject; I've never liked hearing people talk about their possessions. It sounds as if they're bragging, and I hate that. Yet, these possessions *are* a part of my life.

I was asked in 1989 to appear on television's *Lifestyles of the Rich and Famous*. I said "No, thanks" to their invitation.

While I don't feel false pride for what I have, I do feel real gratitude. In my lifetime, I've found I can say thanks just as sincerely under a ceiling that's lofty as under one that leaks.

Our two-story structure is stately. It carries the echo of serious

148

business talk, but more often, it has rung with the laughter of Todd and his friends. We have set Waterford crystal on an antique Chippendale table—and wiped crumbs of corn bread off of it. The buildings' exterior lines are architecturally magnificent, but in the foreground is Todd's treehouse. *Its* design could be called "rectangular routine." Yet, I love it and spent a lot of time up there with Todd when he was younger.

I live around the corner from both Minnie Pearl and the governor of Tennessee.

One day in 1985, Joyce and I came home to find a 25-foot hole in the wall that surrounds our property. Hundreds of bricks had been knocked out, but mysteriously, there were none on the ground.

The hole was large enough to drive a bus through.

The next morning, the local newspaper solved the mystery. A tour bus loaded with fans crashed through the wall after its brakes failed. Passengers hurried off the bus, and gathered bricks as souvenirs. We had no idea what happened until we saw the newspaper photograph of stranded bus riders sitting on our lawn.

The place where anyone grows up is forever special, whether its design is regal or routine. On the other hand, although I'm sentimental about Homer's cabin in Meadow Branch, I don't regard it as "home." For one thing, others have lived there since I have. Also, the place is falling down now and is unfit for human habitation. Finally, I lived most of my childhood at the Governor Morehead School in Raleigh, so I really had two boyhood residences, neither of which carried a sense of permanence for me. The first sense of family roots in my life came with our first house in Memphis.

In the spring of 1969 I had entered into an eighteen-month management contract with two men in Memphis. One owned and managed T. J.'s, and the other was my record producer. I was to pay a 25 percent commission for management services on the rare occasions that they arranged for me to play out of town.

The contract was pretty standard. It indicated that I was to pay a commission on the gross of any money I earned. But the wording concerned me, since it appeared that I would have to take a 25 percent reduction in the salary I was already earning at T. J.'s each week. I had not been paying a commission on it. Did this new contract mean I would have to start paying such commissions? I distinctly recall that the manager of T. J's said he *wouldn't* take a commission for booking me in his own club.

He went on to verbalize what I had felt all along—that T. J.'s was my "home base" to work until my career took on new national proportions. The idea of my paying commissions for future engagements there, or for past ones, was ludicrous, he said. I agreed, and who wouldn't? I had never heard of a house band paying a performance commission to the owner of the house.

That was one reason I took the man's word and signed the contract. The other was that I had been regularly doing honorable business with him for six months. Why wouldn't I have trusted him?

The trust would prove to be misplaced, and provide a priceless lesson that would cost me everything I had.

I eventually would feel more than "taken," not just because I had trusted someone, but because I pride myself in meticulously attending to my financial affairs.

Another disagreement regarding my finances occurred in Memphis in 1972.

I came home one afternoon before work and was met at the back door by Joyce who was visibly upset. There were three Internal Revenue Service agents in my house. They had frightened her, and she was crying.

The men had come by unannounced. They had virtually barged into our house after pounding on the door, loudly demanding to know the whereabouts of Ronnie Milsap. It was a scene straight out of a police movie where cops barge in on bad guys.

The agents told Joyce they were there to collect our income taxes for the previous year.

Joyce told the men I wasn't home, but that she would try to reach me by telephone. She told them that I kept the family financial records, but that she was sure I had paid the 1971 income taxes. They said she was wrong, there had been no payment, and they told her they wanted a check right then and there!

When Joyce said she would not write a check, they said that if she didn't, they were going to find me and take me to jail and the next time she would see me would be behind bars.

Joyce, who by nature is gracious and polite, was outraged.

Ronnie and Gladys Knight during the taping of a Milsap television special. (*Melody Gimple*)

Ronnie and Ray Charles during the taping of a Milsap television special. (*Melody Gimple*)

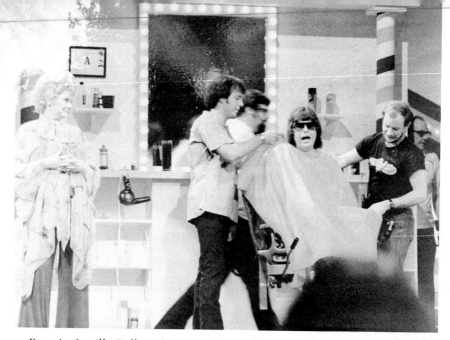

Ronnie, Lucille Ball, and assistants during the taping of "Lucy Comes to Nashville." (*Hope Powell*)

Ronnie and Dick Clark on the set of *American Bandstand*. (*Dick Clark Productions*)

Ronnie and Johnny Carson on the *Tonight Show*. (*NBC*)

Ronnie and Faron Young.

Clint Eastwood and Ronnie at the premiere party for *Bronco Billy* in New Orleans in 1981. Ronnie sang the title song on the sound track. (*Neal Preston*)

Ronnie receives help on his stage show from friend and network television music composer Mike Post.

Glen Campbell visits Ronnie backstage in Las Vegas.

Joyce's favorite photograph, taken in June, 1981. (*Norman Seeff*)

Ronnie and Donald Reeves check concert engagements with (*far left*) the late legendary talent agent, Dick Blake.

Ronnie at a Grammy Awards rehearsal in February 1986 with Huey Lewis and the News, the Five Satins, and Carl Perkins. (*Alan Berliner Studio*)

Ronnie and Larry King on King's syndicated radio show.
(*Rick Henson*)

Ronnie on the set of the "Lost in the Fifties Tonight" video shoot.
(*Melinda Sue Gordon*)

Ronnie enjoys hearing from fans. Looking on are RCA executive Joe Galante and the Nashville Network's Shelly Mangrum.

A favorite family photograph, taken for a Christmas card in December 1985. (*Melody Gimple*)

Dick Clark's "New Year's Rockin' Eve." *Left to right:* Jermaine Jackson, Ronnie, Anson Williams, and Lynda Cornell. *(Dick Clark Productions)*

Ronnie and Jane Pauley inside the Milsap home for the *Today Show*.

Keyboard comrades Ronnie Milsap and Paul Shaffer during a television production break.

Ronnie and Kenny Rogers (*left*) rehearse a duet, while producers Rob Galbraith and Kyle Lehning (*right*) look on. (*Beth Gwinn*)

Ronnie at a TV taping with talk show host Ralph Emery, the Judds, and the O'Kanes. *Seated, left to right:* Wynonna Judd, Ronnie, Naomi Judd. *Standing, left to right:* Kieran Kane, Ralph Emery, and Jamie O'Hara.

Lineberry Hall, where classes were held at the Governor Morehead School for the Blind.

Ronnie on a return visit to the Governor Morehead School in June 1988. *Left:* On the steps of the dormitory that now bears his name. *Right:* With writer Tom Carter and former schoolmate Pat Thompson.

Ronnie with his grandfather, Homer Frisby in June 1988, at Homer's house in Hayesville, North Carolina.

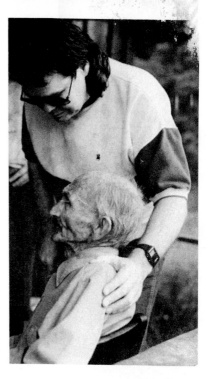

The renovated Meadow Branch Primitive Baptist Church Ronnie attended as a child.

A "remodeled" version of Ronnie's childhood home.

The gateway to Ronnie's present home.

Three men she didn't know had burst into her home to demand money she didn't owe.

Little Todd was asleep. Joyce was concerned that the raised voices would awaken and frighten him too so she got on the telephone and began dialing every place I might have been that afternoon.

The agents were now threatening to affix a lien to our house. Joyce's tension was rising as high as their voices. Eventually I walked through the door. The uninvited goons began their same spiel to me, although their tones softened. I didn't push as easily as a young and frightened mother alone with her baby.

Joyce told me at the back door before I met the men what was going on. I got hot. I bounded into the living room, where the agents tried to introduce themselves, pushed past them, and went directly to a file cabinet in another room where I kept my records. From the cabinet, I produced a canceled check for approximately $3,200, payment in full for our 1971 income taxes.

I went into the living room and laid it on the table in front of the men. Seeing the check, they backed off. They said they would need to take the canceled check with them to clarify their records. I, of course, would not allow that, as the canceled check was my only proof of payment.

Their records, they said, indicated that no such payment had been made, and they didn't know how they could have been mistaken.

They never said they were sorry.

Instead, these fugitives from Hitler's army said they wanted to come and see me at the nightclub where I was working. Their phony conciliatory tone was actually a hypocritical apology for their blunder and behavior. The foes had suddenly become fans.

I said to them, "You sons of bitches, if you ever step foot inside the club, I'll have the bouncers throw you out!"

I usually control my emotions, but this time was different. These idiots had made Joyce cry.

"You came in here and upset my wife, by saying that you were going to take me to jail!" I exploded. "You get out of my house, and if you ever need to see me, then find me, but don't you ever force your way into my house again!"

To this day, I'm audited every year by the IRS. I send my accountant, but I won't attend. I get too angry. I'm very strict about keeping personal records. The IRS knows that about me, and still my staff and I go through that humiliating audit every year.

I think of Jerry Lee Lewis and his tax problems. The IRS, in seizing his assets, reportedly took the gold and platinum records, with no value to anyone except Jerry Lee, from his wall. What are they going to do with them?

I know we have to have taxes, but every time we have an increase, Congress just spends it.

Even without financial pressure, merely trying to make it in music can be so frustrating. You can consistently come so close, yet remain so far away from your elusive dream of hitting it big. The encouragement of artists who have already made it can mean a lot. In my case, it helped change my career.

Take, for example, my first meeting with Charley Pride. I was booked to perform out of town. Chips Records was being distributed by Capitol Records. Chips and I thought that such major distribution would be the break I needed. Capitol seemed sincere and wanted to showcase the entertainer who was recording on the new label they were distributing. They suggested booking me into the Whiskey A-Go-Go in Los Angeles.

It was there that I met Charley Pride. You can imagine how encouraging such an encounter is to someone who thinks his career is on the brink of breaking through.

Joyce and I were staying at the Continental Hyatt House on Sunset Boulevard. Joyce was on the elevator one morning, and so was Pride. He said "Good morning," and she said, "Aren't you Charley Pride?" In the course of conversation, she told him that her husband was playing at the Whiskey-A-Go-Go. He asked her what my name was. When she told him, he said he remembered hearing about me from people who had seen me at T. J.'s, in Memphis. He told Joyce he'd like to say hello to me. He asked for my room number.

When I answered the telephone, no one spoke a word. Instead, a voice sang "Is anybody going to San Antone or Phoenix, Arizona . . . ?"

"I don't know who you are," I said, "but you do a damn good impression of Charley Pride."

He said he wanted to come see me at the Whiskey A-Go-Go that night, and he did. So here I was, knocking on the door of success and meeting a man who had knocked it down.

Funny how things like that can be so pivotal. That night, because Pride was there, I sang one country song, "Today I Started Loving You Again." To my surprise, the crowd loved it. And the most successful country singer in the world at that time told me afterwards to forget singing anything but country music. I would soon take his advice seriously.

Capitol Records persuaded people influential in the music business to see my two-week engagement at the Whiskey A-Go-Go. Besides Charley Pride, one of the hottest female rock 'n' roll singers in the world came. She would eventually record country albums, rock albums, and albums of old standards with the late Nelson Riddle, and she would star in a Broadway musical. Time, and her accomplishments, have only increased the admiration I felt that night in September 1970 for Linda Ronstadt.

She came by my dressing room after the show and told me she was astonished to see that I had received a standing ovation.

"This is a hard room to play," she said, implying that the crowd had seen a surplus of great entertainers perform there. "These people just don't give standing ovations."

I regret to say that was the only time I've ever met Linda Ronstadt. Yet her words did wonders to encourage me at the time.

That year, 1970, was an interesting one. I worked more often outside Memphis than at any other time during my four-year Memphis residency. My managers booked my band and me into that job at the L.A. Whiskey A-Go-Go, as well as at Al Hirt's club in New Orleans, and at Roger Miller's King of the Road Club in Nashville for two weeks.

I played the King of the Road job on the hotel's roof—literally. It was on the building's ninth floor, part of which was open to the sky. It was indisputably the most popular club in Nashville in May 1970.

Most of the out-of-town engagements were intended to promote Chips' new label. With the exception of moderate chart action on "Loving You's a Natural Thing," most of the promotion didn't pay off. There was no other significant hit record for me during that time. Chips' interest in me, my talents, and his own record label seemed to wane. He told me he didn't know what else he could do to accelerate my career. He cited all the recording and personal appearances he had directly or indirectly arranged, to limited success.

Chips stopped coming around his own studio. He even gave me permission to record an album with producer Dan Penn for Warner Brothers in 1971. Although that was a good record, nothing commercially significant came from it, except the undeniable conclusion that Chips had lost his enthusiasm and optimism about my future success.

In the fall of 1970 my management contract expired, but I wanted to continue working out-of-town engagements to expand my career and avoid getting into a rut with those two clubs in Memphis. So I called my brother-in-law, Billy Reeves, in Georgia and asked him to move to Memphis. I wanted him to help me with the out-of-town bookings, working out of my house. So Billy, his wife Diane, and their baby daughter, Alyson, moved to Memphis the following week.

This was a depressing time for me. Many nights I would lie in bed just wondering and worrying, frustrated with my past, disappointed with my present, and terrified of my future. I listened once again to the faraway disc jockeys who played the plaintive vocalists singing as sadly as I felt. The country songs I'd grown up with as a child were touching home.

I told Joyce I was sick and tired of it all. I wondered if I shouldn't just quit the music business altogether. I went so far as to have her get some brochures from broadcasting schools, thinking I might have a career in radio. I sometimes wondered if I hadn't done a dumb thing by declining the scholarship to law school years earlier. My thoughts often controlled me more than I controlled them. I don't know which is worse: depression or uncertainty. I only know I had both.

I was watching the Country Music Association awards on television on a Monday night in October 1972. Country music had always been such a big part of my life. The program made me wonder if Charley Pride hadn't been right. Maybe I should be singing nothing but country, and maybe I should be in Nashville, like the folks on my television screen at that moment. These thoughts and others were running wild through my mind. Each time I heard the names of award nominees, I wondered if that could someday be me.

And it wasn't as if country music was foreign to me. I had grown up with it, and with the kind of people it was written for and about.

I loved country music. If it was going to be my last resort, it wouldn't be a reluctant resort.

I sent Billy to Nashville to explore job possibilities, and the first week of November, 1972, he booked me into a place called The Villa. We played there for two weeks, and during that time, a man came in and introduced himself as Don Davis, the new manager of the King of the Road Hotel, where I had played in 1970.

He said he would give me steady employment—and, of course, it would be in Nashville.

I felt like Brer Rabbit. "Don't throw me in that briar patch," I said to myself.

A move to Nashville was my last chance to make it in music. At least that's how I felt. After all, I had moved to Memphis from Atlanta. Would a move to Nashville make a difference?

These are questions I asked myself each night after work at T. J.'s, and the Thunderbird Lounge, the last place I played in Memphis.

Joyce telephoned Tom Collins, who at that time ran Pi-Gem and Chess music companies for Charley Pride and his manager, Jack Johnson. Collins had seen me at both T. J.'s and The Villa. Joyce told Tom about my offer from Don Davis. Tom told her to encourage me to move to Nashville, where, he said, he too could help me get a foothold in the country music industry.

On December 15, 1972, my already restless thinking was clouded by the ringing of the telephone. I don't remember who called, but I'll never forget his message.

"Ronnie," said the faraway voice, "your daddy is dead."

He had been for three days. The call came the day of his funeral.

Years later, my Uncle J.C. told me that my father said, just before his death, "I guess Ron doesn't care anything about me."

Hearing that hurt me a lot. If I had known my daddy was ill, suffering with the lung cancer that killed him, I certainly would have gone to his bedside. Yet my father and I were mutually guilty of not maintaining contact. I had no idea where he was. He was a rambling man in pursuit of manual labor.

He knew where Homer lived, and Homer always knew where I was.

He had remarried, and one of the last times I saw him was when I was sixteen, the time Phenia and I went to his house because his wife had hit him over the head with a frying pan. That was the same day Phenia suffered her fatal heart attack.

I know I had a lot of guilt for a long time about missing my daddy's funeral, and about not even knowing he was terminally ill. But guilt is like love. It's only healthy when appropriately placed.

Today, I have to travel a lot in my work. But I don't let a day pass without talking to my son. It would be years before I would come to a mature and healthy understanding of the circumstances surrounding my separation from my father, and how I wasn't totally to blame. My father and I failed to stay in touch, and the consequences were dire. Nothing I can ever do or say will make a difference now. And so, my guilt toward the matter has died too.

Nashville was my last chance for success in the music business. If I can't make it there, I said to Joyce, I guess I don't belong in the music business after all.

And so the four spectacular Memphis years came to an end. Joyce, Todd, and I rolled into Nashville with a car full of clothes and heads full of dreams on the day after Christmas, 1972. I worked that night at the King of the Road Hotel. The three of us lived in that hotel for three months. After that, we would look for an apartment that accepted children—and required no money down.

19

I had been playing at the King of the Road about a month when a man knocked at my hotel door. I'd never seen him before and never would again. The results of his intrusion would be remembered for a lifetime.

The door was slightly ajar when he asked if I was Ronnie Milsap. He said he had something for me. When I extended my hand, he handed me a sheaf of legal-size papers. It was a summons, a lawsuit filed against me by my former managers in Memphis.

I had psychologically closed the book on my four Memphis years. In seconds, it had been torn open again.

The petition alleged that I owed back commissions for the salary I was paid while working at T. J.'s. The one question I emphasized to my former managers was, "Will my signing this management contract make me liable for commissions on the money I earn working at T. J.'s?"

The manager who owned T. J.'s laughed at the question, saying the idea of paying a commission to him to work inside his club was out of the question.

Yet that was precisely the back commission he was seeking through the lawsuit against me. He and I had talked this whole thing out. He knew the crystal clear agreement. But what he said and what he had written down for me to sign were two different things, in my opinion. I suspect the lawsuit was really a last ditch effort to get me to return to Memphis, and to his career management. He had made as much or more money from my skills as I had. I know he hadn't wanted me to leave Memphis. Persuasion hadn't worked. A lawsuit might.

On the petition he said I owed $50,000 in commissions. I suppose that with inflation, $50,000 in 1973 would be the equivalent of $100,000 in 1990. It could have been $50 million and my chances of paying it would have been no less.

Ridiculous? Not in the eyes of the court. I soon would learn unequivocally that the terms of a signed, written agreement take precedence over a verbal agreement in a court of law.

That is obvious to me today, but in 1973, before I had ever suffered major abuse from someone I trusted, the idea of written versus spoken agreements never crossed my mind. I was that naive.

The summons was served in January; Joyce and I moved our furniture out of our Memphis house to Nashville in April, and I went to trial in June.

I had a two-sided hit that was climbing the charts at the same time I was involved in the court proceedings. Knowing that I had a hit on a major label did wonders to get me through that trial.

"They can't take my hit record from me," I continually and silently told myself, during the three-day hearing. I was driven to Memphis to the court in the daytime, then back to Nashville to sing at the King of the Road at nights. I was doing five shows, sitting for several stressful hours in court, and traveling 400 miles roundtrip.

I sat on the witness stand before a lawyer who grilled me in a way I have since learned is typical. I wasn't allowed to give long answers to his questions. I wasn't allowed to explain myself.

"Just answer the question, Mr. Milsap!" the lawyer would bark. When I would try to do just that, he would often cut me off in mid-sentence and order again, "Just answer the question!"

I had done thorough preparation for my defense. The twisting of my words, and the harshness of the questioning, frustrated me. I couldn't communicate as effectively as I was capable.

I had believed I would get a fair shake in court. I thought that when the judge heard my side, the court would be the vehicle that would ensure justice, and this squabble would be put in the past.

Obviously, I had been watching too much Perry Mason.

The only person who had heard the plaintiff and me make our verbal agreement was Chips Moman. Although Chips was one of the plaintiffs in the lawsuit, he did not testify against me, nor did he testify on the behalf of the other plaintiff.

I was the only defense witness. The plaintiff had other witnesses, and he had that contract.

The verdict was pronounced, the judge's gavel fell, and so did my spirits.

The plaintiff had asked for $50,000. The court arrived at a compromise settlement of $15,000. While that was a substantial reduction, it was still far more money than I had.

It was decided that the court would sell my house to satisfy the judgment. Joyce and I lost the first house we ever owned, into which we had put all our money and love. It was sold to satisfy a judgment that was unfair regarding an agreement I didn't make—all based on a contract.

I formed an immediate disdain for lawyers. I couldn't believe I had ever wanted to be one. When I saw firsthand how guilt or innocence, or fairness and truth, had so little to do with the hearing, I wondered why anyone would want to be an officer of the court. To me, they were just participants in a sham.

I realized years later how foreign the idea of legal proceedings was to me then. I had been raised in the country, where people in general were a trusting and trustworthy lot. Nobody sued anybody. It just wasn't done. Honorable men ought to work out their differences with talk. If that didn't work, there were always fists or pistols. But you didn't go around asking a man in a robe to listen to a beef that was none of his business. And you sure didn't want outsiders making decisions about something that affected only you and somebody else.

Joyce didn't attend any of the proceedings. I wouldn't let her. I knew she would become too upset. Instead, she watched me in the courtroom through the glass door. She couldn't hear what was going on, but she monitored my reactions nonetheless.

Our legal fees, beyond the judgment, were $10,000. I had less than $1,000 to my name. I was living in a hotel, not a house of my own whose equity I could have pledged as collateral to secure a loan to pay my lawyer.

I learned another valuable lesson during this ordeal. When you're in a bind, your best friend can sometimes be someone you've yet to meet. That's how I felt later about Clarence Reynolds, a Nashville banker, who gave me a signature loan to satisfy my lawyer's fee.

The man said he liked me and that he was going to take a chance on me. I had never done business with him. He has been a friend to numerous Nashville musicians. I never forgot that.

Joyce and I could have sold our house for a lot more money than the court got for it. But the court wouldn't wait, and it sold the house well under market value. The sale of the house and the satisfaction of the judgment went like lightning. It had taken five years of marriage to work up to home ownership. It took only weeks to have it taken away.

People have asked me why I didn't give up when I lost that house, just as I have been asked why I didn't give up in connection with other major traumas in my life. I never give up, because I know the opposite of dark is light. I know that if I will wait, something good will happen. Often, perhaps usually, the good things will outnumber the bad. I was taught to think that way, I believe in that way, and for me, it works that way. I have been down but never out. I have lost battles, but never the war. I refuse to.

Don't get me wrong. Joyce and I were devastated at the loss of the house, and the ruling in general, the gist of which implied that we were at fault. It's maddening to be declared officially wrong when you and your accuser know you're right.

But I had gotten through worse. And I knew I'd get through this. And that meant getting on with my life.

It was encouraging to have a record climbing the charts at the time. In many ways, it was equally encouraging to have a job at the King of the Road.

I loved it.

Here I was, an out-of-town singer in a country music city, and the world's leading country stars were popping in routinely to catch my show. My band members would whisper, "Faron Young's in the audience" or "Ray Stevens is in the crowd." There were legends such as Porter Wagoner, who at the time starred with Dolly Parton on his own syndicated television variety show.

I soon learned how to play the celebrity crowd. One night when my guitarist told me Faron Young was in the house, I quietly asked, "What color jacket is he wearing?"

"Green," he replied.

At the microphone, I said, "Faron, I sure like your green jacket, and it goes with that stripe in your necktie."

"You ain't blind, you son of a bitch!" he thundered across the room.

The crowd fell out with laughter.

A couple of years later, when Faron and I were doing a show together, he told me, "Milsap, I don't feel sorry for you because you're blind! Now if you sang like Webb Pierce," he added, "then I'd feel sorry for you!"

Around 1970, Faron Young was one of the most powerful men in Nashville and all of country music. He'd had a stellar recording career that by then spanned more than two decades. He was a pillar of the city's business community. He owned the Young Building, where a lot of the music companies had executive offices.

Faron also owned the *Music City News,* a monthly tabloid that was the bible of country music. If, as a newcomer to Nashville, you could get Faron Young's acceptance in 1973, you had a leg up in the music business.

Others who came to see me at the King of the Road included Dottie West, David Clayton Thomas, Mickey Mantle, Buford Pusser, Jack Greene, and Jeannie Seely, to name a few.

Although I rarely play them now (except in Nevada), I can't count the number of nightclubs I've played in my career. Even in the early days of my RCA Records success, beginning in 1973, I had to play what entertainers call the "skull orchards." They were knife and gun clubs much like some of the dives I had played a few years earlier as a rhythm and blues artist. I've also played the elegant showrooms where gentlemen were admitted only if they wore a tie, and only if it was black.

But among those thousands of after-dark playgrounds for adults, it was the King of the Road that was more important to my career, and stands out more vividly in my memory, than any of the others.

Funny, I can still remember little things about the big stars who stopped in there. I recall my first meeting with Conway Twitty inside the nightclub. He was kind and complimentary, and then he offered some off-the-wall advice.

"When you make it big," he said, "don't buy an airplane. They're more trouble than they're worth. Travel on a bus. You'll save money and travel a lot more comfortably."

I later saw a lot of major country stars try flying from appearance to appearance in their private planes. Most regretted it and took a loss on the planes they eventually sold. Who knows, I might have tried the same thing were it not for that tidbit of advice that night from Conway.

Back then, there were probably only a few hundred people working at the publishing companies, record companies, talent agencies, and other country music–related businesses on Nashville's notorious 16th and 17th avenues. As a matter of routine, almost as a matter of ritual, many of them ended the workday by starting (and sometimes finishing) the night on the King of the Road roof.

I could never have gone to Nashville if I had not had that waiting engagement at the King of the Road. That job gave me the security I needed to establish my credentials as a country singer. There was no place then, and there is no place today, where a would-be country entertainer could get better exposure to the powers that be. Hundreds of million-dollar deals were made over a cocktail and under the starlight at the King of the Road on the roof in Music City U.S.A.

I'll never know the real reason why it closed. The crowds, every night, were either big or gigantic. It wasn't unusual, even on a weeknight, for people to stand in line around the building to get into the nightclub 90 feet above them. The hotel was named after the enormous hit record by Roger Miller.

A sighted person, being playful, will slip up behind a guy and put his hands over the eyes of the guy in front, then say, "Guess who?" To this day, when Roger Miller sees me, he slips up behind me and says "Who is it?" as he covers my ears.

Anyhow, I played on the roof at the King of the Road Hotel from December 26, 1972, until January 5, 1974. We were a four-piece band playing five nights for $1,600. During that time, I signed with RCA Records, signed with one of the strongest career management firms in Nashville, and recorded my first and second national top-ten songs.

My drummer and best friend at the time, Steve "Hawk" Holt, and I put together a band whose song list had a lot of Nashvillians confused. Our repertoire went from Stevie Wonder to Webb Pierce. Hawk often stood up when he played the drums, which was something most folks in Nashville hadn't seen. Hawk was friendly to everybody. If he liked somebody, male or female, he called them "baby." He was so outgoing, and funny, that all the fans liked him. He's an impish clown whose broad smile melted color boundaries.

We grew accustomed to sit-in musicians. Every nightclub house band expects that. Our sit-ins included the world's most famous country music celebrities. Every night was an event at that club, wondering which big name would pop onto the stage.

Charlie Rich sat in one night. Charlie is a former winner of the Country Music Association Entertainer of the Year award, the highest award in all of country music. In 1973, he recorded a song that became an American standard called "Behind Closed Doors." The night he came into the King of the Road, he had just released what became another monster record called "The Most Beautiful Girl in the World."

The guy was a big star.

He walked up to the bandstand, and in a voice slurred with alcohol, said to me, "Would you let a poor boy sit in and play the piano?"

I said, "Sure, Charlie," and got up from the piano bench and moved to the electric piano, so he could play the grand.

Charlie started his song and, midway, decided he wanted to stand up and sing. As he was singing, he passed out. I heard the mike hit the floor; then I heard Charlie hit the floor. He's a big man, and he hit the bandstand with the crash of a human oak.

His head fell into Hawk's drums. It landed way up inside the bass drum.

Charlie was down. We just tried to cover it up as best we could, and we went right into our next tune, Stevie Wonder's "Superstition."

Now that's a hard song to play, and it has a heavy, heavy drumbeat. Hawk was pounding his bass drum, with Charlie's head still inside. The decibel level inside Charlie's ears had to be painful but he kept on dozing.

We got to an instrumental break in the song, and the band was cooking, precise and loud. Charlie was still down. Thinking that no one could sleep through that, I was afraid he was dead. I mean, hotel guests used to call the front desk from the sixth floor to complain about the music's volume on the ninth. Here was Charlie Rich with his ears under assault, not near the big drum, but inside it! But he still wasn't coming to. I just knew a legendary entertainer had died on my bandstand.

I kept playing, and as discreetly as I could, I yelled above the music to Hawk.

"Hawk, is Charlie all right?"

"He ain't moved, baby," Hawk bellowed.

We did an extended version of the song. I wanted to drag it out thinking that Charlie would come to and remove himself from the stage. I guess I was thinking he could crawl off when no one was looking, and not add to his embarrassment.

The song ended. The only sound was the crowd's laughter, and Charlie's snoring. I came from behind the electric piano, Hawk came from behind his drums, Johnny Cobb laid down his bass guitar, and the three of us rolled Charlie off the stage like a sack of feed.

We went right back to playing, and Charlie went right on sleeping. I don't remember if they carried him out when the club closed, or if they just turned the lights off and left him inside.

There was another reason I didn't stop playing when Charlie fell out. If I had, somebody would have told Don Davis, the club manager. He wouldn't have cared that the up and coming Entertainer of the Year was passed out on his bandstand. His only concern would have been that the music was nonstop.

In 1971, I recorded an album for Warner Brothers Records. There was a song on that album entitled "I Didn't Know the Cat was a Junkie." I was still living in Memphis at that time, and my one shot on Warner Brothers didn't pan out. The song did nothing.

It was a medium-tempo rock 'n' roll number about a guy who didn't know his friend was a drug addict. I would do a forty-minute version of the tune, incorporate a passionate narration in the middle, and make the thing into a real production.

Don Davis told me time and time again not to perform "I Didn't Know the Cat Was a Junkie." He hated that song. After the first time I played it, he told me if I ever did that awful song again, I was fired.

One night, people were hollering for me to do the song. I tried to ignore their requests, but they kept taunting me to do the song.

Finally, I asked the bartender, "Where's Mr. Davis?"

"Oh, don't worry, he's in Memphis," was the reply.

For him to be in Memphis wasn't unusual. The hotel's corporate offices were in Memphis. Still, I didn't want to leave anything to chance.

So I asked a waitress, "Where's Mr. Davis tonight?"

"He's in Memphis," she assured me.

A few of the customers began to chant, "He's in Memphis! He's in Memphis!"

That was a green light for me. Against the sternest of warnings, I broke into "I Didn't Know the Cat was a Junkie."

Twenty minutes into the song, I heard somebody screaming, "Stop! Stop!" I could hear the furious voice of Don Davis approaching the bandstand. I could hear the complaints of customers as he pushed them out of his way and made a path up to my side.

In western movies the gunfighter walks into the saloon, and everybody immediately gets quiet. No laughing. No whispering. Maybe just the clatter of glasses.

The same kind of nervous quiet fell over the club, where ten seconds earlier the laughter and music were deafening.

Then, in front of 300 hushed and confused customers, in a voice like a sonic boom, Davis fired me.

"I told you not to play that song!" he shouted. "You're fired! You're fired! Get out! You're fired!"

He knew the crowd liked the song, too, and he threatened to throw every one of them out.

He finally worked himself into such a lather that he turned on the houselights and yelled, "The club is closed!"

The next morning, at 9 a.m., an unheard of hour for a nightclub musician, I was at Davis's office door. I approached his secretary and said, "Please tell Mr. Davis that Ronnie Milsap is here to see him."

Before she could, from the next room I heard, "I don't want to see him, I told him not to play that song!"

I asked her to please let me see him. She asked him to see me. He told her, in a voice loud enough for me to hear, that he wouldn't see Ronnie Milsap, and that she should tell Ronnie Milsap to go away.

Like the old *Temptations* song "Ain't Too Proud to Beg," I asked her to ask him to let me have my job back. Her head must have looked like a swivel, turning to hear me, then turning to talk to Davis, who was hollering his response back to her.

Finally, Davis and I just bypassed her.

"Mr. Davis, you've got to give me my job back," I pleaded. "I need this job. You know I moved up here from Memphis because of this job. You know I've got a family to support. You know I have band members who need to work. Let me have my job back, and I'll never play that song again."

There was a long silence.

"Come on in here," he thundered.

Davis then did ten more minutes of screaming. He said that if he gave me my job back, and that if I ever played that song again, not only would he fire me, but he also would bar me and my band from the hotel.

So, I got my job back.

Now, the above scenario, our playing against his wishes and getting fired, happened six times. We were fired six times in thirteen months because we played "I Didn't Know the Cat was a Junkie."

It became a standing joke, the frequency of my firings by a man whose nightclub I was filling to capacity every night. The funny thing is, I'm convinced the man liked me. And I liked him. I'd enjoy seeing him today. He just didn't like that song.

In April of 1973, Joyce, Todd, and I moved into Sutton Place, a Nashville apartment complex. I had gone to bed around 3 a.m. one Sunday morning, whipped from another week of music making. About 6 a.m., there was a knock at the door.

Who would be coming by, unannounced, at that ridiculously early hour, on my day off? At first, I tried to ignore it. But the knocking grew louder. I finally staggered out of bed and went to the door.

"Who is it?" I shouted.

"It's Don Davis!"

What could he be doing here at this hour? I wondered.

I opened the door and he came inside.

"Wake up, Milsap," he said. "Let's go to Hendersonville. I want to buy a car, and I want you to help me pick it out, and I want to see you drive it."

I couldn't believe it.

Some time earlier, I had told Davis the story of my driving the van on the military base.

"Don, it's my day off, man," I said. "I want to spend the day with my family, you know. Thanks anyhow, but I'll see you later."

"I don't want to hear it," he snapped. "We'll go to Hendersonville, and I'll buy a car. We'll have a big time...."

Again, I politely told him that I should be in bed; my family was, and when we all arose, we were looking forward to spending our Sunday together.

He was unrelenting, insisting now that I drop all my plans, shake myself from sleep, and go with him.

I was unrelenting too. This was my day off; I wasn't on his time now, and I wasn't going to go.

The bickering went on for perhaps five full minutes. There was silence. Then he said, "Milsap, do you like your job?"

"Of course," I said.

"Do you need your job for your family?" he asked.

"You know I do," I said.

"Do you want to keep your job?" he finished.

"Let's go buy a car," I said.

He kept me out all day. That night, instead of taking me home, he took me to the King of the Road, the one place I didn't want to be on my day off. He insisted that I sit in with the band that was playing in the lounge. He closed the club and dropped me on my doorstep around 3 a.m. Monday. I had missed the entire day off.

"Boy, we sure did have a good time today, didn't we?" Davis said. And he drove off into the night.

Can you imagine working for someone who fired you so frequently, that that's what you and the customers at the club remember most about him? People would telephone the club and ask, "Is Ronnie Milsap playing, or is he fired tonight?"

In 1976, after I'd been with RCA for three years and the King of the Road was long behind me, I was on tour with a stop in Louisville, Kentucky. Somebody came to the stateroom on my bus.

"There's a guy out here to see you named Don Davis," he said.

I said to send him in.

As I sat in my quarters, I could feel the bus shaking with Don's heavy footsteps as he came down the aisle toward my room in the back.

Then from nowhere: "Milsap, you're fired! Damn it, you're playing too loud! You're fired!" We hugged each other. We swapped King of the Road stories and laughed away the afternoon.

20

There is a certain momentum in the music business in Nashville. There is a pace involved in making records, negotiating personal appearances, meeting the press, and handling all the rest of the responsibilities that can overload an entertainer. There is struggle to further one's career; there is struggle to fulfill one's dreams.

Yet, in describing my career in 1973, the word "struggle" would be misleading. My career took off that year more than it ever had. And the things I was experiencing for the first time were very exhilarating. Life for me was far more fulfilling than fatiguing. At the time, it seemed the hardest of the hard times were behind me. My success was beginning to unfold.

A few years earlier, I had fought insomnia from worry and stress. Now, I sometimes couldn't sleep because I was just too turned on by all the things that were happening to me.

Nashville, like New York or Los Angeles, is an entertainment city whose machinery seems to stop during winter holidays. I opened at the King of the Road between Christmas and New Year's, so it wasn't likely I'd get an audience of music business executives soon.

I was happily surprised when Tom Collins said he was going to bring the entertainment manager Jack Johnson to hear me the second or third night after my December 26 opening. One night, when the place was filled with holiday spirit, Tom and Jack came through the door.

Jack Johnson was perhaps the most sought-after personal manager and booking agent in Nashville at the time. He was the booking and managing genius behind Charley Pride. He heard me, said he liked what he heard, and came back a second night to hear me again.

On the afternoon of January 3, Joyce, Tom Collins, and I met with Johnson. It all happened that fast. He said he would eventually work me as an opening act for Pride; he said he would get me signed to a major recording label.

I signed a personal management agreement that very afternoon. For managing, booking shows, and directing my career, Jack would receive a 20 percent commission from my gross earnings.

Almost before the ink was dry, I heard Jack push his chair from his desk and lean back.

"Ron-i," (pronounced "Ron-eye") he said, "I can't make you a star. You'll have to do that yourself!"

"Jack," I said, astonished, "why in the hell did I just sign this contract?"

He didn't answer. Eventually I would understand that no big entertainment manager can make you a success. . . . you've got to want it yourself.

Jack did arrange for me some of the biggest career breaks I've ever had.

Jack is a likable and gruff old show business buccaneer in the tradition of P. T. Barnum or Col. Tom Parker. He's tough to deal with. Eloquent profanity rolls from Jack's mouth, and yet he's a wonderful throwback to the old school of manners.

He was fiercely loyal and protective of his clients. I was doing a show for the Music Operators of America in Chicago. I had gotten permission to use another entertainer's sound equipment. The sound was great until I went on! Then the owner of the equipment changed his mind in the middle of my show! He changed it by literally pulling the plug on me. In front of thousands, I suddenly had no audio!

Furious, Jack walked over to the guy at the soundboard and grabbed him around the throat. As Jack was choking him, he pushed him down over the audio console.

"Turn him back on," he growled. The sound came back on, and the audience could hear me again.

The afternoon he signed me, the meeting was very positive. We ended the meeting with my sitting at a piano in Jack's office, singing some songs, including a tune that had been written by Dan Penn called "I Hate You."

I sang it as an example of the kind of traditional country music that I could do, despite my reputation as a rock 'n' roll and rhythm and blues singer. I told Jack that I would like to record the song for whatever label he was able to sign me with.

He and Collins liked my idea and then went on to say that they had some songs of their own they'd like me to record. Collins came up with "All Together Now, Let's Fall Apart," written by Johnny Coonts, and "That Girl Who Waits On Tables," written by Bobby Barker.

Both were good songs, and both were published by Pi-Gem-Chess Music, the publishing company owned by Charley Pride and Jack Johnson.

Over the years, I recorded many Pi-Gem-Chess songs that would become hits. Jack and Charley's publishing company that had operated in the red began to see black.

In late January, three weeks after my signing with Jack, he arranged for me to get into a recording studio with some of Nashville's premiere musicians. The idea was for me to record some songs so Jack could present them to a major label.

I hadn't been living in Nashville a month, and I was working nights at the most popular nightclub, and already working days on a recorded product to be presented to the world's leading record labels.

Our recording session was what used to be called a "standard session" in Nashville. We had three hours to record as many songs as we could. We got down the two Pi-Gem-Chess songs first. We had twenty minutes left of studio time, and ran through "I Hate You." The Nashville players, with their typical excellence, picked up the song immediately. We recorded two takes of the song. Who knows, we might even have had a minute of studio time left.

That day, I recorded with studio legends, including Pig Robbins on piano, Kenny Malone on drums, Joe Zenken on bass, Charlie McCoy on organ, Lloyd Green on steel guitar, Billy Sanford on guitar, Chip Young on acoustic guitar, Tommy Williams and Jim Buchanan on fiddle. As I sang, I played electric piano. A group called the *Nashville Edition* sang background. I was having so much fun that the three songs and 180 minutes were over before I knew it.

Today, in my own state-of-the-art studio, I have been known to spend three days recording just one song. That's not necessarily the standard in Nashville recording studios, but the days of recording three songs in three hours are gone. Things have changed a lot in the country music recording industry.

I eventually left the management of Jack Johnson. We reached a point where we couldn't agree on things as often as I'd like. It doesn't matter who was right or wrong. In show business career management, what matters is teamwork. Jack and I got to a place where we were no longer teammates. But working with Tom and Jack on that first album was magic.

Tom remains one of my producers to this day, having coproduced with me seventeen of my twenty-one albums. Ours has been a long and good relationship. We had a plan from the start. We would make the best country records we could, and stay away from anything that had a feel of rock 'n' roll or rhythm and blues. The goal was to establish me firmly as a country artist. We would be surprised later on to see my music branch out into other areas.

Tom taught me, in our early days, a lesson about country music and its credibility. He said that country fans believe that what a singer sings comes from his personal life. He told me not to sing songs about drinking or adultery, since neither is part of my life, though both are popular country music themes. In the first years of association with Collins, we actively sought positive country songs, which were an oddity, since the majority of country songs back then were sad. In the next few years, we would find, record, and hit with tunes such as "Pure Love," "Daydreams about Night Things," "What Goes On When the Sun Goes Down," "I'm a Stand-By-My-Woman Man," and "Let My Love Be Your Pillow."

Collins and I had a second criterion for selecting songs.

I'll never record a song that puts a woman down, I decided. I respect women, and we were wise enough commercially to realize that women buy most of the records.

Jack pitched those first three songs we recorded to Jerry Bradley, then president of RCA Records in Nashville. Collins says today that Jack had his greatest influence with RCA at the time because Charley Pride was on RCA. It just stood to reason that RCA would give a listen to me.

Bradley, however, was a practitioner of one of show business's biggest curses: typecasting. Bradley had heard me sing a couple of years earlier at T. J.'s in Memphis.

"Milsap ain't a country singer," he told Jack Johnson. "I heard him at T. J's. He's a rock 'n' roll singer."

Jack twisted Bradley's arm, and he agreed to come by Jack's office to hear the three tunes I had recorded. Jack played the songs on a good stereo through big speakers. There was a long silence when the last song had played.

"That son of a bitch *can* sing country!"

In April of 1973, I signed an exclusive recording contract with RCA Records. The result has been thirty-five number-one songs and twenty-one albums. The folks at RCA tell me that's more number-one songs than anyone else has recorded for the label in its history.

In May 1973, a month after my signing, RCA released my first single. The A side of the release was "All Together Now, Let's Fall Apart." The B side was the song we had done in less than twenty minutes, "I Hate You."

"I Hate You" was the bigger hit of the two. The success of that song reaffirmed my confidence in my judgment about country songs.

By August, when I was beginning my eighth month as a resident of Nashville, RCA gave me the green light to go back into the studio and record seven more songs, so that they would have ten songs in all.

They needed that many to release my first album. It would be on the record store shelves in time for Christmas shopping.

What a year I was having!

I recorded those seven remaining songs in three days in RCA's legendary studio B, which today is a tourist attraction because of its rich heritage. Jim Reeves, Don Gibson, and other legends, including Elvis, recorded there. Believe me, thoughts of those giants were running through my mind as I recorded my first album in the summer of 1973.

One day, while on break from a session, Tom Collins heard me doing an interview. I said, "Country music is really where my heart is." He liked the phrase "where my heart is," and said, "That should be the title of your first album!"

That album, "Where My Heart Is," had a production cost of $8,500. Today, a ten-song album would cost an established country artist about $150,000 to record.

I didn't have my first number-one single until the spring of 1974. Collins was looking for a song to kick off this "positive country music" campaign. One day he called me to come into the office, all excited about a new singer-songwriter he had just met the night before. His name was Eddie Rabbitt. Tom mentioned to Eddie that he was looking for a "positive, up-tempo song" for Ronnie Milsap. Eddie played "Pure Love" for him.

The song originally had about seven verses, but I used only one of them.

I remembered the name Eddie Rabbitt from a few years earlier in Memphis, when I had sung and played on Elvis's "Kentucky Rain," which Rabbit had co-written with Dick Heard. Now I was recording one of Eddie's songs on Elvis's birthday, January 8, 1974.

A few months later, I was sitting in Jack Johnson's office, a place I liked to hang out during those days. Elroy Kahanek, then head of promotion for the country music division of RCA, called.

"Ronnie," he said, pausing, "I want you to know that 'Pure Love' will be number one in *Billboard* magazine next week!"

That's how simple the announcement was. After years and years of dreams about the elusive number-one record, the announcement was made in seven seconds. Some folks remember exactly what they were doing when they first heard that man had set foot on the moon. I remember, too, but my excitement about the moon was nothing compared with finding out that I had a number-one single on RCA Records.

I was so fired up, I asked Joyce to write a thank-you note to the program directors at country music radio stations who had played my record. We got the list of directors, and we wrote. We had a number-one song on the radio, and our spirits were as high as those guys on the moon!

In addition to the thank-you notes, I began calling radio stations regularly from the RCA conference room. I'd make spot announcements for the disc jockeys, and say things like "This is Ronnie Milsap, and when I'm in Tulsa, I listen to KVOO Radio."

I loved doing that sort of thing, and got to do it in person when

I first participated in the disc jockey convention, an annual week-long bash held each October in Nashville for the hundreds of country disc jockeys. Today, it's called the Country Music Association convention, open to all its members, disc jockeys, show promoters, talent buyers, and basically anybody who plays a role in the country music business. But in 1973, it was still primarily for disc jockeys.

I was sitting at the RCA table along with some big celebrities. On my immediate right was Canada's Hank Snow. Here I was, the newest artist on the RCA roster, seated next to a legend. There were long lines of disc jockeys with tape recorders. They wanted to do brief, recorded interviews to take back to their home stations, and they wanted the artists to make station endorsements. I was really enjoying being a part of it all. I know it sounds corny, but I was so glad to be there.

When it at last was over, I stood up to leave and someone said to me, "Ronnie Milsap, you're great, and I hope you make a million dollars," then kissed me on the cheek.

That was my first encounter with Dolly Parton. It knocked me out that she took time to speak to me. I've always related to her because we're both from the Smoky Mountains, and I've always been a fan of hers. When I really got into the business, I thought about what Dolly had said at our first meeting; I found out making a million dollars was possible. But after salaries, road expenses, show costs, taxes, and all kinds of other expenses, I wish she had said, "Ronnie Milsap, I hope you get to *keep* a million dollars!"

I participated in my first RCA Fan Fair that year. Fan Fair is an annual event in Nashville to let the fans see their favorite country music entertainers. By 1989, there were 25,000 fans who paid $65 each, plus their food, lodging, and transportation, to come to Nashville to attend this bash.

I love to participate in those week-long galas, and I have some fond memories. My first fan fair was in June 1973, at Nashville's War Memorial Auditorium. My first record had been out just a month. I was supposed to do only a few songs, because there were so many other big acts on the program. Since my song list was so short, the stagehands apparently decided it was too much bother to position my piano at center stage. They said I could do my songs with the piano sitting back with the band.

The idea was that the audience could hear me, even if they couldn't see me so well. Well, Jerry Bradley, the head of RCA, hit the ceiling. He stopped the show and said it would not resume until the stagehands put me front and center, where he thought I belonged. I really appreciated that he wanted me well presented.

I sang three songs that day: "All Together Now, Let's Fall Apart," "I Hate You" (my current record at that time), and Merle Haggard's "Branded Man." The audience responded with a standing ovation. The next morning, a newspaper reported that the Ronnie Milsap portion of the show was "magic." Since then, I've been fortunate enough to headline the RCA Fan Fair show many times.

One of the highlights of my career during this time was an invitation to do the syndicated Ralph Emery radio show. I've always had a great affinity for radio. Ralph had the greatest radio voice I had ever heard. And he had credibility. He sounded good, but he also knew what he was talking about. He brought more dignity to country music broadcasting, and the industry in general, than anyone I knew. I had fantasized all my life about making it in music, but somehow, I never dared to fantasize about making it to the *Ralph Emery Show.*

I was taken to the old WSM radio studios in Nashville to do a tape-recorded interview with Ralph to be broadcast over WSM-AM and several hundred other stations.

You'd have thought that with the whirlwind of wonderful developments that were happening to me, I wouldn't have been nervous. But merely getting to meet the dean of the all-night airwaves had shaken me up. I felt as though my career was staked on one roll of the dice.

"What if I say the wrong thing?" I asked Joyce. "He won't like me, and I won't make it in this business."

Ralph's celebrity was based on his live, all-night broadcast, but he also had a syndicated radio show. That's the show I was booked on. It consisted of five segments, one aired each day, Monday through Friday. All of the five segments were recorded in one sitting with Ralph.

I wasn't well enough established to be a solo guest, so I shared billing with the singer Mac Wiseman.

I was determined to be as alert and responsive as possible. I even wanted to make notes during the show and thought about taking my

Perkins braille writer to the studio. The machine's size prohibited that, however, so I instead took along a braille slate and pointer for making notes.

The interview began with harmless chitchat. Ralph was magnificent at putting me at ease. He had never seen a slate and pointer. During a break, he commented about the little noises that occurred when I punched in the individual dots that enabled me to read.

"What are you doing over there?" he asked, as I sat writing.

"I'm just making notes in braille," I replied.

"Oh," he said, "it sounds like a chicken pecking."

The show's recording proceeded, and by now we were in the Friday segment of the program. My debut on the legendary *Ralph Emery Show* was coming to a close, and I packed up my slate and pointer.

Then Ralph unintentionally caught me off guard.

"Ronnie," he said, "I was thinking, back some time ago, about you writing in braille. I'm sure all the people listening know you're blind. Why don't I put the microphone down close to where you're working and let them hear how it sounds when you write in braille.

My throat tightened. My palms moistened. My mouth dried up.

Ralph wanted me to use the apparatus that I had just put away, and the audio tape was still rolling. I knew broadcasters hated "dead air."

I scurried to get my slate and pointer out of my briefcase and searched for an explanation. Subconsciously, I must have remembered Ralph's saying that my braille writing sounded like a chicken pecking.

"Wait a minute, Ralph," I said. "Let me get my pecker out!"

Mac Wiseman, who is an enormous man, had been leaning backwards in his chair with his feet propped up. He exploded into laughter and fell over backwards out of his chair. Billy Reeves, who had taken me to the station, struggled to set Mac upright. Ralph, the consummate and unflappable professional, began laughing too hard to talk. The engineer yelled "Cut, cut!" The tape was stopped until he and Mac regained their composure.

My comment was never broadcast, but I saw Ralph recently, and he said he still has it on tape. He and I had a good laugh about my debut on his show.

But I wasn't laughing at the time. I went home and told Joyce I had blown it—I would never again be asked to appear on the *Ralph Emery Show*. I said, "I just made the biggest mistake of my career."

When I told her the story of what had happened, she laughed and said it wasn't nearly so serious as I thought.

I have done the *Ralph Emery Show* many times since, both on radio and television. Each time I'm scheduled to appear, he asks me to bring along some high-tech device that aids the blind, but he's never asked me to bring the slate and pointer.

The year 1973 was the year of big shows for me, including a package show with Jeannie Pruitt and Don Gibson in Atlanta for radio station WPLO. It was a homecoming for me. I had played so many years in Atlanta, and was returning with a record out on RCA. Tom Collins and Joyce went with me. Tom was struggling to find his way around the busy city, and because I had once lived in Atlanta, I gave him driving directions. I don't think he was too sure he should rely on my directions, and when he saw that he could, it really shocked him.

Shortly after that, Tom and I went to Dallas. It was a package show for WBAP radio, Fort Worth, held at the Texas Rangers baseball stadium. Collins and I stood in the wings as Hank Williams, Jr., went on stage, to the roar of 35,000 fans.

The organizers told me I could sing "I Hate You" and one other song. That was fine with me; I'd gladly wait around for Hank to do his show. And, man, what a show he did!

He performed for about an hour and a half, singing all those Hank Williams songs I'd always loved.

Then he jumped off the stage and kissed the ground. He was pulling out all the stops to excite the crowd, and it worked. They went crazy; then most of them went home.

Tom said there must have been about 3,000 people left when I at last went on around midnight on a weeknight.

I sang "I Hate You," and the word "you" echoed in the near-empty Stadium. For all practical purposes, the show was over. Hank had slain the audience and left. Singer Wayne Kemp followed me, and by the time he went on, the show had run into the morning hours.

My first national television exposure occurred that year as well. I was on the *Mike Douglas Show* in Philadelphia, with Charley Pride as the cohost.

Pride told Mike all about me, and it was a very strong shot for my career. Since it was my first appearance on the show, I wasn't asked to sit on the couch and talk with Mike but just sing two songs. Before I was to go onstage, I became so nervous I got a case of "cotton mouth." Tommy Williams, a fiddle player with the Pridesmen, who had also worked on my first Nashville recording session, got me a cup of water. He was trying to calm me down and make me relax.

Once I sat down at the piano and started singing, I was fine. I sang my first single, "I Hate You," and my second single, "That Girl Who Waits On Tables." Charley's band, the Pridesmen, backed me.

That year, in the fall, I made my debut on *Hee-Haw*, then America's highest-rated syndicated television show. That was my first realization of the staggering power of national television. After my appearance, people called RCA, they called Jack Johnson's office, and they even called my unlisted home telephone. I heard from folks I hadn't heard from in ten years. I heard from folks I'd never heard of. It all happened from singing just a few minutes on television.

In November 1973, I did my first show with the tremendously popular Charley Pride. I had been in Nashville eleven months, during which I had signed with Jack Johnson, signed with RCA, had a two-sided hit record, appeared live before thousands of people, and had done my first national television shows. A year before, during the holiday season, Joyce, Todd, and I had moved to Nashville with our dreams. Now, Thanksgiving day was upon us. For me, thanksgiving had been the order of every day for almost a year.

21

I began touring as the opening act for Charley Pride in January 1974. Music fans and the folks who ran the country music industry kept my head in the clouds. Somehow, my feet miraculously stayed on the ground. And I was learning from the best. In 1974, Charley Pride was one of the best and most popular country entertainers in the world.

I became one of Charley's opening acts because he and I were on RCA Records and he and I were under the career management of Jack Johnson. A *Grand Ole Opry* quartet called the Four Guys filled out the bill. The three acts made one commercially successful and critically acclaimed show.

Pride paid me $600 a day to do approximately thirty minutes onstage. The money was more than I had ever earned as a nightly fee. Yet, it wasn't enough for me to afford a band, so I took one musician with me, my old friend and drummer from Memphis, Steve "Hawk" Holt. I needed the familiarity of Steve's presence onstage. I also needed a friend to travel with me.

Todd was just a baby, so Joyce had to stay home with him. Steve Holt became my eyes, as I began a style of life that is still going on today, playing for thousands of fans night by night, one town at a time.

When Pride was on stage, Hawk and I would stand in the wings, watching him work the crowd. My timing and pacing skills were sharpened as I listened to Pride perform. Charley had very strong convictions about showing up on time, professional stage behavior, and avoidance of alcohol and drugs. I shared that philosophy, so it was easy for me to fit into the show.

Each night, after the concert, we went back to the hotel on a chartered bus. The next morning we would crowd into a customized Fairchild F-27 airplane that Charley leased for touring and fly to the next city, where the routine and rigor resumed.

Charley had two outstanding pilots: Bob Sowers, the captain, and Fred Acciardo, the copilot, whose skills reduced, but did not eliminate, my fear of flying. They flew the plane with such precision that they made even me feel safe.

It was aviation strictly by the book during this one time in my life that I relied primarily on an aircraft to get from show to show. One stormy night we had to land in Chicago, en route to Waterloo, Iowa. The pilots felt it was unsafe to proceed, but Pride wanted to go on anyhow.

He was annoyed when the pilots announced that the entourage should spend the night in Chicago.

"I want to go on to Waterloo!" insisted Pride.

"You got it," one of the pilots said, and he handed Pride the airplane keys.

Pride was impressed with their dedication to flying and their refusal to fly the plane in bad weather. We flew to Waterloo . . . the next morning.

I had been with the Pride package about six weeks when we played Charlotte, North Carolina, on February 19, 1974. North Carolina is my home state, and that date was my first appearance there since signing with RCA. I was coming home, coming with two hit records under my belt, and coming to the Charlotte Coliseum on the Charley Pride Show. I was proud to be sharing my success with the home folks and I felt somehow as though they were a part of it.

Sometimes when you're planning something really big, some little thing raises it ugly head to try to mar it all. Joyce had bought me a new denim jacket, and Sherry Cobb, the wife of my former bass player, had sewn studs and rhinestones on it. They thought it looked spectacular.

As I was getting dressed backstage, Pride's band leader, Gene O'Neil, told me to take off the jacket.

O'Neil and all the Pridesmen, including Charley, wore conservative suits on stage. O'Neil was against my wearing denim, although denim was very fashionable at the time.

Now here I was, the new guy on the block, and I'm listening to a lot of bosses, and trying to please them all. In the middle of the discussion, Dick Blake, the promoter of the show, approached O'Neil and me. He was the guy paying everyone's bills.

"Let him wear the coat!" Blake told O'Neil. "It's flashy, and we *are* in show business, you know."

I got to wear my jacket for the home state crowd.

This was the first time that a lot of my former Governor Morehead classmates had seen me since I had graduated, almost twelve years earlier. I'm certain some of them had wondered what ever happened to me.

My desire to please this gathering was enormous. I wanted my part of the show to be letter-perfect. Perhaps I was thinking about some of the teachers who resisted my going into this career. Maybe I was thinking about that scholarship to law school I had turned down years earlier. And maybe I was thinking about all the old friends who had believed in me and my pie-in-the-sky dreams of making it in music.

I had these thoughts and more in mind as Hawk and I, backed by the Pridesmen, stormed the stage. Our spirits were high, and it must have shown. The house came down.

What a homecoming!

It was hard to leave the stage. If it had been my own show, I probably would have sung for hours.

There is an old rule in show business that says the hometown crowd is the hardest to play. The Charlotte show wasn't a hometown event, but it was mighty close. The reception given to me could have been reserved for a foreign head of state.

I don't mind telling you I was emotional—and grateful. I sought their approval and had been showered with their love.

The *Charlotte Observer* columnist Kays Gary wrote a glowing review.

A STAR IS BORN

They were all applauding, yelling, stomping or whistling and maybe half of the 9,000 people were out of their seats and on their feet when the big man with the baby face slowly ambled off stage, feeling his way down the steps toward the dressing room.

"Boy!" he breathed, beads of sweat rolling off his cheeks, "Some crowd. What an audience!"

The black man with the smooth, finely-chiseled features, reached out and grabbed a shoulder.

"Well, you really gave it to them," he said. "They're just giving it back. Great show!"

It was an accolade from Charley Pride, the star, The Man, to 31-year-old Ronnie Milsap, blind and awash now with the big, new sound—the roar of the crowd.

Pride meant it. He'd been peeking under the canvas backdrop out onto the stage where spotlights blazed into the upraised glistening face of Milsap, joyously pounding the piano and singing, winging, flying through an encore of a Jerry Lee Lewis medley.

Pride liked what he heard and saw. The crowd was warmed up for the No. 1 man, yet to make his appearance. Later, even as he was similarly baptized by the accustomed accolade, he must have felt it a shade subdued by comparison. When Pride, near the end, graciously acknowledged appreciation for the Milsap performance, there was that roar again, decibels above anything he'd heard since coming on stage.

A new star? Ronnie Milsap right up there with Haggard and Pride?

Ronnie stood in the center of fans crowding into the backstage area, smiling, thanking everybody and murmuring about "That crowd . . . it sure turned me on. . . ."

Classmates from his days at the North Carolina State School for the Blind plucked at his sleeve to ask: "Remember me?"

"Lewis Modlin! You wanna wrestle? Dorothy Black . . . Billy Davis . . . Charlie Helms!" Hands touched each other, moved to shoulders and stayed there and there was a whole lot of hugging when the Boyce Atwell family of Pineville came in.

"I reckon you'd call them family," Ronnie said. "I spent happy times with 'em."

"Like my son," Mrs. Atwell said. "He and Larry were roommates. They did so enjoy each other. Larry died nine years ago and Ronnie—Ronnie's here—We're so proud."

"When they brought Larry something, they'd buy me something," Ronnie said. "That's like family."

He was glad so many people were proud. It hasn't always been that way.

Born blind in Graham County's mountains, he remembers the arms of a father, of his grandma and grandpa. Loving arms. But some arms were missing and he tried not to think about that. When he reached, though, Grandpa Homer Frisby's hand was there. He was wishing, this night, that Grandpa were here.

"I'd like to have him out there on the stage, that great old feller. He's in his 80's . . . happy up there in Hayesville with his chickens and whittlin'. I sure do wish he could hear this. . . ."

After nine years of playing clubs, rock and pop and country—whatever—Ronnie's star began to rise nine months ago with his first Nashville record: "I Hate You" and "All Together Now, Let's Fall Apart." Top Ten. He landed on "Hee Haw" and the Mike Douglas Show. Credit, he says, his manager, Jack Johnson, the man who also put Charley Pride up there.

"I just listen to him, that's all. This isn't a job. This is living. It's fun. I'm trying to get used to big crowds now. Oh, this is great."

There are no tears for Ronnie. Not any you can see anyway. Early on, he decided to enjoy.

He had a scholarship to Emory Law School but there was too much music in him, too much need to play and sing and make the happy scene soaking up people. The focus finally came to country music because "It tells all the stories that everybody feels and hears and understands. And then country music people, the fans, are the most faithful. You can't get 'em down. Mostly I'm singing other people's songs, but maybe someday I can sing the way I feel."

Ronnie Milsap doesn't worry about "getting down" himself, about whether the star will dim or fizzle. He has a wife and a little boy in Nashville and no regrets except . . .

North Carolina, he says, is most generous and "great" in its treatment of handicapped people except he wishes all blind kids could just start in regular school like everybody else. "You're taught that you'll be accepted when you leave the State school but it doesn't work out that way. Sighted and blind people are kept apart too long during important years. It's not their fault but it's a gap that just can't be closed later. It's a segregation that hangs on, hard as everybody tries."

That said, he called for Steve and introduced him and said. "He's my main friend. Keeps me straight. Great drummer, too."

"Can't get away from this fellow," Steve Holt said. "We've been together five years. I love the man."

With that, Ronnie took the arm of black Steve Holt and, threading their way through the fans, headed for the exit.

"Don't forget," he called over his shoulder, "I got a new record coming out. It's called 'Pure Love.' That's a plug, son!" He was laughing.

Kays Gary, Feb. 19, 1974, *Charlotte Observer*

That was one of the select nights in my career when I knew that becoming a professional musician had unquestionably been the right thing to do after all. There had been doubt. That night, applause laced with love was the great eraser. There had been years of hard times. That night, I couldn't have recalled one.

Not long after the Charlotte show, I played the Felt Forum at Madison Square Garden in New York City with Bobby Bare and Dolly Parton. Dolly had recently left the *Porter Wagoner Show* to pursue a solo career.

That night in New York she was without Porter, and with her own Family Band. Two brothers, two sisters, and a cousin made up the band. The sibling harmonies were unbelievably powerful.

What I felt in New York with Dolly as she closed the show that night, and what I felt in Charlotte when I opened for Pride, was a hurricane of emotion I hadn't felt since those childhood days at the Meadow Branch Primitive Baptist Church. That's the only thing I can compare it to. I will relish, and be humbled by, that feeling, anytime it should want to repeat itself, anywhere on the globe.

During those months with Pride, I was introduced to another group of people who evoked strong emotions in me—working people who were poor and often down in spirit. They would ask for my autograph and tell me how much my music meant to them. And they weren't talking mere entertainment. They were talking about inspiration, the positive effect my work had on them.

Maybe they had physical handicaps. Maybe they were bound by poverty. Maybe they had recently undergone the death of a loved one. Whatever the hardship, so many of them seemed to want to tell me about it. Then they would tell me that hearing me on the radio, and seeing me in concert, had been uplifting to them. That it had all given them renewed strength. They would tell me that seeing me press on in my own life had given them the strength to do the same in theirs. This was frightening to me. I can only call the emotion a blend of appreciation, humility, and fear. Words couldn't describe it.

Today, my life and career largely comprise publishing companies, studios, record contracts, and big businesses that sometimes make me feel like a one-man conglomerate. Given the magnitude of the success I have been blessed with, a lot of folks wouldn't think I miss the comparatively simple days. But I do. They'd never believe that in the midst of my chaotic life, when I least expect it, I still hear a song or something equally simple that really moves me.

I'm often robbed of personal contact with the fans. And I miss that. I miss that a lot.

But it can't be helped. Today I travel with three buses, twenty-two people, and a tractor trailer that carries a 7-foot grand piano and the production equipment. It takes six hours to set up the equipment, three hours to take it down, and untold hours to move it hundreds of miles to the next town. I do that on a daily basis when I'm touring. I can no longer give up three or four hours in each town to sign autographs. Staying overtime in one city makes me late for the next. I hate that.

Of all the spectacular things that happened to me in 1974, the best was yet to come.

I was sitting in Jack Johnson's office one day between trips, when his assistant, Melva Matthews, said she had some news for me. "You've been nominated by the Country Music Association for 'Male Vocalist of the Year'."

Man, what a surprise!

I had been with the RCA label for little more than a year. Here I was, an opening act who didn't even have his own band, nominated for Male Vocalist of the Year.

Furthermore, the other four nominees were established artists, one of whom would be named. "Entertainer of the Year" that night.

I called Joyce on that summer day in 1974 to tell her about the nomination. I was almost too excited to talk. I kept saying, "I won't win Joycie, I won't win, but I've been nominated!"

Joyce was as excited as I was, and much more optimistic. She said I could win, that I was the best.

"Being in love with someone makes you a little prejudiced," I laughed, "but it's still good to hear!"

The CMA awards show is held in October each year and televised on CBS. To be sitting in the audience with all those performers I admired so much was a dream come true, but to be nominated was unbelievable.

Joyce held on tightly to my hand as they called the names of the nominees for male vocalist, and when the presenter said, "The winner is . . . Ronnie Milsap," I think I went into shock.

Joyce threw her arms around me and said, "You won Ronnie, you won!"

I was in a daze. I rose to my feet, and Jack Johnson and Tom Collins rushed over and each grabbed an arm and pulled me to the stage, where I was presented the award.

I stood in front of the microphone, and all I could think to say was "Thank you! I love you!"

That was the extent of my acceptance speech before millions of viewers on national television.

The audience didn't mind; they knew how I felt. It was obvious, and their response told me they understood! A day or two later, I thought of all kinds of things I would like to have said, people I would liked to have thanked. But that night, my emotions overruled everything.

The significance of what had just happened finally hit me! That same night, Olivia Newton-John won "Female Vocalist of the Year." *Grand Ole Opry* legend Roy Acuff presented the award and mispronounced her name! She had scored with giant crossover records, such as "I Honestly Love You," "If You Love Me Let Me Know," and "Let Me Be There." But Roy apparently had never heard of the Australian singing sensation.

In announcing the winner to the world, he called Olivia—"Oliver" Newton-John.

I had a record out at the time. It was a Don Gibson song, "(I'd Be) a Legend in My Time." After I won the award, the song went to number one almost instantly.

The country music awards have been called a "popularity contest," and in a very real sense, they are. If someone wanted to call them a popularity contest, and that meant my acceptance by the country music community, then that was just fine.

One day in March 1975, I was called to a meeting with Jack Johnson and Charley Pride. They felt my popularity had outgrown my affordability to the Charley Pride Show. After I had won male vocalist, Pride raised my performance fee to $1,500 a night. Jack thought he could get $5,000 a night for me, and that was more than Pride wanted to pay for an opening act.

It was time to leave the man who had put me in front of thousands.

My mind was a maze of confused thoughts. I had been very secure as part of Pride's show. I was just settling into that nest, and now he and Jack were advising me to leave it.

I thanked Charley for all he had done for me, for all he had taught me.

There was a long pause.

"Son," he said, ". . . just pass it on."

Throughout the years, I have tried to do just that. I have had opening acts on my show who have gone on to achieve their own headline status, including Alabama, Reba McEntire, Ricky Skaggs, and the Judds.

I hope I have followed Pride's directions and "passed on" the kind of treatment and teaching he gave me.

It was a fascinating time. Pride taught me about show business success. The fans were teaching me about love. And above all, I learned there was enough of both to go around for everybody.

22

There is a lot more responsibility headlining your own show than there is as a feature act on someone else's. When I was an opening act for Charley Pride, my travel and lodging arrangements were handled for me. There were folks who told me when and where the bus would leave for the show, and what time it would depart for the airport.

Today, all of that is handled for me again. I have my own personnel to do it. But such tasks were unaffordable to me about the time I formed my first touring band. Instead of being taken care of, I suddenly was the one who was taking care of others; it was now my responsibility to arrange travel schedules and lodging for everybody.

My first band with RCA was just five pieces, including me. I've had several musicians work for me since 1975 whose technical skills were better than those of that early group, but what they lacked in technical skills they made up for in feeling. I didn't just hear their music, I felt it.

Putting together a really good band can be difficult for a new artist. The great musicians you've heard about already have jobs with established entertainers, and it's hard to compete with that. But I was lucky. I already had a great drummer in Steve Holt. Johnny Cobb, who had played bass with me at the King of the Road Hotel, called and said he'd like to be a part of the new band. Johnny's wife, Sherry, joined us later as a background singer. I still needed full-time musicians to play guitar and steel guitar.

Tommy Williams, Charley Pride's fiddle player, told me about a great steel guitar player named Dicky Overbey, who had played behind many of the great country singers. Tommy didn't know where Dicky was living, but definitely thought Dicky was the man for the job.

Now, just before I moved to Nashville, a new recording artist named Mel Street was really catching on in country music. He was one of the inspirations for me to move to Nashville. I'd hear him on the radio and think, "Man, that's what I ought to be doing!"

Mel sang a lot like George Jones and had some songs I loved, such as "Borrowed Angel" and "Lovin' on Back Streets."

In early 1975, Mel and I worked a few shows together. One night on one of those shows, I was standing backstage, waiting to go on, and listening to Mel. I commented to Hawk how good Mel's steel player sounded and asked who he was. Someone said that Dicky Overbey was sitting in that night. Dicky Overbey! That was the guy Tommy had told me about. I knew Dicky wasn't playing for Mel full time, and I decided right then and there that if I wanted him in my band I'd better talk to him now.

Mel finished his set, and there was a short intermission before I was to go onstage. I knew Mel's bus would probably leave before I came offstage, so I would have to speak to Overbey during the intermission.

When Dicky came offstage, Hawk saw him go into the men's room. I immediately thought of Elvis and the people that followed him to the restroom, where he was a captive audience. Those people were asking for money or a job. I decided to reverse the bathroom ploy. So I walked into the restroom, where Dicky was standing at the sink, washing his hands. "Dicky Overbey, I'm Ronnie Milsap. I heard you out there playing steel tonight, and you sounded great!"

"Hey, thanks, man," he said, as he reached for a paper towel to dry his hands, "Nice to meet you!"

"I'm putting a band together," I said, "and I'd like you to play steel." I told him I would like him to meet me at my manager's office in a couple of weeks, if he was interested. Then I went out of the restroom and onto the bandstand. Overbey went down the highway with Mel Street. I didn't know if he was going to show up for the appointment or not.

Before the scheduled appointment, Dicky saw me play a show at Randy's Rodeo in San Antonio, and told me later that after seeing my show, he he wanted to keep that appointment.

Dicky went to work for me playing steel guitar in March 1975. After some time off, he returned to my show in 1989 and is still with me today.

Of all the people I have worked with, I learned more about country music from Dicky Overbey and my friend singer-songwriter Darrell McCall.

They both have huge record collections. I knew country music, but my interest was limited to the major artists of the day, such as Buck Owens, Merle Haggard, and Conway Twitty. They knew the guys on the off-beat circuit, the singers known to country's counterculture of enlightened listeners.

In 1976, Dicky introduced me to Jack Watkins, who became my guitarist, bandleader, and longest-running, full-time musician. Jack had played for Diana Trask, Tex Ritter, Stonewall Jackson, George Jones, and Jack's former wife, Connie Smith, among others.

Jack and Dicky had traveled with a lot of entertainers before a lot of them had buses to travel on. They rode to shows in cars or station wagons and told me many war stories about the life of alcohol and "Old Yeller" stimulant pills.

I assured them that life on the road with me wouldn't be that way.

The general public often thinks that we get a hit record, buy a customized bus or two, and hit the road. It isn't that simple, unless you happen to have a manager or agent who'll spring for the money. I never did.

The customized coaches are nicer than some apartments and in fact, are apartments, of sorts, on ten wheels. With beds, bathrooms, televisions, stereo systems, microwave ovens, refrigerators, video cassette players, carpet, and central heat and air-conditioning, all nestled inside tons of steel. The price tags for those coaches can go as high as $500,000. A couple of hit records, which pay delayed royalties, don't pay enough, or pay fast enough for a young touring entertainer to write a check for his most important tool—transportation.

Our first bus wasn't elaborate, and it wasn't really mine. I leased it from Milo Liggett, Sonny James's bass player, for $150 a day. There is no way I'd rather travel from show to show than in a customized bus.

Today, I have three, to which I've added videocassette recorders and compact disc players.

The buses are nicer than some of the hotels I've stayed in. Many times Joyce and I sleep on the bus rather than in a hotel room. We stay on the bus in the hotel parking lot and go inside the hotel to shower. Then it's right back to our personalized suite on wheels. It's much better than air travel, with which you're at the mercy of the airlines' schedules. Instead of having to get up at 5 A.M. to get to the airport, I can sleep on my bus while it purrs right past it.

The band and I were traveling through western Arkansas late one night on Milo Liggett's bus. I was the only one awake. There was a sudden jolt, and I was thrown forward from my seat, as the bus veered and almost ran off the highway. The front left wheel had come off at highway speed. Later, the driver said he watched it speed off into his headlights, while sparks flew over the top of the bus. The noise was deafening as the steel brake drum plowed a trench into the highway. The band woke up, and the guys were screaming as the driver tried to get the bus under control. Finally, we came to a grinding stop. It was the middle of the night in rural Arkansas, and someone had to go for help. I don't remember why we selected Hawk to go. Maybe he volunteered. Knowing that it might take a long time for him to come back with help, all the rest of us could do was just sit and wait.

There was a movie released at that time about a monster from Boggy Creek. The picture just happened to be set in rural Arkansas. Here we were broken down in rural Arkansas. If that wasn't coincidence enough, the band had just happened to be talking about that monster right before we lost the wheel.

Now, Hawk always liked a good time and a practical joke. If we had been thinking clearly, we would have realized that. But when you're stranded in the country darkness, and the only sounds are crickets and hoot owls, and when you're so keyed up that you're actually mindful of the clock's ticking, well, you think about your rescuer, not his personality.

Hawk hitchhiked to a service station, but he was unable to find a mechanic at that time of night. Always the charmer, he persuaded a guy with a pickup truck to drive him back to the bus to rescue the stranded band in the predawn darkness. Hawk asked the man to turn off his headlights some distance away from the bus. Then, black like the night around him, Hawk silently crept toward the bus loaded with nervous musicians, whose talk had resumed about that dumb monster from Boggy Creek.

From outside, there was a deep and slow moan. Its volume over-powered our conversation. The driver turned on the headlights. Nothing was out there.

If it's always darkest before the dawn, it must always be most quiet before the noise. The bus suddenly took on an eerie silence.

Then there was a deafening rapping on the bus's sheet metal side. It was actually more of a thudding, the kind that comes when metal is pounded by flesh.

Someone, or something, was running the length of the vehicle, beating and screaming, and the sound was soon drowned out by our own yelling.

The driver saw the door open, but before he could see who the monster was, Hawk bolted onto the bus with an ear-splitting growl. A boot, hurled toward the growler, missed, and hit the windshield.

Then came the sound of Hawk's laughter, and a chorus of cussing by the frightened band, most of whom, naturally, said they knew it was Hawk all along. He didn't argue with them. He just moaned like the monster from Boggy Creek.

One of the biggest legitimate scares of my life was in January 1978, when the first bus I bought crashed with the entire band and my business manager, Donald Reeves, on board. We had just finished an engagement at Harrah's in Lake Tahoe, Nevada. Joyce and I flew back to Nashville and had just gotten into bed when the telephone rang. It was Donald calling.

The bus had overturned on ice, on a mountain, in New Mexico. Donald quickly reassured me that no one was seriously injured, but everyone was taken to a hospital. It's a miracle that no one was killed, especially Donald, who was not even in a bunk. He was asleep on a couch near the front, where the television and other appliances were. Steel and glass accessories were flying around the spinning room, and so was Donald. Miraculously, none of the flying apparatus touched him. Donald, who also has a fear of flying, later rode all the way to Nashville in a truck we rented to haul our battered equipment. Even after the bus wreck, he still wouldn't fly.

Johnny Cobb was carried out of the overturned bus on a stretcher. Hawk sat up in his bunk, and when a flashlight was shined on him, pieces of shattered glass sparkled in his Afro haircut. He started to crawl out of the coach until he realized the news media was filming the wreck outside.

Then, he asked to be carried off on a cot.

I always felt that my band and I were a family that just happened not to have the same last names. The feeling of family was driven home to me the instant Donald's faraway telephone voice awakened me to tell me about that wreck. I remember my sense of relief as I talked individually to each member of the group that night. The doctors and officials told me they were all right, but I couldn't rest until I heard it from them personally.

Along with the bus wrecks there is also the monotony of the road. Even though I travel in cushioned comfort, I'm not immune to frustration.

Simon and Garfunkle described it in the 1960s in "Homeward Bound": "... each town looks the same to me, the movies and the factories, and every stranger's face I see reminds me how I long to be ... homeward bound." Even with all the amenities I've mentioned, there are times when I just wish I was home.

I now had the band, I had the booking agent, I had the bus. What I needed was a business manager.

So I hired the man who has been a Ronnie Milsap employee longer than anyone, my brother-in-law, Donald Reeves. Donald and I had been friends for many years. I always told him that when I could afford it, I wanted him to come and work with me and head up my organization in the music business. So in August 1975, Donald, Brenda, and their four children, Kim, Donna, Donnie, and Paula, packed up and moved from Georgia to Nashville.

Donald and I started in a little house we used as an office in Brentwood, a suburb of Nashville. Donald, in those days, opened all the mail and answered the telephone. The conditions were a far cry from those inside my two-story office complex with its staff today.

If my career had a mastermind, it was Donald Reeves. I'm hesitant to say he has "managed" my affairs. He has instead "sculpted" them, with all the care and concern of a master craftsman.

He couldn't be more conscientious. The only thing that surpasses his conscientiousness is his competence. The only thing that surpasses his competence is his loyalty. If he ever leaves my employ, I'll leave show business.

Donald Reeves oversees a multimillion-dollar cash flow for me annually. I would not entrust that to anyone on the strength of his last name. He has the job because he can cut it. Since I wouldn't give him the job just because he's my brother-in-law, why should I withhold it because we're related.

Charley Pride taught me years ago the value of having my own in-house organization. In years to come, I would hire my own accountant and press agent and more. But the rock-solid nucleus of my organization, its skeleton, came with the hiring of someone who combines the wisdom of a board chairman with the loyalty of a family member.

Another career milestone came along in 1975—a guest shot on the *Grand Ole Opry*

There I was, as a guest of *Opry* regular Jeannie Pruitt, playing the world's longest-running live radio show (now in its sixty-fourth year). And the funny thing is, they have yet to hold a rehearsal.

I never got to play the old Ryman Auditorium, home of the *Grand Ole Opry* for over thirty years in downtown Nashville. I attended two shows there in my youth, one with a friend named Bobby Vinson. The show was sold out, and people were lined up outside. Bobby told someone at the door that I was blind and that we had come all the way from Atlanta to hear the *Opry,* and the man let us in.

We walked down the jammed aisle of the Ryman, and the first sound I heard was the incredible voice of Connie Smith singing "Once a Day." Later that night, Roger Miller brought the house down when he sang his two hit songs "Dang Me" and "Chug-A-Lug." And then the most popular country band in the world at that time was introduced—Buck Owens and his Buckaroos ran down the aisle to the stage! What a night of memories.

By the time I first played the *Opry,* the legendary Ryman Auditorium had been closed down, and the *Opry* had moved to Opryland Park in suburban Nashville. I was milling backstage with some of the *Opry's* veteran performers: Bill Carlisle, Minnie Pearl, Roy Acuff, Little Jimmy Dickens, and others. I had listened to those entertainers on the *Opry* as a student at Governor Morehead and during my childhood in Meadow Branch. Who would have ever thought I'd get off that impoverished mountain and be backstage of the renowned *Grand Ole Opry?*

In the center of the modern *Opry* stage, there is a circle of wood, cut from the old stage at the Ryman Auditorium. That piece of old wood supported the likes of Hank Williams, Patsy Cline, Jim Reeves, Ernest Tubb, Johnny Cash, Willie Nelson, Merle Haggard, George Jones; the list goes on and on.

I walked onto the stage, and was overpowered by *Opry* ghosts. I was consumed with memories of the late Jim Reeves and the late Patsy Cline. I was where they had been. In one simultaneous rush of emotion, I felt grateful, humble, and terrified!

I did "Daydreams about Night Things" and "Just in Case." Then Jeannie Pruitt brought me off stage.

In February 1976, after I had done five guest spots on the *Opry*, I was asked to become a member. Roy Acuff introduced me.

"We've got a new *Opry* member here, and I want to tell you about him. He's been coming up here for the last few months as a guest. He can't see, but I want to tell you something, give him another time or two, and he'll be running out here on this stage just like everybody else. Ladies and gentlemen, let's make welcome our fifty-eighth member of the *Grand Ole Opry* . . . Ronnie Milsap!"

The *Opry* is the undisputed mother church of country music. Were it not for the *Opry* and its radio broadcasts, country music might not be as popular in some of the areas where I perform.

I think the *Opry* is country music's greatest AM radio ambassador.

23

In the latter part of 1970, I became part of a package show with the Statler Brothers and Tammy Wynette.

We worked from the fall of 1976 through the end of 1977. Those months of live performing were the most thrilling time of my career.

A package show should be more than a group of various acts. It should be a collection of entertainers pulling for overall effect.

The Statler Brothers, who today are known as the Statlers, were the headline attraction. They had their ideas about what each act should contribute, and the result was a well-rounded, show-stopping presentation of live music.

The emphasis was on professionalism. The Statler Brothers were a rarity back then, because they were one of the few country acts to conduct a sound check before each concert. I did that too, and I still do today.

There aren't as many package shows touring out of Nashville today as there once were. The few that remain seem to put the artists in competition with each other, vying for star billing, the biggest dressing room, or the longest performance set.

Modern managers are telling some of their artists that the thousands of people in the auditoriums have come solely to see them. They're advising their acts to demand better billing, or a higher performance fee. Consequently, the entertainers (some of whom have been in the business long enough to know better) are getting inflated opinions of their worth. When that happens, the artists and fans both suffer.

I've worked on tours in recent years where the performers barely spoke to each other, although they were traveling thousands of miles each month in the same entourage. The name of the game in the Statler Brothers–Wynette-Milsap program was not competition. It was camaraderie. On that tour, we all had breakfast together each morning with the late legendary concert promoter Dick Blake. We held meetings to improve the show, and many times each of the acts gladly surrendered or extended stage time to meet changing schedules. We even traveled on each other's buses just so we could visit. The morale on that tour was wonderfully high. It was a perpetual party.

I once stepped onto Tammy Wynette's bus and found she had two of my tapes. The "first lady of country music" was very complimentary, and told me I had the talent to perform any kind of music I wanted to; she said I could do television and explore other avenues of show business. I was ignited by such words from an artist of her stature.

The Statlers host an annual Fourth of July festival in Staunton, Virginia, their hometown. About 40,000 people attend every year. The proceeds go to charity. They asked Joyce, Todd, and me to ride in their parade preceding the 1977 concert. It was fun for all of us.

One of the few dates I worked away from the Statlers' tour in 1977 was a Hilton Head appearance in South Carolina. Jimmy Buffett and I were booked at a national convention for Record Bar, a chain of retail record stores. The good news was that RCA financed the trip for my band, family, and some RCA executives. The bad news is they expected all of us to fly.

As I've mentioned, I'm not overly fond of flying, and Joyce still hates it. The night she spent in a bathtub when we were newlyweds is still fresh in my mind.

Joe Galante, who today is president of RCA's Nashville division, was aware of her apprehension and took measures to put her at ease. He made plans to fly us in a private aircraft and asked the plane-leasing firm to send her a photograph of the plane we'd be using.

A lovely photograph of a sleek and picturesque jet was sent. It was attractive and looked safe, but it wasn't the same aircraft that showed up the day of the flight.

What came was a DC-3, a loud, old plane flown during World War II. Dicky Overbey said the thing looked exactly like the planes in those Tarzan movies . . . right before they crash in the jungle!

The band and I first played a show in Iowa, where we were picked up in that rickety contraption. We then flew to Nashville. Joyce and the others were waiting near the runway to join us for the flight on to Hilton Head.

When the plane landed, Joyce saw it and said she was glad that she wouldn't be flying on that dented, gray junker. She waited for her plane to come along next. When I got off the old plane, Joyce declined my invitation to join me back on the plane.

I began my reassurances.

"It's OK, Joycie," I said. "I flew down from Iowa, and it's fine; now, come on and let's go."

I wish I had never said a word. Joyce's reluctance to board that aircraft turned out to be clairvoyance. That flight was not only the worst I've ever had, by far, but also the only time I've been positive I was going to die.

Joyce finally agreed to enter the airplane. Because the front of the plane was higher than the back, when we boarded, we walked uphill toward the front, right into a wall of giant amplifiers and electronic equipment. It didn't feel like a passenger plane; it felt like a cargo plane.

The noise of the engines was deafening. We had to scream to be heard. We strapped ourselves in, the noise swelled to the volume of a volcano, and that rusted, riveted patchwork of tin shook forward.

We taxied to one end of the runway, the engine raced again, and the old heap began to trudge forward, slowly picking up speed—too slowly. Someone yelled that we weren't going fast enough to get off the ground. Ruth, our stewardess, was standing alone at the rear of the aircraft. She had the rear passenger door open, as if she were going to jump should the plane not clear the runway.

We kept picking up speed, but Ruth wouldn't shut the door.

I yelled, "Ruth, close the door; Ruth, close the door," and it became a chant. In seconds, every passenger on the plane had joined in, while the speed quickened.

And at last, we were airborne.

Things were fine, briefly, until we got over the Blue Ridge Mountains of South Carolina. We flew smack into a thunderstorm. We were told that the DC-3 could not fly high enough to go over the turbulence. So we went right through it.

And the roughness was overpowering. If we hadn't been strapped in, we would have been bucked out of our seats. The plane seemed to fall hundreds of feet in a split second, then be thrust upward by mountain air currents. It was like riding a giant roller coaster, only much faster, and with larger dives.

To ease the terror, I pretended to be having fun. I began to yell like someone on a carnival ride each time the plane rose and fell. The band picked it up, and that too became somewhat of a chant. Then I noticed Joyce was crying, and I yelled for the band to stop.

Joyce and Jack Watkins happened to look out the window and saw oil spewing from the right engine. Joyce pleaded with me to notify somebody. I told someone to go into the pilots' cabin to tell them the engine was losing oil. The messenger walked into the cockpit, and found the pilot sitting on top of two telephone books. He was too short to reach the controls.

The frightening and sickening claps of thunder, the stomach-twisting thrusts of that worn fuselage, the pelt of blinding rain and brilliant flashes of lightning, all blended with the overpowering roar of those antiquated engines, and I thought it was all over. I was sure we were going to die in a mountainside crash.

When we landed safely, spontaneous cheering broke out as soon as the plane's wheels touched concrete. I could have kissed the ground. Some in the band did.

We were met by Joe Galante, who couldn't apologize enough for the trauma we had undergone, but I sensed a deeper remorse in him.

"Elvis Presley is dead," he said. "They found him today at Grace-land."

We had nearly lost our lives in a violent mountain storm. Elvis had lost his quietly at home. I was especially grateful to be alive. With the announcement of Presley's death, the fiery crash of Ronnie Milsap and his entourage probably wouldn't even have made the evening news.

That afternoon, as Joyce and I walked into our hotel room, we found the telephone ringing. Donald Reeves had been at the Nashville airport when we boarded that junker. He had taken it upon himself to book Joyce, Todd, and me a return flight on a commercial airline and was calling to let us know.

The band and I did the show that night, the Record Bar folks gave us a standing ovation, and it was a fulfilling concert for everyone.

Billy Coren, my production manager at that time, flew back to Nashville with the band on that same plane that had terrorized us going out.

But the plane never reached Nashville.

It took off from Hilton Head and managed to get out over the Atlantic Ocean; then the engine that had been leaking oil before went out altogether. Billy, who was still in shock when he phoned us, blurted into the telephone that the plane had crash-landed in a field. Actually, the crippled plane had returned to the airfield, landed, and taxied off the concrete into the grass. The band was taken off the airplane, shuttled by bus to Savannah, Georgia, and flown on American Airlines to Nashville. So far as I know, the airplane is still sitting in South Carolina in the weeds.

There are times when everything goes right, and that sums up 1977. I was a part of a colossal tour. My recording of "Almost like a Song" (one of the biggest records I've ever had), was number one on the country charts for several weeks and eventually went to number fourteen on *Billboard* magazine's pop chart. But my greatest thrill was yet to come.

I was standing at the sound board during an afternoon equipment check in the Fairmont Hotel in New Orleans when the CMA's executive director, Jo Walker, came up to me and said she wanted to congratulate me for being a nominee for "Album of the Year," "Male Vocalist of the Year" and the Country Music Association's highest award, "Entertainer of the Year."

Each of the nominations was exhilarating, but the one for Entertainer of the Year was especially so. I was overwhelmed, but had no thought that I would win. I was nominated along with Merle Haggard, Dolly Parton, Waylon Jennings, and Kenny Rogers.

Sixty million viewers in North America and overseas watched the CMA awards. When I was awarded Male Vocalist of the Year, I walked from the front row of the *Grand Ole Opry* house, where I was sitting with Joyce, Donald Reeves, and his wife Brenda, and stood onstage in a state of shock, accepting the award while thousands of people applauded and a forty-piece orchestra played.

When I next won the Album of the Year award I was practically speechless.

With five minutes or less left in the CMA broadcast the Entertainer of the Year nominees were read. A song excerpt by each was played, as his or her face was projected on an enormous overhead screen. The presenter was Mel Tillis, the previous year's Entertainer of the Year.

I knew that my face, along with the faces of the other four nominees, would be projected on a split screen around the world. I knew that I'd be in a "reaction" shot, whether I won or not, so I was thinking composure.

"Your chances are one in five," I told myself.

"You have a 20 percent chance to win. Don't show disappointment if you lose. Applaud for whoever wins."

In the few feet between my seat and the stage, I could hear what the television audience couldn't—the hustle of hurried cameramen easing toward the footlights. I don't care how seasoned or cool a performer might be, he can never escape from this kind of pressure.

"And the winner is ..." the words rang through the hall. There was crackling of the envelope holding the winner's name. I heard the sheet of paper, bearing the announcement, leave its container. What was taking so ...?

"RONNIE MILSAP!"

I'm not sure which was louder—the sounds of deafening music and applause, or my heartbeat. My otherwise shy and reserved sister-in-law, Brenda, put a flying hug to my neck that was more of an affectionate strangle hold.

Joyce and I walked to the stage. Joyce had been at my side when no one else was and she was there that night when everyone seemed to want to be.

I might have had a speech prepared somewhere in the back of my mind. I've talked to other winners, and they did exactly what I did—prepared a speech, then forgot it in the excitement.

Joyce, to this day, is afraid of microphones. She did the Phil Donahue show with me once. She was so nervous, she answered each question only with the words "yes" or "no." No matter what Phil asked her, she would say only "yes" or "no."

So there we were onstage, the clock ticking, airtime costing thousands of dollars a second, the local news about to go on in every market in America, and I couldn't remember my speech.

So I yelled.

I just opened my mouth and let it out.

The guys in the sound booth said my holler was so loud they had to yank their headsets away from their ears and turn down the volume.

Then I remember saying, "A lot of people think I'm an overnight success. It's been ten years, so it's been a long night, hasn't it, Joyce?" Joyce said, ". . . long night."

In moments, we were off the air.

Overnight, performance offers came from everywhere, at fees that were four times as much as I'd been getting, and there were endorsement opportunities. For a few days, the mailman made more than one trip from his vehicle to my office door, carrying letters of congratulation. Folks I hadn't heard from in years wrote. I heard from friends of friends, and I didn't know either one. Our telephone answering service was jammed with messages. The momentum from that win mounted all year, until the following October, when I was again nominated, but lost to Dolly Parton.

After the CMA awards show that night in 1977, RCA threw a party in my honor at the Roy Acuff Theater at Opryland. It was a black-tie affair with ice statues and linen napkins. Donald, Brenda, Joyce, and I left the party that night as we had arrived, in a white stretch limousine. We took the rented car, in tuxedos and long gowns, to Krystal, a fast-food chain in the Southeast that serves hamburgers slightly larger than a silver dollar. We ordered forty of them.

We wanted to go somewhere to celebrate that was nonalcoholic and private. The back of the limousine with a sack full of Krystals seemed perfect. We were maintaining a tradition that began when I won my first CMA award in 1974.

The band left the next day for a show in Florida. Jack Watkins, my band leader, called to say that I was front-page news when he transferred flights in the Atlanta airport, and that he had seen my photo again when he arrived in Tampa. Joyce said she could hear the excitement in his voice. The wonderful thing about success is being able to share it with those who supported you. Jack is one more of those folks who is an unshakable pillar of my band and overall organization.

At home, we were up early, not long after the newspaper was delivered. The headline on the *Nashville Tennessean*'s front page screamed, "Milsap Sweeps Three Top Awards at CMA Show." That afternoon, the headline on the *Nashville Banner* read, "Milsap Gets CMA Crown." There were photographs of Joyce and me. The type was as big as the letters announcing the end of a world war.

But the public has a short memory. Most record-buying country fans couldn't tell you who the current Entertainer of the Year is. Only close friends, relatives, and the most dedicated of fans could tell you it was Ronnie Milsap in 1977.

In 1976, 1977, and 1978 I acquired three more valuable employees: Nancy Overbey, my personal assistant; Phil Jones, my road manager; and Billy Coren, my assistant production manager.

Nancy Overbey became part of my organization in December 1978. We had known Nancy since 1975, when her husband, Dicky, came to work with me playing steel guitar. Unfortunately, her marriage to Dicky ended, but fortunately for Joyce and me, she immediately fit right into the family.

Over the years, she has become a valuable employee as well as a trusted friend. Nancy has the trait that is a prerequisite for working with me—loyalty.

She has her own place on the grounds of our home in Nashville. Her duties over the years have become so varied and so many, I affectionately call her my "aide-de-camp." To say she's invaluable, would be an understatement. She's family.

Phil Jones is a former professional football player and weight lifter, whose muscular frame is critical as we negotiate thick crowds and tight places. He was an experienced road manager when he came to me in August 1977, having worked for Johnny Rodriguez. His greatest value to our operation lies in his ability to coordinate the movement of twenty-two people, three buses, and an eighteen-wheel truck around North America and overseas. He checks the group in and out of hotels with ease. Most of my people never even see a desk clerk or registration desk, since Phil handles all of that for them.

When we pull into a town, most of the band is still asleep on the bus. When they get up in shifts, they merely walk into the lounge, where their hotel keys and a room list awaits them. I've seen Phil move our giant entourage through bustling international airports without anyone having to check his own luggage. Once, my personal bus driver quit his job one hour before a twenty-hour trip. Phil, who had been up all day because he didn't expect to drive, drove the entire twenty hours without relief. We made the show on time.

Billy Coren joined me in February 1976, after I met him in Hendersonville, North Carolina. He used to come around whenever I played North Carolina and tell me that he wanted a job—any job— just to be a part of my show. He has been with me ever since.

He is a former military photographer who knows a lot about lights and photography. There was a period when he single-handedly set up and tore down what sound equipment I had, and loaded and unloaded it onto and off the bus. Today, I have five sound and light technicians in the show to do the same task.

In one of our routines, we began the show with a tape recording of the theme from "Superman." Right where the suspense of the music climaxes, I was supposed to bolt onto the stage amid an array of swirling lights and canned fog. It was supposed to be very theatrical. But one night Billy accidentally unplugged the tape machine with his foot just as I was making my grand entrance. The music ground to a stop like audio molasses, and I appeared onstage to that amplified dying sound and the giggling of 10,000 people.

I'd be hard-pressed to name a closer friend. Billy's presence simply calms me. I love to have him around before I go onstage. That kind of closeness, coupled with his obvious creative talents, makes him an invaluable asset to my show and life.

One thing that both Phil and Billy have, which is mandatory when part of a touring show, is a sense of humor. They can laugh at circumstances, and laugh at themselves. Their attitudes are lubricants that help grease the wheels of my machinery.

I have always felt strongly about giving the crowd a visual as well as an audio presentation during a concert. I was determined to make each one-night show the equivalent of a network television special. Billy's idea for bombs onstage fit right in with my plans.

I was the first country act to use pyrotechnics (controlled explosives) as part of the stage show. We used them through much of the late 1970s, and took them out of the show in the mid 1980s.

Billy and Phil have each set up and ignited the explosives at one time or another, and because neither is a licensed pyrotechnician, there were mishaps at first.

Billy didn't buy the bombs we used. He couldn't have, since he was not licensed. So he made them.

He filled a metal box with blasting powder, hooked an electric wire to the box, and plugged in the wire. An electric short was created and the box ignited. On a couple of occasions, so did the stage curtains.

Our first homemade bombs were really unpredictable. The intended electrical shorts we created sometimes overloaded breakers. Musicians' amplifiers went out, auditorium fuses blew up, and houselights failed. We weren't a popular attraction with some building maintenance supervisors.

There was also a problem with the mix of blasting powder. Depending on the climate and atmospheric conditions, and how well it was packed, the stuff was more explosive at some times than others. We played a show at Rupp Arena, the biggest hall in Lexington, if not all of Kentucky. That time, Phil Jones overfilled the makeshift bombs. One blast shook the entire 24,000-seat fieldhouse. The place quivered as if it were in an earthquake. Don Williams was on the show that night. His group had placed their amplifiers in the wings. When our bombs exploded, so did Don's amplifiers. I had to lend him mine to do his show. I bought new amplifiers for his band. I was glad to do it.

One summer I played a matinee show, at the Opry House, in Nashville. The president of Tanzania was in the audience as a guest of the United States government. The U.S. Secret Service was on hand. Along with the Service there were security dogs, trained to sniff out explosives.

The dogs sniffed each member of the band as a precaution when we came in backstage. The animals sniffed around the stage. No one escaped the scrutiny of those dogs. It was for national security, so everyone cooperated.

Well, the animals found no weapons. And they found no bombs. And that was too bad, because my crew had brought the pyrotechnics into the Opry House. We didn't give a thought to the emphasis on security, or that we were doing anything out of the ordinary.

The show went off without a hitch. The bombs went off on cue. The African dignitary went under his seat, shoved there by Secret Service men, who immediately brandished pistols. Meanwhile, the applause was thunderous, as it usually was when the bombs signaled the end of our show. The noise overpowered the barking dogs, which I'm told had to be restrained.

Billy discovered that he could make the explosions louder if he used a concussion mortar. It was actually a 6-inch pipe, 3 inches in diameter. Once again, he had no official instructions on how to load the cylinder. He experimented by filling the steel shell with compacted powder. The tighter he packed, he discovered, the louder the blast. He continued to ignite it by using a standard, two-prong ac plug. Eventually, he built a box with light switches. When he wanted to ignite a bomb, he hit a switch.

The switches weren't working the night we played Leslie, Georgia, near the home of President Jimmy Carter's family. Attending the show that night was Lillian Carter, the president's mother. She was seated prominently in the front row.

In some towns, we work with local stage attendants. Most of them are nice guys who want to be helpful. That was the case in Leslie. The bombs were packed and strategically located in hidden areas of the stage and, as usual, were attached to electrical cords.

The sound check had been done. The crowd was seated. It was show time. Billy was on the stage, and that particular stage had no stage curtain. He was putting last-second touches on the equipment in full view of the audience. Offstage, a well-meaning stagehand noticed an unplugged electrical cord. He plugged it into an outlet.

Onstage, Billy happened to be leaning over the explosion pipe the very second the stagehand plugged in the cord. It blew up directly into Billy's face.

He was wearing glasses, and that's all that saved his eyes. The blast was so hot, it melted the plastic lenses. His beard burned away with the flash, and his skin was seared.

The audience was taken by surprise. When the crowd looked toward the stage, Billy, staggering incoherently around the bandstand, ambled toward the edge, beyond the footlights.

Donald Reeves saw Billy holding his face, just about ready to walk unknowingly off the front of the stage. Donald sprinted from the wings and caught him a split second before he would have fallen into the lap of Lillian Carter.

A nurse applied cream over his burned skin, and he returned to work the sound for the show. He was the only person there who knew what I wanted for the audio, and he went on without a word of complaint.

He couldn't hear a thing. He mixed the whole show by looking at the settings on the dials.

After the concert, Mrs. Carter asked to see the young man who had nearly blown up the place.

"Son, what were you trying to do?" she asked. Billy blushed beneath his burns and acquired a nickname. Everyone knows him now as "Boom."

My son Todd traveled with us during summer vacations well into his teenage years. By the time he was six, he wanted to be a part of the setup of the show. Billy agreed to let Todd help with production. Todd very quickly learned my keyboard setup and, even as a child, was truly a help. Needless to say, that little boy wanted to be involved in the part of the show that made the big noise.

Billy told Todd he could throw the switch on the show's final bomb. In those days, I ended my show by standing atop the piano, winding up the Rolling Stones' "Honky Tonk Women," bathed in bright lights. I'd leap from the piano bench, and while I was airborne, the bomb would be triggered and the houselights would fall. The enormous explosion was my cue to exit the stage in the swirling smoke. The last sound from the stage was always that ear-splitting explosion. Billy's cue for that was my final jump. It was a very simple thing to do, and very dramatic.

So Billy carefully explained to Todd, on the first night Todd was to ignite the bomb, that he was to hit the switch when I jumped from the piano bench. Todd understood, and he did his part right.

But I got mine wrong.

For some reason, I got unusually happy that night. In the middle of the closing song, not at the end, I leapt from the piano bench. That was the cue Todd was waiting for.

He hit the switch.

I've explained how those bombs affected an unsuspecting crowd. You should have seen how a bomb affected an unsuspecting band. That thing went off 2 feet from them, and it went off perhaps a full minute early.

Jack Watkins, the lead guitarist, managed to drop his instrument, even though he wore a shoulder strap. Hawk fell off his drum stool.

The crowd didn't know what was happening. We were in the middle of a song, but playing with half the instruments. I just kept pounding it out on piano, the other instruments fell in, and we finished the show. We never did explain to the confused audience what was going on.

The fact that Billy fiercely stuck it out through the pyrotechnic days was a sign of his determination and loyalty. I guess the greatest example I saw of his devotion happened in Boston, in 1986. I was on the eighteenth story of a hotel. Billy was in the lobby when a fire alarm sounded. The elevator instantly shut off, so Billy ran up eighteen flights against scores of excited hotel guests who were running down. His sole purpose was to rescue me.

In 1978, I was booked into Disneyland on a show with Crystal Gayle. We alternated with three, thirty-minute shows. There was an enormous revolving stage. Crystal was set up on one half of the stage, and I was set up on the other half. While she was onstage singing, my half of the stage was behind the curtains, out of sight of the audience.

Before my first set, I happened to touch the piano. It was terribly out of tune. It was my first California show of the year, and Disneyland is a pretty important venue.

Crystal was onstage singing, and I was about to have that revolving platform wheel me in front of the fans in just a few minutes. There was no one to tune the piano, so I did it myself. The trouble was, without my knowing it, the sound was leaking onto Crystal's set.

Nothing sounds more monotonous than tuning a piano. You take a single note, and hit it, "ding, ding, ding . . . ," over and over.

On stage, Crystal was trying to establish a mood. She spoke in velvet tones. She began her first number, and from out of nowhere came a faint "ding, ding, ding . . ."

Crystal tried to recover. She went into her enormous hit, and eased into the chorus, "Don't it make my brown eyes . . . ding, ding, ding."

Crystal, with good reason, was mad at me for disturbing her show. I could tell by the note she sent backstage. I'm sorry it happened, Crystal. I didn't mean to offend you.

Along with the bombs, standing on my piano became another trademark of the show. We hit on it while fooling around in 1976, and it's still part of the act. I was doing a show in Terrell, North Carolina, with a weird performance schedule. We'd play for thirty minutes, then break for a half-hour, then go on again for thirty more minutes.

I kept wondering what we could do next that was different each time we came onstage. Once I came out without a shirt. The fourth time we went on that afternoon, I was doing a Jerry Lee Lewis tune. I was pounding away on the keyboard, and stood up the way I'd been told Jerry Lee does.

Something possessed me to jump up on top of the grand piano. And the audience loved it. Billy Coren observed the crowd's enthusiasm and later said he knew we had hit on something.

I've done it thousands of times successfully. I've done it once disastrously.

We were on a European tour in 1979, doing a half-dozen shows, including a stop in Gottenberg, Sweden. As part of my act now, when I finish my dance steps on top of the piano, I leap onto the floor. It's about a 4-foot drop.

During this show, I did some footwork on the piano top, then jumped to the stool, and then to the floor. I forgot that the stool had only three legs. I jumped down, the stool jumped out from under me, and I tumbled headfirst into a bank of amplifiers and monitors.

Stagehands and people in my entourage were there to help me up. I didn't know what to do next, so I did what came naturally. I found that piano bench, sat it upright, and went on to finish the show.

After the show, I noticed my finger hurt badly. When people shake your hand after a show, they're often excited. Even tiny women grip like lumberjacks, but the pain was so bad, I knew something was wrong. When I got back to Nashville, the doctor told me I had worked the rest of the tour with a broken finger.

24

My love for the recording process has been with me practically all my life.

My third-grade teacher in Raleigh, Mrs. Lewis, had a wire recorder; Larry Atwell, Walter Lackey, and I (dubbed the "three fat boys") would record our own skits and plays on it. We made sound effects and talked with dramatic, radiolike voices.

Later, J. Spell and I borrowed a Wollensak or a Voice of Music recorder to tape jingles for our "on campus," outlaw radio station, or to record rehearsals of the Apparitions. So making recordings has been fun for me for a long time.

During my two years of college, I got my first real recording studio experience at the LeFevre's studio in Atlanta. Recordings there were made on a three-track Ampex machine. When I went to New York to record for Scepter Records, they used a four-track machine.

During my first session in New York at Scepter, in April 1965, I recorded three songs: "Never Had It So Good," "Let's Go Get Stoned," and "Win My Love and Break My Heart." All three songs were written for Florence Greenberg by Nick Ashford and Valerie Simpson, who were staff writers for Scepter at that time; later they would have gigantic songwriting careers at Motown, and they eventually became the hit singing duo they are today.

I was scared to death on the day of the session. Pat Hughes, my disc jockey friend from Atlanta who had brought me to New York, tried his best to calm me, but I was so excited the day of the session I just couldn't settle down.

The tracks for the three songs had been recorded a couple of days earlier. I had everything all brailled out, and I had been rehearsing the songs, so I'd done my homework. I didn't play piano on those three songs; I just stood at the microphone and sang. So all I had to do was walk in the studio and sing the songs—but I didn't know if I could do it. Fortunately, Valerie Simpson came to my rescue. She went into the studio with me and sat at the piano during my session, giving me encouragement, hints, and musical advice, and my nervousness disappeared. Thanks, Valerie, for making my debut recording session in New York a success.

While I was still living in Atlanta, I would occasionally go over to Bill Lowery's studio to see my friend Cotton Carrier. I would get to hear things that Joe South and Billy Joe Royal were working on, but most of the time I just visited with Cotton. Before I had any money, he bought me many a lunch. I was hoping to get to play or sing on some of those records coming out of Atlanta, and eventually Freddy Weller brought me in to play piano on a couple of sessions.

My real studio savvy came from working at American Studios in Memphis for Chips Moman. When Chips was not in the studio, he encouraged his staff of musicians and writers to get involved there. I hung around and played and sang on all kinds of stuff at American: songwriters' demos and live master sessions—and late at night, after I finished at T.J.'s club, I even got to record my own demos. Some of those late-night demos were mixed, packaged, and released, without my knowledge, on albums with other master material after I became successful. At American Studios I got to record with many of the great artists, including Elvis, and I saw the multitrack recording process go from four-track to eight-track and on to sixteen-track.

By the time I got to Nashville, I had quite a bit of studio experience, a knowledge that became very helpful to me on those early sessions at RCA Records when I was getting started in country music. My first four albums at RCA were recorded on the sixteen-track, 2-inch tape format with no noise reduction. Those early sessions for RCA, under the guidance of my producer at the time, Tom Collins, were magic.

In May of 1975, Tom and I were working on a 6 p.m. session at RCA studio A. Many of Nashville's best musicians were there. Three songs were recorded in that three-hour session: "Daydreams about Night Things," "Play Born to Lose Again," and "Just in Case." Man, what an evening! I mean, I was so caught up in the outcome of the session, I couldn't sleep that night. I could hardly wait 'til the next morning when Tom and I could hear what we'd done with those three songs.

The next morning, Tom and I met at RCA in Jerry Bradley's office. Jerry had a rough copy of the session on his tape machine ready to play. (Jerry Bradley was head of RCA, Nashville, at that time.)

"Hey, Jerry," I said, "Wait'll you hear what we did last night! This just may be the best stuff I've recorded for RCA!"

"OK," Jerry said, as he leaned back at his desk and pushed the play button on his tape machine.

The music started. Something was wrong. There was distortion on the bass . . . and on the drums, and there was some distortion on my voice. The fiddle came in, and it too was distorted. What was happening?

"Sounds like you've got a bad tape copy," Tom Collins said.

Jerry stopped the tape, picked up his phone and called downstairs to studio A, where he spoke to one of the engineers. "Get out the multitrack tape of the Milsap session you guys did last night," he said. "We're coming down to give it a listen."

Downstairs in the control room of studio A the multitrack tape had that same distortion we'd heard in Jerry's office. It was determined that somehow too much level had gone to tape; the distortion was there and it couldn't be fixed.

"Oh, Lord," I thought, "There goes my record—and what about the cost of all this?" The cost of that session was probably around $4,000.

As if Jerry had read my mind, he said, "Don't worry about the cost of this session, Ronnie. I'll make sure it isn't charged against your royalties. Can you and Tom go back in and do all of this again?"

"I don't know," I said, wondering about how I would recreate musically and emotionally what we had done.

Tom got the musicians together a couple of days later, but RCA studio A was booked and not available. We re-recorded the three songs in RCA studio C, where there was barely enough room for all the musicians. We were practically piled on top of each other. I can remember sitting at the electric piano, and with my arms outstretched, I could touch Haywood Bishop on drums and Bobby Wood on acoustic piano. Right behind me was Mike Leach with his bass bumping me in the back. The studio was too small for the Jordanaires, so we over-dubbed their part after the musicians had gone. But everything turned out fine; the sound on "Daydreams about Night Things" still holds up when I hear it on the radio today.

In the latter part of 1976, Tom Collins gave me a song to listen to that would change my career as a recording artist. The song was "It Was Almost like a Song," written by Archie Jordan and Hal David. It took me a few months to establish an arrangement for the song, but during Christmas of that year, sitting in my own living room, I figured it out. I called Tom, and when he came over to my house, I sang the song for him, using the piano arrangement I had worked up. He was as excited as I was, so in early 1977, we went to the studio to make a record.

The session took place at Woodland studio B. (I was not recording at the Nashville RCA studios anymore, because they had been sold.) Les Ladd, who has worked with me on many album projects, was chief engineer for the session. We did several takes and, eventually, got the performance Tom and I wanted, although the fifth octave E-natural unison on the piano was slightly out of tune. I still notice it when I hear the record on the radio, but when a record becomes a hit, nothing like that matters. And what a hit "It Was Almost like a Song" turned out to be.

I learned in 1981 that albums are not cut in stone. I had finished an album and had delivered it to RCA. There was a song on the album, called "It's All I Can Do," which was slated to be the first single. My friend, Rob Galbraith, who has produced many albums with me, brought me a new song called "There's No Gettin' Over Me," written by Walt Aldridge and Tommy Brasfield from Muscle Shoals, Alabama. I absolutely loved the song! But I had already turned the album over to RCA, and records were being pressed.

I rushed into the studio with "There's No Gettin' Over Me." I remember we did twelve takes of the song, but take number one was the magic one. I called Jerry Bradley at RCA and told him that I had just cut a song that I was very excited about. "This is a big one," I said. I asked him if I could come over and play it for him.

"Milsap," Jerry growled, "this had better be real good. Come to my office in the morning at 8:30."

The next morning I took my rough mix of "There's No Gettin' Over Me" to Jerry's office. When he heard it, he loved it as much as I did. But there was a problem . . . that day, folks at RCA were stuffing envelopes with deejay copies of the single "It's All I Can Do." That was supposed to be the first single from my new album. When Jerry heard "There's No Gettin' Over Me," he picked up his phone, called the pressing plant in Indianapolis, and literally stopped the presses. He told everybody to hold everything until he could release a new record that Milsap had just cut.

"There's No Gettin' Over Me" went on to be a big crossover hit in the summer of 1981, and wound up at number five on the pop charts for four weeks in a row. I might have made it to number one if it hadn't been for "Endless Love."

Today I record in my own studio, Groundstar Laboratory. The building at 12 Music Circle South in downtown Nashville houses a complex of business offices and the recording studio. I have done most of my recording at Groundstar since the fall of 1978. The studio part of the building was taken down to the bare concrete walls and rebuilt according to my specifications by Rudy Breuer from California.

Since I'm not a recording engineer, and don't want to be, I certainly need the help of others to work in the studio. I just want to sing and make music. And although I want to be involved in record producing, I certainly don't want to produce my records all by myself. So I've been fortunate to have qualified producers to help me. Rob Galbraith, Kyle Lehning, and Tom Collins have assisted me with different projects. I've been working with Rob and Tom in some capacity ever since coming to Nashville.

I started working with Kyle in early 1983. I value his judgment and his friendship. As a producer and engineer, he is meticulous; he listens better than anybody I've been around. As a human being, he's a good guy, fun to be with—one of my all-time favorite people.

In 1984, while Joyce and I were basking in the sun by the pool at the Century Plaza Hotel in Los Angeles, Rob Galbraith brought a demo tape of a new song, "Lost in The Fifties Tonight," written by Mike Reid and Troy Seals. When I heard it, I was very impressed with the song, but with all those background voices, I thought it would perhaps be more suited to a group like Alabama or the Oak Ridge Boys. The song was never recorded by any of the groups in Nashville, so in early 1985,

I recorded it. My friend Bruce Dees, who plays guitar on most of my records, also sang all those background parts with me. Twenty-two tracks of background parts in all, as I recall.

In June 1986, I recorded my first Christmas album. Much of the album was recorded live with about fifty people in the studio, counting the musicians and background singers. Most of the music was arranged and conducted by David Clydesdale. The album was recorded and mixed in two weeks.

Bill Barnes, in Nashville, designed the cover with me as a jack-in-the-box wearing a Victorian costume. Bill said he needed three small children to be with me in the picture. Joyce's sister, Kay; her husband, Dr. Roy Powell; and their three children, were in Nashville. I told Bill about the children, and when he saw them, he said they would be perfect. Somehow, having Josh and Lindsay and Andrew with me on the cover made the album feel Christmassy to me.

In the 1980s Rob Galbraith and I were also involved in the music publishing business. Because of that, I had the opportunity to work with one of the greatest songwriters I've ever known, Mike Reid.

Mike is an interesting guy, and for those who may not recognize the name, at one time he was a professional football star. He was all-American at Penn State; then he played pro for the Cincinnati Bengals. Mike is also a pianist trained in the classics. Musically, we have a lot in common.

I've recorded many songs that Mike wrote or cowrote, including "Inside," "Stranger in My House," "Still Losing You," "Prisoner of the Highway," "Lost in the Fifties Tonight," "In Love," "How Do I Turn You On," "Where Do the Nights Go," and a song he and I recorded as a duet, "Old Folks."

My friend, Ben Harris, the recording engineer at Groundstar, is the guy who gets it all on tape. We've been working together now for close to twelve years. Because he knows me so well, I'm comfortable working with him, which allows me to concentrate on the music.

Keith Odle is studio manager at Groundstar. He is an engineer who is highly capable and knows the technical side of the studio inside out. He also keeps Groundstar financially in the black.

Groundstar is a state-of-the-art facility with a Neve 8128 audio console with flying fader automation, two Otari DTR-900 thirty-two-track digital tape recorders, a Studer A800 twenty-four-track analog tape recorder, numerous two-track analog tape recorders with ¼-inch and ½-inch formats, a vast array of outboard gear (tube and solid-state), digital and plate echo chambers, the JVC VP-900 digital two-track system, the Sony PCM2500 professional DAT machine, the Sierra playback monitor system, and Lord knows what other goodies in the control room.

The studio part is intermediate-sized, but there is plenty of room for just about any situation. The Yamaha 9-foot grand piano is isolated in a room all to itself.

They say that the difference between men and boys is the cost of their toys. Well, Groundstar Laboratory for me is one heck of a playground!

25

I have recorded twenty-one albums for RCA records, and I'm frequently asked if I have a favorite. One that heads the list of potential favorites is a tribute album to Jim Reeves I recorded in 1980. Jim Reeves was one of my all-time favorite vocalists, and one of that handful of artists whose performances influenced mine.

The album was recorded live in the studio. That means that I recorded with minimal electronic overdubbing of sounds. I had a burning conviction to give the project my best, and I'm immensely proud of what we came up with.

Yet I did that entire album at less than full force. I had a throbbing pain in my right eye, my "real" eye at the time. I tried Tylenol and Excedrin, but to little benefit. I finally admitted to Joyce how bad the pain was, and she insisted that I see a physician, who prescribed pain medication. The painkiller, which gave only partial relief, had codeine in it, and that was awful! The codeine nauseated me. I'd get up in the morning, drink juice because I had no appetite, take the codeine, go to the studio, then rush to the bathroom and throw up. I'd go into my office and wait 'til I felt better, then go back into the studio and press onto the next version of the next song, which often was also interrupted by my running to the bathroom because I was sick again.

About the same time that I was undergoing this nonstop sickness, Donald Reeves noticed a swelling around my eye. He questioned me about it, and I told him the problem I was having with the pain. Donald searched out one of the nation's leading ophthalmologists, Dr. Bruce Shields at the Duke Eye Center in Durham, North Carolina.

During my first visit to Dr. Shields's office, in the fall of 1980, I jokingly asked him if medical science had come up with a bionic eye. "If they have, I'm your guinea pig." I quipped. "If they can do it for the Six Million Dollar Man, then they can do it for me."

Dr. Shields is a caring surgeon, as compassionate as he is competent. He has a soft-spoken disposition that is very reassuring. It's particularly soothing when one is thinking about having the last "good" eye, and the last chance for sight, surgically removed.

After the examination, that's what Dr. Shields recommended. "I hate to have to tell you this, Ronnie, but when you asked about the possibility of a bionic eye, that was more realistic than any chance you'll ever have to see from this eye. The eye is useless to you; it's deteriorating, and it's contaminating your physical system. You would be much better off to let me remove it."

He had asked earlier why I wanted to keep the eye. I told him that I hoped some day science would come up with an eye transplant procedure that would work for me.

"And if they come up with that procedure," I said, "I thought they would probably need the whole eye to tie into. Or perhaps through laser surgery or whatever, they could attach a new eye to the old optic nerve."

I guess I was desperately presenting an idealistic hope. Dr. Shields was tactful and delicate about why I should have the eye removed. Bless his heart, I know his was an argument he wished he could lose.

"I know that doctors replace the heart and liver and other organs, but that just isn't like replacing the complete eyeball," he said. "The eye and the whole sense of sight is so complex. In your lifetime, the possibility for you to surgically receive a new and workable eye is nil. To alleviate the pain you're going through, and to get yourself off this medication that makes you sick, well, you should let me help you. You should let me remove your eye."

I knew they could never repair my eye if I let them remove it. The removal would unquestionably mean that I would be blind forever. As with my other eye, for years I had listened to encouragement, not from the medical community, but from a small voice inside that told me someday, someway, I would undergo a medical miracle that would enable me to see. This doctor was asking me to forgo the miracle.

Agreeing to do so was one of the hardest decisions I've ever made, but I made it before I left his office that day.

Dr. Shields scheduled my surgery for December 16, 1980.

During our initial conference, I mentioned having a blockage in my nose and eustachian tube. Dr. Shields arranged for me to see another doctor by the name of Boyce Cole, who diagnosed my problem as a deviated septum. He said surgery was the only way to correct it.

The doctors wanted to perform the operations on two separate occasions. I told them I wanted them to do both procedures during the same session. They insisted that would be too much of a strain on me. I explained that I had to finish the Jim Reeves tribute album, the deadline for which was fast approaching, and that I had a full schedule of concert dates waiting for me in late January 1981. So for the first time in the careers of Dr. Shields and Dr. Cole, eye enucleation and deviated septum surgeries were scheduled for the same patient on the same morning.

I was told that, following my surgeries, I would not be able to fly back to Nashville. Pressurization of an airplane cabin could cause damage. I was advised to arrange for ground transportation for the twelve-hour drive, so, Todd, Phil Jones, Donald Reeves, Joyce, and I rode my customized touring bus to the Duke Eye Center, so the bus would be available for the trip back home.

That afternoon we had lunch at Dr. Shields's home; then I checked into the hospital. Dr. Jerrell, the chief of anesthesiology at Duke, came by my room later that afternoon to discuss the procedure he would use for the operations. He told me that Dr. Shields and Dr. Cole had requested general anesthesia; that is, I would be put to sleep for the two major operations. But after visiting with me for perhaps an hour, he decided not to put me to sleep. General anesthesia would require putting a tube down my throat. Such a procedure, he said, could leave me hoarse for months. He felt that I would have enough trauma recovering from the two surgeries. With all that stress, he did not think I should have to worry about when I would be able to sing again. I appreciated his thoughtfulness in making that decision. Since having two operations performed with a local anesthetic was unusual, Dr. Jerrell said he would stay with me himself throughout the operations.

I remember a lot about the operations and my recovery. But Joyce remembers more than I do. She never left my side, and her memory was not dimmed by the medication and painkillers that were part of my life for the next several days. So I've asked her to finish this chapter, and tell you about the events surrounding all this.

"Ronnie was awake before daylight on December 16. My brother Donald, Phil Jones, and I crowded around Ronnie's bed, and Todd, who was eleven, sat on the bed, near his daddy's chest. There was a sadness in the room that I could feel physically. I was determined to be strong for Ronnie, but I was gripped by emotion. I looked over at Phil, and that hulk of a man had tears in his eyes. Donald's eyes were glistening, too. The man I love was accepting this better than all of us. Ronnie, the strongest human I've ever known, had whipped poverty, maternal abandonment, and unscrupulous businessmen, but he couldn't whip sightlessness.

"Ronnie always knows when I'm hurting. He can sense it. And he always thinks of me more than himself, and he did so again that morning, minutes away from going into the operating room.

'I wish all of you people would cheer up,' he said. 'I'm not dying, I'm just going in there to have my eye removed. Everybody act happy! Look how lucky I am! I had this done when I was fifteen, and I wasn't even in a hospital. I was in an infirmary, and I didn't have anybody then that cared. There was nobody. But look how lucky I am today. I have all of you folks here with me! Everything is going to be fine, so let's laugh a little bit.'

"Our son laid his head on his daddy's shoulder. It was as if he couldn't get close enough to him. I couldn't help but think how terrifying this operation must have been for Ronnie when he was fifteen, when no one was there to support him. I realized more than ever how solitary my husband's young life had been.

"I didn't want to say anything. I didn't want Ronnie to hear the sadness in my voice. There has always been a special closeness between us. I knew I couldn't fool him by trying to raise his spirits when mine were touching bottom.

"Ronnie again began making jokes and small talk, trying to reassure those who had come to reassure him. A nurse came in to give him a shot. Ronnie asked what was in the syringe and was told only that it would make him happy.

"As they wheeled him through the operating room doors, we heard him singing 'Hit Me with Your Best Shot,' and for the first time that morning, everybody laughed.

"He was on the operating table for two hours, awake, and throughout both procedures he heard the surgeons and nurses discussing their work.

"Shortly after Ronnie came out of recovery, while he was still heavily sedated, a telephone call was put through to his room from a disc jockey. The D.J. was live on the air and had promised his listeners that he would be talking to Ronnie Milsap, who minutes earlier, had undergone surgery at the Duke Eye Center. Since Ronnie was too groggy to be coherent, I handed the telephone to Dr. Shields, who with no preparation for the interview, went live on the air to explain the surgical procedures to the fans of North Carolina.

"That night, when the anesthetic began to wear off, Ronnie became ill. He got out of bed and started walking to the bathroom. I told him that he wasn't supposed to be up and told him I would send for a nurse. I tried to help him but he wouldn't hear of it. He said he could find his own way to the bathroom. Then I saw him do something I had never seen him do before. And I've never seen it again.

"He put his hands out in front and tried to feel his way to the bathroom. This was the man I had seen countless times bound into a room unescorted. I had seen him run up and down stairs in our house and offices. I had seen him string a guide wire onto a platform so that he could go on- and offstage by himself. Now, he was groping for his way inside this small hospital room. The sight chilled me to the bone. I yearned to be his hands and eyes, and to tell him that he would never be without sight as long as I lived. I also knew that he could never see through my eyes anymore than I could walk in his shoes at that moment.

"I kept insisting that he shouldn't be standing, as he took weak, short steps toward the bathroom. He had no idea how much medication he'd been given, and how it might affect his balance.

"He stopped and after a moment of silence, said, 'Joycie, for the first time in my life, I feel blind.' The words trailed into a silence that cut like a knife. I was trying not to cry, but I could feel the tears welling up in my eyes.

"Ronnie made it into the bathroom, where he began violently

throwing up blood. That was it. Whether he liked it or not, I was going to call a nurse, and I did.

"The nurse said the situation was serious, and immediately summoned a doctor. Ronnie was having an allergic reaction to the morphine he was given. He had no medical history with that drug. He has such a pronounced aversion to drugs, he had little or no prescription history for doctors to draw on when they administered the morphine. They switched his medication to Demerol, and shortly the vomiting stopped.

"A couple of days after the surgery, Donald had to return to work and Todd to school, so they went back to Nashville. I never left the hospital, and stayed with Ronnie day and night.

"The doctors told us he could not make the long trip to Nashville without a nurse to accompany him, so we called Lee Ann Glisson, a longtime friend and private nurse in Nashville.

"Lee Ann flew down a few days early to consult with the doctors about Ronnie's care. She laughed about her role as his private nurse, saying the other nurses had hoped they might be the one to accompany Ronnie home.

"We considered ourselves very fortunate to have such an unselfish friend as Lee Ann, to leave her family at Christmastime, and come to Duke to help us.

"On December 23, Ronnie was dismissed from the Duke Eye Center, earlier than the physicians had recommended. He wanted to be home for Christmas, his favorite time of the year. We left a room overflowing with flowers, fruit baskets and telegrams from caring friends and fans. Radio stations had sent huge posters covered with get-well wishes from Ronnie's fans. Ronnie had told us earlier, before the surgery, how lucky he was to have so many people who cared, but I think even he was shocked to learn just how many did.

"Dr. Shields escorted us from the hospital, and after our good-byes, Ronnie stepped up onto his touring bus for the long trip home.

"With our bus driver at the wheel, Phil, Lee Ann, Ronnie, and I started out for Nashville. The trip was trouble-free—for sixty miles. The bus broke down near Greensboro, in the cold, the freezing cold! The driver was able to get the bus off Interstate 40 to a small garage, where the mechanic on duty said that because of Christmas, it would take him several days to get the parts needed to repair the bus engine. We waited on the bus while Phil telephoned to find other transportation. Fortunately, the bus generator still worked, and we had heat. Phil couldn't find a customized touring bus but did finally come up with a passenger bus, with upright seats on which Ronnie could lie down sideways. We couldn't travel in a car, because Ronnie was supposed to be lying down.

"When the leased bus arrived, it had a very inadequate heating system. Lee Ann feared that Ronnie, in his weakened condition, would catch cold. We covered him with blankets and tried to make him as comfortable as possible. Given Ronnie's size, there was barely enough room on the seats for him to *sit* comfortably much less lie down. He tried anyway and was jostled on the seats' stiff springs. I knew the vehicle's suspension sent pain into his face with every bounce. I saw him grimace as the coach bumped up and down, and I worried that the packing inside his nose would loosen, but he didn't complain.

"We arrived home late that night, exhausted and hungry. When we walked through the door, the air was saturated with spruce, cinnamon, and all the wonderful aromas of Christmas. Nancy Overbey surprised us by decorating the house beautifully for our return. She knew how special Christmas was to Ronnie, and she wanted it perfect. She and Todd had decorated the tree with all our special ornaments, and all the presents were beautifully wrapped and placed under it. Christmas music played on the stereo, and a fire crackled in the fireplace. What a homecoming!

"Ronnie knew how many hours it must have taken Nancy to decorate the entire house, and her efforts touched him deeply.

"After two days, Ronnie decided to stop taking his Demerol. He said he had to know how bad the pain really was. I'm sure that's true, but I also think his decision had something to do with his dislike for drug dependency.

"The parting admonition given to Ronnie at Duke Medical Center was for him not to sneeze. A sneeze, he was told, could disrupt the healing of his nose and could cause a blood clot.

"One night, however, in his sleep he sneezed. He began to bleed profusely. We kept cold packing on his nose, to stop the bleeding, until Lee Ann came the next morning. Ronnie didn't want to awaken her in the middle of the night. Lee Ann packed in new dressings, but that single sneeze in his sleep set back Ronnie's recovery by three weeks, his doctor said.

"I have been married to Ronnie Milsap for almost a quarter of a century. Yet each day, I am amazed in some new way at the man's inner fortitude. He is so accomplished and so determined, I can't imagine all that he could do if he could see.

"I remember an incident that happened when Todd was in the first grade. His teacher, Nell Fowler, told me about the children having to share a special story with the class one day. When Todd told his story, it was about his dad. Mrs. Fowler loved the story and knowing what Ronnie was capable of, wanted to make an impression on the class. So she said, "And, Todd, your dad did this?" Todd thought she was questioning the truth of what his Dad could do. She said his brown eyes shot sparks, and he replied angrily, "Mrs. Fowler, my Dad can do *anything* better than anybody else—except drive a car!" Her point was made.

"I also remember the time we visited the Governor Morehead School with Ronnie. He had lunch in the school cafeteria with the students, and later did a 'miniconcert' in the auditorium. After the performance, he stood in the auditorium and met and shook hands with every student. Each one was special to him, and he answered every question. The one student who was most memorable to me was a little girl about seven years old. Ronnie got down on his knee to hear her. Her question was, 'Mr. Milsap, when you were seven, were you afraid to grow up?' Ronnie put his arms around her and spoke softly and said 'Afraid of growing up? Goodness, no! I looked forward to every day and the new things there were to do. Life is exciting! And you can do anything you set your heart and mind to. Don't you be afraid—OK, Honey?' She put her little arms around his neck and hugged him and thanked him. We all had tears in our eyes.

"Ronnie's philosophy is believe in God and yourself and there's nothing you can't accomplish. Many people have told us what an inspiration he has been to them. He has visited with many dying children through the 'Make a Wish' Foundation, but will never allow any publicity about it. Ronnie is quite simply, the most unselfish and caring man I've ever known."

26

My career and personal life have had more ups and downs than a runaway roller coaster. But the 1980s were the years of dreams come true—with one calamity. A bad business decision nearly ruined me financially. From 1982 until 1987 I worked to pay off a seven-figure loss. It had to do with an amusement park which bore my name. There were published stories and unpublished rumors about what went sour. I want to set things straight here.

In 1980 I was earning more money than I ever had before.

My advisers urged me to make a major investment.

If your business is music, you'd better be careful about getting involved in a business you know nothing about. That was the bitter lesson I learned from an amusement park investment in Kentucky.

To promote the park, I performed there. I drew more than 30,000 people to my Ferris wheel and tilt-a-whirl wonderland at one show. That was less than a year after my partners and I bought the place. I lost $800,000 within months after the purchase.

I was president of the corporation. We hired managers. They told us what we were doing wrong, and they charged me for the advice. I consulted with other managers, who told me to fire the first, then charged me for that advice.

I was in demand for concerts as never before, but found myself passing up high-dollar engagements to return to Kentucky to check on that problem-plagued amusement park. I could hurl some accusations about the people who ripped me off. I was naive about the business and even more naive in overrating human character. In my opinion, what those people did to me amounted to theft. No charges ever will be filed. The fight to keep afloat a sinking investment came close to breaking me within two years. I had people on payroll, I had money coming in, and I had debts that absorbed more than what I was earning.

I wondered, more than ever, what my rat-race lifestyle for financial success had been about. What had been the purpose of all those miles and motels, of stale sandwiches and cold coffee, of being away when Todd pulled his first tooth, of sacrificing my sanity for financial gain? More than any other time in my life, I realized that there was something worse than not achieving your goals. That was to achieve them, only to lose them. The most valuable thing I had left was the house in Nashville, and, thank God, I never really ran the risk of losing it.

I was nearly depleted emotionally when I huddled with Bob Zeigler, a gravel-voiced Nashville bankruptcy attorney. He barked into the telephone with a sandpaper voice that sounded like morning cigarettes before coffee.

"Who cares what this guy has got to say," I thought. "He's just going to send me a bill, too."

"Do you want to declare bankruptcy?" he snapped.

"No sir, I don't," I replied, fatigue in my voice.

"Well, how do you propose staying out of it?" he demanded.

"I don't know how to stay out of it, sir," I said, "but it goes against everything I was ever taught."

Bob Zeigler introduced me to Joyce Rice, a Nashville banker, who put together a consolidated payoff plan. I certainly thank my friends Joyce Rice, Bob Zeigler, and Nashville attorney Aubrey Harwell for their help in getting me out of that financial jam.

I don't have a monopoly on bad investments in Nashville. The same thing has happened to many country music artists. Most of us have avoided bankruptcy, and have clung to the tradition of our teachings and paid off our debts. We all make mistakes, and we pay the consequences. Some consequences cost more than others.

Anyway, I learned a new lesson about life. I learned it from losing, not from making, money. Money is a tool. Some people think it's a necessary evil in a capitalistic society, like a car or a telephone. I do know that money is a means to an end, and it is nothing more than what it will buy. It should serve its owner, and not vice versa.

One can't put a price tag on something like the tried and tested love Joyce and I have. I can't measure in dollars and cents my good health I miraculously maintain despite the lifestyle of a marathon man. There is no way to evaluate conversations I've had with my son. Those are the things that really do matter.

But do I regret the monetary loss? You know I do. I'll make sure it never happens again. But if it ever does, God forbid, no matter how much I lose, all I'll lose is money. I'll never again lose my mental health or put a price tag on things that *really* matter, for something as fleeting as dollars.

On the other side of the coin, there were highs for me in the 1980s as well. In 1982, *Billboard* magazine named me "Adult Contemporary Artist of the Year." Other awards, including Grammys and Country Music Association awards came my way. I had the greatest crossover success of my career; that is, my songs registered, not just on country surveys, but on other popular music surveys as well. At our concerts, folks driving pickups parked next to BMWs. We played the *Grand Ole Opry,* and we also played *American Bandstand*.

To meet and work with the "broadcast dean of rock 'n' roll," Dick Clark, was a thrill. I have been a fan of his for more than thirty years. At the Governor Morehead School all the blind students gathered around the TV every afternoon to catch American Bandstand. What an influence he's been on all our lives.

Dick came backstage to talk with me before the show went on the air and said, "I only have one question. Why have we waited so long to work together?" His remark helped to put me at ease. I appeared on two telecasts of "Dick Clark's New Year's Rockin' Eve" show during the 1980s.

In the 1980s, I had records on the country charts, such as "Don't You Ever Get Tired of Hurtin' Me," and I had crossover records such as "Smoky Mountain Rain," "There's No Gettin' Over Me," "I Wouldn't Have Missed It for the World," "Stranger in My House," and "Lost in the Fifties Tonight," the title song from an album that produced two Grammys. It also won for my band and me a fifteen-minute segment on the Grammy awards show, a salute to 1950s music with Huey Lewis and the News, Carl Perkins, and Freddie Parris and the Five Satins.

I appeared twice on the *Tonight Show* with Johnny Carson in the early 1980s and once on the *Merv Griffin Show,* and appeared for the entire hour on the *Phil Donahue Show.*

In 1983, I was the subject of an ABC television network feature on *20/20* with Barbara Walters and Hugh Downs. Susan Lester, the producer, and Bob Brown, a reporter, traveled with me for a week, and even went to the Governor Morehead School for a video portrait of me that I thought was superb.

In December 1983, I had my own two-hour television special, which is still in reruns in 1989. I was enthralled working with guests like Ray Charles, Gladys Knight and the Pips, Glen Campbell, Leon Russell, Janie Frickie, the Whites, and Bobby Jones and New Life Singers. We taped the whole thing in two days at the Tennessee Performing Arts Center in Nashville.

Country legends like Patsy Cline, Jim Reeves, and Eddy Arnold retained their country music roots and yet branched out to other kinds of audiences. That's exactly the kind of artist I wanted to become, and that's exactly what happened in the 1980s.

This was also the period in which I began using a choreographed, female background trio. Marie Tomlinson, Barbara Wyrick, and Suzy Storm first appeared with me in June 1980, in Gatlinburg, Tennessee. Those ladies sang flawlessly, as if they had been a part of my show for years.

We eventually worked up an ending for the show that we called the "fire medley," singing "Fire" by the Pointer Sisters; "Ring of Fire," the old Johnny Cash hit; and Jerry Lee Lewis's "Great Balls of Fire." Flame throwers erupted on each side of the stage, and the trio did some hip-slinging steps across it.

I also played autoharp in the show, and Marie and I sang an acoustic version of Emmylou Harris's "One of These Days." Jay Spell, my old friend from the Apparitions, heard Marie and me sing it in Las Vegas and told me the mood of the performance brought tears to his eyes.

"Milsap, I never heard anything that moved me so much," he said.

I'm often asked about the singers. I truly miss the impact they had but they are gone for a simple reason. They grew tired of life on the road. We don't always get to stay in the nicest of hotels. There isn't always a restaurant nearby. We do all we can to make our tours as comfortable as possible for everyone—but, it isn't home.

*   *   *

My stage shows during the eighties were put together by my good friend Mike Post, the man of many talents I mentioned earlier, best known as a music composer for television. Mike, without a doubt, has influenced my career. He is always swamped with work, but anytime I have asked him to help me with a show, he has been kind enough to do it.

I loved doing concert tours involving a team effort. From 1983 to 1985 I performed about eighty shows with Merle Haggard and Ricky Skaggs for Marlboro cigarettes. The shows came off with the efficiency of a Swiss watch.

My band today is all any recording artist could hope for and more. My guitarist and band leader, Jack Watkins, has been with me since July 1976. Jack is a great musician. Chet Atkins wanted to produce an instrumental album with him. Jack has played on many of my records over the years, and he's as solid today as he was when he joined my band.

The man who introduced Jack Watkins to me, Dicky Overbey, is back playing steel guitar in my band. Dicky was out of the music business for several years, but now he's back. Dicky is one of the two or three really great stylists on steel.

Warren Gower, who played bass on my records as early as 1978, became a part of my touring show in 1980. He lays a bottom to our music that is rock solid.

Alan Kerr is a drummer with a back beat that's unmatched. He joined my band in May 1981. Alan sets and monitors the tempo to our show and music with invaluable precision.

Keyboard players Shane Hicks and Adam Hampton mastered the contemporary, computerized music for my show. They joined my band at the beginning of the 1988 touring season. In addition to being excellent keyboard players, they are also incredible singers.

In March 1988, guitarist Jamie Brantley joined my band. I had heard about Jamie for years; people in the business told me that he was not only a scalding guitar player but also a fantastic singer. He's turned out to be everything that I heard he was.

I didn't use a fiddle player until 1989. I tried two that same year before finally settling on Hank Singer. Hank does a lot of recording session work around Nashville, and was playing with George Jones before he joined our group. He is one of the few fiddle players that really plays with soul. He is also one of the most precise fiddle players I've ever heard.

These guys make up the best band I've ever worked with on the road. Not only are they accomplished musicians, but they are good guys. I mean, they're fun to be with. They're part of my family.

I couldn't mention the band without spotlighting my five-man production crew. They are the best. They probably have the hardest jobs on the road, because they are the first people to get to the show venue and the last to leave. They are Mike Sullivan, production manager; Jeff Fawbush, stage technician; Mike Frogge, lighting director; Bernie Velutti, stage monitor; and Randy Gardner, house sound engineer. Randy also assists me as an engineer in the studio on my album projects.

Betsy Grooms joined my organization in 1980. She is our in-house accountant, who does the payroll, pays the bills, keeps the books, and basically keeps track of everything pertaining to any of my businesses. To be a successful businessman I've learned that you have to employ accountants, tax advisers, investment advisers, and several attorneys, and Betsy Grooms is part of the glue that holds all of that together. Betsy is loyal and hard-working and is a real joy to work with.

Tommy Kerkeles joined my organization in 1981. He immediately took over the selling of Ronnie Milsap souvenirs out on the road, and made that a very successful business. He has worked for me in many capacities: as an agent, booking and scheduling my performance engagements, and as a tour coordinator, making sure that everything out on the road goes smoothly, and he still goes with me on the road occasionally to work the box office at the show to make sure I get paid what's coming to me. He is a team player who many times works along with Donald Reeves in dealing with the day-to-day problems.

Paula Imes works in my office, and I guess I could best describe her as my girl Friday. One of her main duties is working with my public relations firm to coordinate interviews and information.

Mrs. Eunice Brusseau, Kenny Kerkeles (Tommy's son), and Ricky Whitefield all help Joyce and me at our home.

John Bettincourt, formerly at RCA in New York, breathed life into many pop acts, such as the Pointer Sisters, and Hall and Oates, and my own group. John, and my friend Joe Galante at RCA, Nashville, taught me the value of doing in-store record promotional appearances in conjunction with the releases of new albums.

Joe encouraged me to continue a practice I developed in the 1970s of personally calling music journalists and radio station programmers. I went countless times to RCA, where I spent the entire day on the telephone with music media personnel around the country.

I certainly thank Joe Galante for his help and advice, and for continuing to believe in me and my records. Joe and his nationwide team are the best in the business.

Life on the road can really wear you down. It's difficult just keeping up with the pace. But pacing your time is the key. In the midst of all that work, you have to find ways to relax.

The band and I found a way—we jogged. After concerts, long after the traffic had subsided, we'd get out of our buses on some lonely interstate highway. The drivers would take the buses about two or three miles down the highway to wait, leaving us huddled on the road's shoulder. The semitrailer trucks would rumble by, as we ran along beside the darkened highway.

My road manager, Phil Jones, works out with weights and has a lot of stamina. He and I rigged up a running system involving a belt. We each held an end and he ran ahead. Down the highway we'd go, with the band and some of my staff in tow. It became fun, and often resulted in a foot race. It made us feel good, it relieved the otherwise unending stress, it got us in shape, and it almost got us arrested.

One night in Minnesota it was blue cold. Our feet were pounding the frozen pavement with the force of a herd of horses. Despite the noise, I could hear a car approaching from behind. Phil stopped and the galloping fell off to a trot, along with a lot of coughing and broken breathing. I heard a car door slam.

Phil said, "It's the police!"

The officer thought we looked suspicious, after all, it was after midnight, near zero, and we were dressed like refugees from an eskimo camp.

I told him that these folks worked for me and we had just played a big show earlier in Minneapolis, and that I was pleased to meet him, and I was Ronnie Milsap.

"Sure you are," he said, and asked to see my identification. I had none. I explained that we were just out jogging and that our tour buses were waiting just up the road for us.

"Boys," he said, "it's a $40 fine for running along this interstate."

The running suit I was wearing had no pockets, so I didn't have a dime on me, and no chance of softening this officer's iron will. We were wearing ski masks, which gave the officer more reason to be suspicious. The officer asked me to lift my ski mask.

"Well, you don't look like Ronnie Milsap," he said.

"Maybe," I said, "it's because I don't have my glasses on."

The officer agreed to follow us down the highway to our buses.

I got on the bus, put on my glasses, and handed him some of my latest albums and tapes. He looked at the front of the album and said I looked just like my pictures. And then he let us go.

Needless to say, we no longer jog along interstate highways. Considering the dangers, I can't believe we ever did.

During this period, I saw my son ease from childhood to adolescence and on to young manhood. At the decade's beginning, he was still young enough to play in his treehouse. By the decade's end he was living in a real house of his own. I have no brothers or sisters of my own, so his was the only life I ever intimately observed as it blossomed into adulthood.

The first clue toward the transition came when Todd called me "Dad." He had always called me "Daddy." The loss of that one syllable was a warning that my boy would soon think he was grown up—before he actually was. Yet it all happened too soon for me.

I remembered Todd as a toddler sitting on my knees as I played piano. I remembered his high voice when he tested microphones for me about the time he learned to walk.

I never had to miss one of Todd's birthdays. We planned our personal appearance schedule around them. When he turned fourteen, I was committed to a date in Raleigh at the North Carolina State Fair. I arranged to have Todd flown up there. I called him out onstage, and 15,000 people surprised him by singing "Happy Birthday." Backstage, a huge birthday cake awaited him with fourteen candles.

School boards were cooperative in planning parent-teacher meetings at times I could attend. I have always had daily telephone contact with my son, and we have shared a mountain of homework and prepared for countless school examinations via AT&T.

I'm sentimental about my son. Joyce often says that I'm overly so. When he was in the fourth grade, he was assigned to write an essay about the man he most admired in the world. His classmates wrote about former presidents, athletic greats, and the like. Todd wrote about me, and never told me. His teacher did, however. Joyce read the work aloud, while I felt a wonderful and bittersweet stirring of sadness and joy. I thought of all the sterling things Todd had said about me, and wondered if I always would hold that stature in his eyes.

I have a library of memories of my son, and as the song says, "little things mean a lot." I remember one time when a friend of his spent the night, and the boy left a hall closet door open.

"I can't believe you did that," I heard Todd scold. "What if my dad came down the hall? He would hit it!" Even when he was small, Todd never left his toys in my path. Consideration was instinctive for him.

Those little things are indicative of a large love to me. I have deep convictions about fatherhood stemming from lessons I learned during Todd's transition into manhood.

I've told you, as honestly as I know how, of the emotional loads I've shouldered in my life. I can tell you with the same candor that my son grew up carrying a load I never had to. It was one he had to shoulder alone.

Psychologists have written much about the "famous father syndrome." It's a very real thing. Buck Owens talks about it freely regarding his son, Buddy Allen, and Hank Williams, Jr., in his autobiography described the incessant comparison, son with father, that made him suicidal.

Very often I have heard Todd referred to as Ronnie Milsap's son, instead of Todd Milsap. Had I gone to public school as a child, I might have been made fun of because I was poor. I've seen Todd persecuted because his father is a public figure who has been blessed with a prosperous career.

There was a time when I knew nothing about such discrimination. But watching Todd courageously shoulder the load of his heritage has taught me much. My pride swells and my heart breaks in the wake of his personal traumas and triumphs.

There were times when I was filled with guilt about Todd's paying for my popularity. I used to think I had gotten Todd into this and then wasn't always at home to get him through it.

Todd never wanted to exhibit his prosperity. Joyce and I wanted to give him nice things, but we learned a painful lesson about imposing our values or desires on him.

We put Todd in a private school, because a prominent national study indicated that Tennessee's public schools, at the time, left a great deal to be desired, and we knew he would be looked after more carefully in a private school.

One morning, when Todd was eleven, he came downstairs dressed for school wearing a Dallas Cowboys football jersey. The school's dress code prohibited shirts without collars. Joyce told him he couldn't wear the shirt to school but answered honestly when he asked her if she personally saw anything wrong with the shirt.

She said that wasn't the issue, and that school rules forbade the shirt. Todd argued that the shirt was tucked inside his trousers, that I had bought it for him, and that if I was at home, I would let him wear the shirt, and that it was a dumb rule anyway.

Todd won the discussion and probably hadn't been gone an hour, when the telephone rang. Joyce and I knew the school administrator on a first-name basis. Before the official had a chance to explain the reason for the call, Joyce told the woman she knew why she was calling.

But what the administrator told Joyce went beyond the question of a dress code infraction. She said that Todd, after being dispatched to her office, asked to be expelled from school. He told the educator that the quality of education at her school was good, but that the students were snobs. He said that the children who had more, discriminated against those who had less. My eleven-year-old son told the head administrator at one of the most esteemed private academies in Tennessee that her students, in his word, were "snooty."

In the wake of the public school ratings report, hundreds of students switched to the private academy. Many of those parents had to work at more than one job to afford the tuition. They consequently could not afford the expensive clothes that some of the students wore.

Todd empathized with the children of modest means. Many of them were his friends. He wanted to wear his Dallas Cowboy shirt to dress down so as not to discomfort students who had less. And he was punished for it.

Later that day, Joyce found Todd in his room cutting off the designer emblems on his shirts. It was a little boy's effort toward hiding the prosperity his father was providing. And it was a lesson for Joyce and me.

The school administrator was as impressed as Joyce and I were touched. "Here was a child sitting across from me telling me about these snooty kids in school," she said. "Yet when we go on field trips, we ride by the brick wall surrounding his big house. This child has a lot, but he doesn't have a snooty bone in his body."

Joyce called me on the road and told me the story and then let Todd tell me, so I was ready for him when he asked me to remove him from the private school. I was impressed with the school's security and didn't want my young son in public school until he was older. I told him that I would let him go to public school if he would stay at the academy until he reached high school age. I asked him for that compromise.

He asked me if he could stop wearing the shirts with designer emblems. Joyce, only days before, had been to California where she had bought dozens of designer shirts for the little boy we loved to dress stylishly. Todd packed every one of them into a box and gave them to a friend that attended public school. That child must have thought there was a Santa Claus, and that his name was Todd.

We never forced Todd to dress in accordance with our desires again. To this day, Joyce says Todd sometimes dresses unconventionally. She thinks it's because he's making a fashion statement. The statement is, I suspect in part, that while he's Ronnie Milsap's son, he's nobody's snob and I'm proud of him.

He was often spanked harder than other youngsters by a teacher who admitted as much because more was expected of Todd. There was another incident in which several youngsters were unruly, but only Todd was reprimanded, and the supervising teacher said she had singled out Todd because his father was famous, so she had no trouble remembering the boy's name.

These were major traumas for a little boy who didn't chose his last name, but who was always proud of it.

Joyce and I are fortunate to have Todd. When he exhibited his stand-up character, we thanked God that we had done something right as parents. Ironically, we read a lot of books on child rearing when he was an infant, but we paid little heed to the instructions. Besides, I don't think any prescribed method of child rearing will take the place of love—and example.

Todd never saw alcohol, tobacco, or drugs in our home. He knows neither of us uses those substances, and I think that's largely why my son shuns that stuff today. I never told Todd that if he did, I would disinherit him or punish him severely. I just told him where substance abuse leads.

When he was in high school, he came home one day and told me he had become a member of the mayor's campaign against drugs. In the same breath he told me about the drug dealers he had encountered now that he was in public school. Todd recited horror stories about drug abuse, and the sale of substances in the hallways. He even told Joyce and me about one dealer who carried a shotgun into the school building. I could only shiver at Todd's reports, while being thankful that my son and I have a relationship that enables him to be so frank.

Todd is almost twenty-one now and keeps his own schedule. His mother knows that sometimes he's in nightclubs, and she doesn't like it.

"Mom, tell me Dad wasn't in those places when he was my age," Todd will say.

She has to admit that I was, and it kills her, yet honesty is mandatory to sustain the rapport between a traveling father and his only son. It was one of a series of blessings and good fortune but topped everything else.

27

If you asked me what the one highlight of my career has been, I'd have to say I don't know. Sometimes the simplest thing can mean so much.

I remember January 16, 1976, a time before I won Entertainer of the Year; before the majority of my hit records had been recorded; before the long series of network television, Nevada, or VIP engagements. It was when I had only two of what would become eight CMA awards, and before the three Academy of Country Music awards. I had one Grammy award in my early career, but the other five were yet to come. The gold record albums were in the uncertain future, and so were, of course, the platinum albums. They would create a gold braille album, and I'd be the first to receive it.

I can remember circumstances surrounding events in my life, but I can't always remember how I felt at the time. If you had been there for any of those awards, and if you had asked me to cite the highlight of my career, I might have said, in the mood of the moment, "This is it!"

Yet there were other things that didn't grab as many headlines, but wouldn't let go of my heart. Some were very simple. That January 16 I mentioned was my birthday. Todd was seven, and he and Joyce were at home. I wished I was too. I had just spoken with them on the telephone before I walked onstage in Greenville, South Carolina. The entire audience, as a surprise to me, rose to its feet and sang "Happy Birthday" before I even reached the piano. When you're homesick, and something like that happens, it really moves you. It was over in seconds but I'll never forget it.

In 1986 I had been with RCA for thirteen years. Mine is a business in which an artist's popularity usually yields to those coming up, who want, and often get, your slot on the record surveys. I had performed in every music genre during my recording career and I felt I was being taken for granted. I felt as though the disc jockeys and the public felt they knew everything I could do, and that whatever talent I had was expected more than appreciated. Perhaps I was overly melancholy, or brushing too close to burnout, but I didn't go to the CMA awards show that year, one of only two times I've missed it during fourteen years as an RCA act. That was the night they gave me Album of the Year. The award was a direct affirmation that folks were still appreciating what I was doing. I'd definitely call that a career highlight.

In February of 1988, when I couldn't go to the Grammy awards in New York City, Kenny Rogers and I were surprised with a Grammy for "Make No Mistake, She's Mine," a duet we had out in 1987. I was still getting airplay, hits, and awards, and these were certainly career highs for me.

In 1983 I played for President Ronald Reagan and Vice President George Bush at Constitution Hall in Washington, D. C. It was the twenty-fifth anniversary show for CMA. There were close to thirty acts on the show, but the only standing ovation came for a tribute to Don Gibson performed by Ray Charles and me. Ray's piano and mine faced opposite directions. Our backs were practically pressed against each other. When we finished, I heard the house come to its feet. I realized that the President, and everyone in Constitution Hall, was giving us a standing ovation.

In a stage whisper, I said to Ray, "They're standing for us. We've got to get up!"

Ray didn't want to leave his piano bench, but I couldn't take just sitting there while the commander in chief was standing. So I rose, turned to Ray, put my arm under his, and lifted him off the piano bench. We both walked a couple of steps to the center of the stage and took our bows. That moment could be a career high.

Other things, less showy and more human, are important highs. In 1985, we formed the Ronnie Milsap Foundation with the help of a friend in Detroit, attorney Gary Spicer. Our board of directors includes distinguished businessmen, teachers, and medical personnel.

The purpose of the foundation is threefold: to provide scholarships to qualified blind students anywhere in the world who want to go to college but do not have the means to do so; to provide money to the Duke Eye Center in Durham, North Carolina, and the Kresge Eye Center in Detroit for eye research; and to provide assistance to the adult blind by offering help to retrain them for new jobs.

Even if my own blindness had been curable, I could not have afforded the medical attention when I was young. To be able now to assist in a foundation that extends or even gives sight itself is certainly a career high.

I corresponded with a boy named Joey Caton who was blind and had terminal cancer. He was fourteen. I played a fair in northern California in September 1988, and he came to the show. He asked to sing "Stranger in My House" with me that night. We did it, and needless to say, Joey upstaged me. He stole everybody's heart, including mine. This little boy was going to die. He was going to leave this world without ever seeing it. He knew it, and he nonetheless had a song in his heart, the song happened to be one of mine. A year later, Joey died. His final wish was to be buried in a Ronnie Milsap T-shirt. Career high? The mere term sounds disrespectful. But there is no way you can witness, indeed feel, what I felt as Joey sat next to me on the piano bench and not call it a "high." There is no way that I, or the thousands of people there, will ever forget that youngster.

There have been similar experiences involving children dying of incurable diseases. I think of Mitzi from Tulsa, and Holly from Florida. At times like that, I've found myself being so much more to people than an entertainer. To have flesh-and-blood anxieties of my own and yet be the one they lean on in a time of crisis is a terrifying responsibility. But it's equally rewarding, and I thank God if I've been able to help in some small way. At such times, no one can convince me that I did the wrong thing by chasing my musical dreams.

Another question frequently asked is what do I hate? I don't hate anything. I make it a point not to. I can do that, because hate is a voluntary emotion. Anger may not be. Passion may not be. But to hate is to sustain willfully your dislike for something.

There are things I strongly dislike. There are things I will never sanction. But there is no one or no thing I really hate. To hate is to waste good time and energy.

I was asked recently if I didn't hate the man who beat me so savagely that I lost my only "good" eye and, with it, the remote chance that I would ever see. Someone else asked if I didn't hate the former career manager in Memphis, who, through deception, took my house from me. The answer to both questions is "no." If I hated those men, they probably wouldn't even know it. But I would. And hatred is emotional cancer. Hate mostly hurts the hater. If someone does you wrong, and you hate him, you wind up doing yourself additional injury often at no expense to him.

Granted, there are things I disapprove of with strong feeling . . . things that I will fight against. And I disapprove strongly enough to call the feeling a "conviction." Who among us doesn't have convictions against murder, child abuse, rape, fraud, and the like?

Of course there always will be well-meaning folk who want to know if I don't secretly hate being blind. Let me say this: obviously, I would love to be sighted, but I don't hate blindness. I am so adjusted to blindness that it's a way of life. I just accept it, the way I accept the fact that sometime every twenty-four hours, I'm going to have to eat, and sometime each day, no matter how busy I am, I'm going to have to sleep. I don't miss what I've never had. I've wondered what it would be like to have sight, the way some folks wonder what it would be like to have a million dollars. But they happily make do with the money they have. I have more than made do with the four senses I have.

When you can't see, you develop an intuition about people, which many sighted folks seem to lack. I think it's very difficult for someone to lie to me. I can usually hear the lie in the voice. I suppose anyone could, if he would only listen. But listening is distracted by sight. I'm not distracted by a flashy car or a colorful billboard. I listen, and the sound of the human voice is very telling. So I "see" with my ears what's coming out of someone's heart.

I've never been influenced by the color of someone's skin, or the cut of his clothes, or the length of his hair. Discrimination is something I've never had to overcome, because I've never experienced it. I grew up in the South, where racial prejudice in the 1950s was said to be strong. But I was unaffected. It would be as utterly ridiculous for me to dislike someone because he's black as it would be for him to dislike me because I'm blind. I thank God that I was never victimized by discrimination.

I think the ears are the first thing to go with a lot of folks. Many of us have lost our capacity to listen. Perhaps it has to do with the advent of television, and the surplus of visual stimulation that has saturated society. You'd be astounded at what you can accomplish just by quieting yourself and listening.

I almost never involve myself in direct confrontations. I dislike and distrust arguments. They rob me of the truth. I find it's much wiser to listen to folks, even if you suspect they're lying, and let them play out their verbal hand. If you confront them too soon, you can cut yourself off from a lot of information. Truth is always very elusive. It's very hard to find in this life. But the quest almost always is worth it.

I remember one night a guy came to my dressing room in Lake Tahoe and introduced himself as the legendary Merle Travis. He knew enough about Merle to convince me. I gave him two hours because I couldn't see he was an impostor. Eventually, my friend Jack Watkins, who knew Merle Travis, came into the room and told me the guy was a phony. I was angry and put him out. But I learned from that experience, and my sense of listening perceptively was heightened.

Another of my convictions has to do with the inflated importance we Americans attach to the free press. Don't get me wrong, I believe in the First Amendment and freedom of the press. But too often, the press abuses its precious privilege of freedom of speech. They freely print things that are unfair or flat out wrong and untrue.

I think that members of the press should be guardians of the wonderful constitutional right they have. Too often, they take it all too lightly, and a gullible public is misinformed. After all, we in this country have been conditioned to assume that if something is published, it's true.

But that just isn't always the case.

I was outraged by an incident with the press in 1976 when I recorded my first and only live album. The album also was my first to go gold. We did it at the *Grand Ole Opry* house in Nashville. We recorded two shows and electronically combined the best of both for one album.

My friend, Ralph Emery, was master of ceremonies on the album.

There was only one song released as a single from that project. It's almost unheard of to get a gold album with only one single release from the album. But that's what we did, so we must have done something right.

But the celebration was tarnished. A reviewer from *Country Music* magazine came to the show from New York City. *Country Music* magazine was then, and arguably is now, the most prestigious publication dealing exclusively with country music. It is a slick-paged, glossy magazine with corporate headquarters on Madison Avenue. It's influence, at a time when there weren't many sophisticated magazines covering country music, was powerful.

This reviewer was not just covering a concert. He was covering an event. And he let me have it in print.

He said that my onstage movements were awkward. He said that I was off-balance, and that I teetered on the edge of the stage as if I were blind.

At the time that review was written, I had had six number-one records on RCA, and three others had gone "top five." I had toured with Charley Pride. I was the subject of a great deal of press, and press kits, many of which I'm sure had been sent to his magazine.

The guy simply had not done the most basic homework. Not knowing in 1976 that I was blind was like not knowing that Johnny Cash wears black. Or that Kenny Rogers has a beard. Or that Willie Nelson has long hair. The error was that glaring for someone supposedly covering country music.

It infuriated me, and it hurt me. By the time I found out, the magazine had been distributed to thousands of households.

I do everything I can to overcome and underplay my blindness. I used to find my way on- and offstage alone by running my hand along an inconspicuous wire. One night in Pine Bluff, Arkansas, someone left one of the stage monitors, with a razor-sharp screen, in the path of my guide wire. I walked into the sharp grill of the monitor, cut myself severely, and did an encore with blood running down my leg, although I didn't know it at the time. Later that night, I was treated and released at a local hospital, and the incident put an end to the guide wire.

I relate that story as an indication of the lengths to which I'll go to downplay blindness. For that guy to write that my presence was awkward and disoriented, as if I were blind, was an outrage.

If a journalist has a valid and informed criticism of my show, I'm willing to hear it. But how many times do they draw a conclusion that is totally misinformed? How many times do reviewers come to my show, leave early, then write a review that implies they saw the whole performance? That's not only misleading, it's hypocritical. Somehow, I don't think that's what the framers of the Constitution had in mind when they drafted the First Amendment.

How can anybody do a job for which they're unprepared? I think some press people take themselves too seriously. The obvious rule would call for them to prepare for an interview. They think rules are for others, not for them, because they're with "the press."

I remember flying into Baltimore in 1984 from Colby, Kansas. The previous night we had had to drive to Kansas City after a show to catch the plane. Since there were no direct flights to Baltimore, we flew to Washington, where we then rented a car and drove to Baltimore. The trip was an all-night ordeal. We arrived without sleep, but we arrived on schedule for a press conference in connection with a big Marlboro tour. If we could go through all of that to get there, couldn't some reporters have done their homework?

I walked into the room to still another surprise. What was set up by Marlboro as a press conference was in fact a series of individual interviews. The room was overflowing with reporters from important publications, such as *People* magazine and many of the big eastern newspapers. The reporters decided that they were entitled to one-on-one interviews.

Exhausted and spent and stressed out, I sat down for an interview with one of these high-powered journalists.

She didn't ask why I decided to record my latest single release. She didn't ask about my affiliation with the most commercially successful tour in country music at that time, the Marlboro tour. Happily, she didn't even ask the old standby about whether I was born blind. She didn't ask anything. She couldn't, because she obviously hadn't done her homework. She knew as little about me as I know about Russian opera. Maybe I should have told her I was an opera singer from the Kremlin.

So, after my marathon effort to get there, she opened with, "Ronnie, tell me a little bit about yourself."

In other words, she was saying, "Ronnie, I haven't bothered to prepare for this interview, so you prepare me. Will you spoon-feed me?"

I didn't get angry. I simply said, "I'll see you later," and I walked out, leaving my friend and publicist at the time Tom Corley to make an explanation.

I'm sorry I did that to Tom, but I'd do the same thing again. Time is my most precious commodity. In concert, I'll give the audience everything it takes, and as much time as I'm allowed. I'm happy to give time to the press for interviews. If I'm going to do that, I don't think it's asking too much for someone to come prepared to talk to me.

That said, let me add that there are many informed and responsible members of the mass media who know their stuff. I think of Bob Oermann and Thomas Goldsmith at the *Nashville Tennessean*, Michael McCall at the *Nashville Banner*, Jack Hurst at the *Chicago Tribune*, Gerry Wood, Ed Morris, and Marie Ratliff at *Billboard* magazine, Lon Helton at *Radio and Records*, Martha Hume, Chet Flippo, Kip Kirby, and Neil Pond, just to name a few.

Some of my political convictions have changed over the years. In high school, while I was sheltered at the state-supported Governor Morehead School for the Blind, and while sitting in those American history and civics classes, it was easy for me to define my political position. I was a liberal; not far left, but certainly left of center. I was a Democrat, but then just about everybody I knew at that time was a Democrat.

Then, when I went to college and on into the world to earn a living, and started my own business, started paying taxes, got married and raised a family, I wasn't quite so liberal any more. Today I'm registered as a Republican. I'm not ultraconservative, but I'm certainly right of center.

Since the election of 1952, the first national election I followed, I've been interested in politics in this country. I was a Reagan supporter; I voted for George Bush. It's important to be informed and to stay active in our political process.

Today the electronic media are making it easier for the public to get instant satellite access to the news anywhere in the world. Our state and national political leaders in the legislative and executive branches of government are under the microscopic scrutiny of the American voters. Maybe because of all this, we'll get better politicians.

There are a few other things I strongly dislike: alcohol and drug abuse. That, perhaps, is my most passionate dislike of all. In fact, I flat out won't tolerate it among my employees. If I find out someone has a problem, I'll talk to him. I might even subsidize his professional treatment, as I have done in the past. If that doesn't rectify the situation, he's fired.

There has been a great deal of debate over whether substance abuse is a moral failure or a psychological illness. Whatever it is, if you have the problem, you need to get help. I have had to dismiss family and friends in my organization over this. One man had been with me longer than any employee I've ever had. I let him go, then kept him on payroll for a year, hoping he would get help—but he didn't. Another guy went through rehabilitation treatment three times, all of which I paid for. I'll bend over backward to help my people with their problems, but I expect them to help themselves.

Perhaps I seem unduly hard-line about chemical dependency or alcohol abuse. After all, I know how strenuous the road can be. I know what it's like to be tired, and facing a big show that's tremendously important to your career. In such a situation, it's easy to take the easy way out, and take a pill or stimulant. My question is, why get into the situation in the first place?

I find that, with pacing, you can regulate your energy level. That is so basic. If my day is full, and I have a big show to do that night, something has to go from my schedule so that I can rest. It's that simple. What works for me will work for others. So I don't listen to arguments about drug abuse.

I've seen so many creative people ruined by marijuana, cocaine, pills, alcohol, or whatever. The substances make them delusional. They think they are performing their craft well under the influence. In fact, they're performing well under par.

Drugs are desensitizing. That's the purpose of many, such as pain-killers, barbiturates, and other downers. Sensitivity is required for creativity. How can one be continually creative when he is continually desensitizing himself?

I don't allow the consumption of alcohol even in moderation when the band and crew are "on my time." I won't allow them to have it on the bus, not even in the baggage compartment.

The reason is simple. I am an active antidrug and antialcohol spokesman. What if my bus was stopped in one state for illegally transporting alcohol from another? It would make me look like a hypocrite. Also, I don't have to worry about the band or crew drinking too much if I don't allow them to drink at all.

The entertainment business is highly competitive. Drug users lessen their own ability to compete. Drug use cuts down on the competition. If you're an entertainer using drugs, I'll outlast you. While you're making it hard for yourself, you're making it easier for those of us who don't abuse.

The war on drugs is this nation's biggest internal conflict since the Civil War. I understand that the drug war has produced more casualties. As of this writing, for the first time in history, the American military is being used to lessen the influx of cocaine into this country from Central and South America.

That is an extreme effort toward a problem for which I personally have no solution. I don't believe that legalization of these drugs is the answer; I think that would only compound the problem.

There is so much attention put on drug use in the entertainment and sports industries. Let me tell you that some of the lower-profile industries, throughout the private and public sectors, have just as much drug use.

Drugs are in public schools and they're in public libraries, and yet the nation's antidrug sentiments have never been stronger. We are undergoing a war declared from the Oval Office. And many people are undergoing personal wars, fighting their own addiction. I hope they win their fight. I sincerely do. But they'll have to wage that fight on a battleground outside my organization. Maybe this whole thing could be stopped if other employers had the same attitude.

I have another dislike that is just as rigid, although maybe not as passionate. I deeply object to people's underestimating me because I'm blind. I've overcome some pretty big obstacles and developed an impressive career. Yet, to this day, there are folks who think first of blindness whenever they think of me. It even happens within supposedly professional circles, inside my own industry!

Here's an example. The same organization that named me its Entertainer of the Year asked me in 1979 to sing a medley of the five
songs nominated for "Song of the Year." At the rehearsal I walked
onstage twice, counted fourteen steps to the edge of the stage, and
did the songs. It all went smoothly.

Five minutes before the prime-time telecast, the producers of the
show sent word that they didn't want me to walk while onstage.
Couldn't I do the songs seated at a piano? They were afraid I'd fall off
the stage in front of fifty million viewers. Did those people think their
show was the only one I'd ever done? Did they think I hadn't previously
appeared on network television? I was angry and hurt at the same
time.

The first song I was to sing, during the first seconds of the broadcast,
was "Every Which Way but Loose," from the Clint Eastwood movie.
Just before going onstage, I forgot the first two lines. Phil Jones ran
over to the director, who had everything laid out in his notebook. Phil
tore out the page containing those lyrics. He ran back and read me
the two lines. I had trouble hearing him above the announcer's voice,
which already was saying "Here's Ronnie Milsap!" We cut it that close.

I walked onto the stage and into millions of living rooms, singing
the first of the five songs, while counting fourteen steps. I got to my
fourteenth step at the lip of the stage, and remembered how I'd been
mistrusted because I was blind. So I intentionally took a fifteenth step.
I let my foot dangle over the edge. The television audience couldn't
see it. The producers who doubted me could.

I'm an excellent braille reader. Reading braille is a very discreet
thing; I'm inconspicuous when I place my fingers on the paper and
feel the words. Many sighted performers have a lot of trouble when
they try to read cue cards, a lot more trouble than I do reading with
my hands. I've never understood why television producers don't understand that. Maybe that's what I dislike most about my blindness.
It limits and intimidates other folks sometimes a lot more than it
does me.

I'll have to say that one television producer who always gives me
a free hand is Dick Clark, and for that reason, he's one of my favorites.

I have written a great deal about what I like, and I wanted to include
some strong dislikes in this chapter. Above all, I want you to feel that
you know me.

I have written about my religious convictions and my conversion at the age of twelve. I don't go to church as often as I should. I'm not making excuses when I say that my work takes me away on weekends. If you're a touring entertainer, you work nights and weekends. You almost always travel on Sunday mornings.

I believe in, and have a love for, God and His son, Jesus Christ. Mine is a personal relationship with the Savior. I worship and rely on Him on a regular basis.

Mine is obviously a life of faith, as I have never seen Him. Neither have I seen the wind. I have felt God's presence just as strongly as that of the wind.

I think that God is the author of truth, and I think His handiwork will be seen, as truth continues to unfold about modern phenomena such as mental telepathy and extrasensory perception. Two hundred years ago you would not have believed voices and images could fly through the air. Today, we know all about radio and television.

Today, there is still a great deal of curiosity and suspicion surrounding wordless communication with others. I think time will reveal such communication to be a legitimate field of science. Recently, I was thinking of someone I hadn't seen in six months. I had an urgent need to communicate with him. He called me within the hour. Such things have happened to me hundreds of times.

I can't explain it, but that doesn't reduce my belief in something intangible through which we all communicate, and in the future, may communicate more effectively.

It all sounds unlikely . . . as unlikely as a disadvantaged child from the Smoky Mountains rising to reach his dreams.

Epilogue

In the Book of Revelation, a prophet is said to be without honor in his own land; that is, people are taken least seriously by those who know them best. Sometimes, I find myself taking least seriously the person I know best of all: myself. I don't think of my life as dynamic and triumphant. I've spent my life living it, not analyzing it. When I see some of the benefits many people have, who are content to do so little with their lives, I can't help but think of my own deprived upbringing, and the good things that came to be mine.

My deprivations were mostly economic and physical. There always has been, for me, a wealth of will. I trace that directly to the independence instilled in me as a baby by Homer and Phenia, and by the Governor Morehead School for the Blind.

By the time I was nineteen, I was like a human bumblebee. It's impossible for a bumblebee, aerodynamically, to fly. The scientists know that, but the bee doesn't. So it flies merrily along. I have never concerned myself with what I can't do. I try to become too busy doing it. They say love will find a way. I know determination will.

There are some things I haven't done yet that I'm going to do. I'm a singer, not a vocal stylist. My breathing is correct; my enunciation is precise. Because of that, I can sing anybody's music. Yet there are stylists whose technical skills are so underdeveloped they can sing only their own songs their own way. They might be remembered for their hits longer than I am. I'll probably be working longer than they are. I can sing whatever the times and the trends demand.

249

Country fans might stop buying my records. I hope that never happens, but if it does, I'll obviously have to press on.

I might do a multicity tour with a symphony orchestra. I have the background for it; I could do my music along with some of the classics. I haven't really concentrated fully on classical music since I was in high school.

Someday I'd love to be part of a show on Broadway; maybe I'll even do a one-man show.

I've been thinking about karate lessons too, although not too seriously. Still, the idea of self-defense is appealing. Given the regularity of my exercise, and the absence of drugs and alcohol, I'm in pretty good shape.

I might write another book that would share with folks the methods I've found for releasing inner strength. I might someday do a second autobiography. I expect to live twice as long as the years covered here. I'll have a whole new story to tell.

For the time being, I think I just want to enjoy the security I've created for my family and me out of years of risk taking and insecurity in this business of music. We're booked to perform about 150 shows in 1990. I've been asked to play the large showrooms in Nevada. A European tour is in the works, and of course there is the talk-show circuit. But it's not as glamorous as it sounds.

With my name in lights I play venues for thousands of people. But I've told you about the mileage, time, and hard work it takes to make that show look easy. In many professions, the more inexperienced one is, the harder one works to get that experience, and then things become easier. In show business, it's just the opposite. You can wait around for years for that big break. Then it happens, and the more you're in demand, the harder you work to fill the demands. But your life, and the lifestyle, is everything you ever wanted, and it's worth all the hard work.

We were in Jacksonville, Florida, for a big 1989 Fourth of July package show. The roster was mixed, offering entertainers from different fields of music. One of my all-time favorite groups, the Four Tops, was on that show. Let me tell you, Levi Stubbs sings as great as ever.

The concert was sponsored by the City of Jacksonville. There were about 25,000 people in front of the stage, but radio reports said there were up to 300,000 people lining the river next to the park where we performed.

The river bank was a beehive of concession stands, boat rides, fishermen, and all the wonderfully American activities that go with an Independence Day festivity.

For me, it was an especially patriotic Fourth. Just a few days earlier, the United States Supreme Court had overturned a lower court conviction regarding the burning of an American flag in Texas. The high court ruling had been that the perpetrator was exercising his First Amendment rights.

I had thought about that ruling and that man's rights for days. You know, something about his rights and my flag just didn't gel.

I had put it out of my mind to get into the holiday spirit. I love holidays, and I love patriotism, and I delight in the Fourth of July. Joyce's sister Kay and her family drove down from Macon, Georgia.

It was well after dark when the band and I went on. We did our show for an enthusiastic crowd. I did an encore, and was about to do my second.

I was dripping with sweat. I could feel the slight swaying of the stage as thousands of fans pressed against it. I can't explain what it's like to give your ultimate to an audience that gives you love and response in return. There is a two-way street of electrifying energy.

I finished my second encore and left the stage. The crowd was still screaming and wanted more. The band and I stood backstage for five minutes, and finally we decided to go back and do one more song.

I found my way to the keyboard, and thought about that ocean of people I could see in my mind, not far from the real ocean. There is a river around Jacksonville, and I thought about all the old-fashioned boats and schooners I'd been told lined the harbor. I was told how striking their towering masts were, supporting sails that billowed in the salty air. The scene was patriotism set to land and water.

I began to play a C chord on the piano, and then slowly, the noise of the crowd began to subside.

As I played softly, I began to talk.

"You know, today is a special day. It gets me to thinking about how lucky we are . . . to live in a country where you can be anything that you want to be. Where else on the face of this earth would I be able to do what I do today. So excuse me if I get a little bit choked up when I sing this song, but the day wouldn't be complete without it. I hope you'll all sing along with me."

For me, it was the most natural thing in the world to let my voice rise with the lyrics of "America, the Beautiful."

That melody at that moment was magic. No other word will do.

Joyce and some folks from my office had been standing on the side of the stage. They all locked arms and began to sing along.

It just happened. Then thousands of people out front followed suit. Imagine a sea of swaying people, arm in arm, who spontaneously become a giant choir singing "America, the Beautiful." The mood was as intense as it had been unpredicted, and it was wonderful.

I thought briefly of the wonderful irony of Joyce's being behind me there in front of all those people. She had been behind me when no one was, and when we wondered if there ever would be anyone out front.

I thought of the words as I sang, and how they were commemorating a freedom that was so pronounced it would allow an impoverished and handicapped child to come all the way from the hills of Meadow Branch—to that moment. I had come from the mountains to the marquees, and my journey had been possible because of the wonderful freedom common to all Americans.

The last note was played, and as I stood, there was an explosion. The fireworks, scheduled to follow my concert, were timed to ignite via computer. What timing! I couldn't have planned it better.

The sky was illuminated by the flashes of exploding fireworks and skyrocketing bombs.

And then it was over.

We rushed to our idling buses. Then there was that psychological crash that goes with the bedlam of one moment followed by the near silence of another.

I left for still another show, in still another town, thinking about all the spacious skies, amber waves of grain, and purple mountains in their majesty along the way.

Then I climbed into my bunk, pulled the covers to my neck, and thought no more in poetic terms. Another show was over, and in minutes I would be asleep, lulled by the hum of the highway, the highway that was always waiting to take me home.

I'm a prisoner of the highway,
Driven on by my restless soul;
Call me a prisoner of the highway,
Imprisoned by the freedom of the road.

"Prisoner of the Highway," recorded by Ronnie Milsap,
written by Mike Reid, and published by BMG

Postscript

I read in several different ways. Many periodicals, magazines, and novels are printed in braille. Some materials are recorded on cassette tape for the Library of Congress, and I obtain them through the local Library for the Blind in Nashville. When reading novels, I especially like books of high adventure: Robert Ludlum, Clive Cussler, Ken Follett, Stephen King, among others.

I use computers for fun and work. I use an IBM 286 computer. Screen access for me is done in two ways: with a voice synthesizer and with a braille display called the VersaBraille. It's possible for me to read the screen just as a sighted person does, so the computer is a gateway to an infinite amount of information. Through on-line services such as CompuServe, I can read the news, or information pertaining to my specialized interests.

I use the Kurzweil Personal Reader, which is basically an optical character reader. The machine will read practically anything in print, and speak the information with synthetic speech, or I can transfer that information to the computer and store it for future reading.

My personal notetaker is a small machine called the Braille 'n Speak. It's small enough to fit in a coat pocket, and it has synthetic speech and 200K of RAM.

I use the Thiel, a high-speed braille printer from Germany.

For ink printing, I use a Hewlett-Packard laser printer.

I got my novice amateur radio license while I was in high school, my general license in 1968, and my current advanced license in 1970. My ham call is WB4KCG. Although I've collected many pieces of ham gear over the years, I prefer to operate the new computerized solid-state transceivers, such as the Icom equipment. Because of my work, I usually get on the air only in the winters on the 75- and 40-meter bands, and occasionally on the 2-meter band.

I collect old radio shows, a hobby that started about twenty years ago, and I now have thousands of hours on tape.

I'm a record collector.

I also collect old vintage radios. I have several of the E. H. Scott console radios made in the thirties and forties, my favorites.

Discography

SINGLES

Princess Records
Total Disaster / It Went to Your Head 11/25/63

Scepter Records
Never Had It So Good / Let's Go Get Stoned 8/30/65

When It Comes to My Baby / A Thousand Miles from Nowhere 2/66

The End of the World / I Saw Pity in the Face of a Friend 6/66

Ain't No Soul Left in These Old Shoes / Another Branch from the Old Tree 10/66

House of the Rising Sun / I Can't Tell a Lie 10/67

Do What You Gotta Do / Mr. Mailman 9/68

Denver / Nothing's As Good As It Used to Be 4/69

Love Will Never Pass Us By / What's Your Game? 11/69

Chips Records
Loving You Is a Natural Thing / So Hung Up on Sylvia 9/5/70

A Rose by Any Other Name / Sermonette 12/70

Warner Brothers Records
Magic Me Again / You and Me, Me and You 6/72

She Even Woke Me Up to Say Goodbye / 9/20/75

256

A Rose by Any Other Name / 12/27/75
Crying / Blue Skies of Montana 6/19/76

RCA Records

I Hate You / All Together Now, Let's Fall Apart 6/30/73
That Girl Who Waits On Tables / You're Driving Me out of Your
  Mind 11/3/73
Pure Love / Love the Second Time Around 3/30/74
Please Don't Tell Me How the Story Ends / Streets Of Gold 7/20/74
(I'd Be) a Legend in My Time / The Biggest Lie 11/30/74
Too Late to Worry, Too Blue to Cry / Country Cookin' 3/15/75
Daydreams about Night Things / (After Sweet Memories) Play
  Born to Lose Again 7/19/75
Just in Case / Remember to Remind Me (I'm Leaving) 10/25/75
What Goes On When the Sun Goes Down / Love Takes a Long
  Time to Die 3/20/76
I'm a Stand-By-My-Woman Man / Lovers, Friends, and Strangers
  7/10/76
Let My Love Be Your Pillow / Busy Makin' Plans 11/27/76
It Was Almost Like a Song / It Don't Hurt to Dream 5/28/77
What a Difference You've Made in My Life / Selfish 11/19/77
Only One Love in My Life / Back on My Mind Again 6/3/78
Let's Take the Long Way Around the World/I'm Not Trying to
  Forget 9/2/78
Back on My Mind Again / Santa Barbara 12/16/78
Nobody Likes Sad Songs / Just Because It Feels Good 4/28/79
In No Time At All / Get It Up 8/18/79
Why Don't You Spend the Night / Heads I Go, Hearts I Stay 1/12/80
My Heart / Silent Night (After the Fight) 4/12/80
Cowboys and Clowns / Misery Loves Company 6/21/80
Smoky Mountain Rain / Crystal Fallin' Rain 10/11/80
Am I Losing You?/ He'll Have to Go 2/81
There's No Gettin' Over Me / I Live My Whole Life at Night 6/12/81
I Wouldn't Have Missed It for the World / It Happens Every
  Time I Think of You 10/81
Any Day Now / It's Just a Room 3/82
He Got You / I Love New Orleans Music 7/82
Inside / Carolina Dreams 11/82

Stranger in My House / Is It Over? 4/83

Don't You Know How Much I Love You? / Feelings Change 8/83

Show Her / Watch Out for the Other Guy 12/83

It's Christmas / We're Here to Love 12/83

Still Losing You / I'll Take Care of You 4/84

Prisoner of the Highway / She Loves My Car 8/84

She Keeps the Home Fires Burning / Is It Over? 3/85

Lost in the Fifties Tonight / I Might Have Said 7/85

Happy, Happy Birthday, Baby / I'll Take Care of You 3/86

In Love / Old-Fashioned Girl Like You 7/86

How Do I Turn You On? / Don't Take It Tonight 11/86

Only One Night of the Year / It's Just Not Christmas (If I Can't Spend It with You) 12/86

Snap Your Fingers / This Time Last Year 4/87

Make No Mistake, She's Mine (duet with Kenny Rogers) 7/87

Where Do the Nights Go? / If You Don't Want Me To 11/87

Old Folks (duet with Mike Reid) 4/88

Button Off My Shirt / One Night 8/88

Don't You Ever Get Tired of Hurtin' Me? / I Never Expected to See You 1/89

Houston Solution / If You Don't Want Me To 5/89

A Woman in Love / Southern Roots 9/89

ALBUMS

Warner Brothers Records

Ronnie Milsap 10/71

A Rose by Any Other Name

She Even Woke Me Up to Say Goodbye

RCA Records

Where My Heart Is (1973)

Pure Love (1974)

A Legend in My Time (1975)

Night Things (1975)

20-20 Vision (1976)

Ronnie Milsap Live (1976) (Gold)